FILM STRUCTURE AND THE EMOTION SYSTEM

Films evoke broad moods and cue particular emotions that can be widely shared as well as individually experienced. Although the experience of emotion is central to the movie viewing, film studies have neglected to focus attention on the emotions, relying instead on vague psychoanalytic concepts of desire. *Film Structure and the Emotion System* synthesizes recent research on emotion in cognitive psychology and neurology in an effort to provide a more nuanced understanding of how film evokes emotion. Analyzing a range of films, including *Casablanca* and *Stranger than Paradise*, this book offers a grounded approach to the mechanisms through which films appeal to the human emotions, demonstrating the role of style and narration in this process.

Greg M. Smith is assistant professor of communication and graduate director of the Moving Image Studies program at Georgia State University. He is the editor of *On a Silver Platter: CD-ROMs and the Promises of New Technology* and coeditor of *Passionate Views: Film, Cognition, and Emotion*. He has also contributed to *Cinema Journal* and *Journal of Film and Video*.

Film Structure and the Emotion System

Greg M. Smith
Georgia State University

CAMBRIDGE
UNIVERSITY PRESS

CAMBRIDGE UNIVERSITY PRESS
Cambridge, New York, Melbourne, Madrid, Cape Town, Singapore, São Paulo

Cambridge University Press
The Edinburgh Building, Cambridge CB2 8RU, UK

Published in the United States of America by Cambridge University Press, New York

www.cambridge.org
Information on this title: www.cambridge.org/9780521817585

First published 2003
This digitally printed version 2007

A catalogue record for this publication is available from the British Library

Library of Congress Cataloguing in Publication data
Smith, Greg M., 1962–
    Film structure and the emotion system / Greg M. Smith.
        p.   cm.
    Includes bibliographical references and index.
    ISBN 0-521-81758-7
    1. Motion pictures – Psychological aspects.   I. Title.
    PN1995 .S5355   2003
    791.43′01′9 – dc21   2002034987

ISBN 978-0-521-81758-5 hardback
ISBN 978-0-521-03735-8 paperback

Contents

FILM STRUCTURE AND THE EMOTION SYSTEM

DEVELOPING THE APPROACH

1 An Invitation to Feel

W hen nonacademics learn that I am writing a book, the polite conversationalist will ask what my work is about. After I reply that my book looks at film structures and emotion, inevitably their response is something like, "Isn't that an enormous subject? There must be so much written about film and emotion." Because emotions are so central to most people's cinematic experiences, they assume that film scholars must have placed the topic of emotion at the top of their research agenda. Most nonacademics are surprised to learn that there is relatively little written by cinema scholars on film and emotion per se.

But cinema studies is not unique in its neglect of emotion as a topic of study. From the fifties to the seventies, few academic disciplines gave precise attention to the topic of emotions. Cultural anthropologists had difficulty reporting such highly "subjective" states of mind using traditional methods of observation on other cultures. Instead, they focused on more externally observable differences, such as those in language and ritual performances. Sociology's agenda led academics to areas in which socialization was most clearly at work. These thinkers recognized that emotions were manipulated by society, and so they tended to view emotions in a purely instrumental fashion, as means to an end. Social forces relied on fear or love to create prejudice or empathy, but few sociologists questioned the basic nature of these emotions.

In psychology, behaviorism's influence led theorists away from anything located within the "black box" of the human organism. When cognitive science arose to challenge behaviorism with a new emphasis on internal representations, researchers agreed not to consider emotion. Emotions, unlike memory or perceptual tasks, could not be simulated on computers, and so emotions were often considered to be "noise" unique to the human hardware, a possible source of interference with cognitive processes. Similarly, the emphasis on reason within the philosophy of mind kept many philosophers away from "messy" states such as emotions.

In the late 1980s, academic disciplines began to produce a flurry of new research in the neglected topic of emotions, and this work continues today. New anthropological methodologies encourage researchers to examine more "subjective" states in their complexity. In many cases this emphasis on emotion grew out of earlier research problems. Studies of the effects of mood on memory helped open up cognitivists to considering emotion, as research on empathy did for sociologists. The research on emotion in these fields still carries traces of these originating questions.

Like these other disciplines, film theory has historically paid only spotty attention to emotional effects, although almost everyone agrees that eliciting emotions is a primary concern for most films. In the modern world's emotional landscape, the movie theater occupies a central place: it is one of the predominant spaces where many societies gather to express and experience emotion. The cinema offers complex and varied experiences; for most people, however, it is a place to feel something. The dependability of movies to provide emotional experiences for diverse audiences lies at the center of the medium's appeal and power.

Emotions are carefully packaged and sold, but they are rarely analyzed with much specificity by film scholars, particularly in the modern era. Some classical film theorists, particularly Sergei Eisenstein, foregrounded emotion as one of the primary goals for filmmakers, but Eisenstein's broad discussions of emotion did not give other theorists a specific foundation for discussing emotion (unlike his more concrete prescriptions about editing).[1] André Bazin also emphasized that filmmakers should evoke emotion, but he foregrounded a particular means of eliciting that emotion (realism). In the modern era, studying emotional responses to films became the task of quantitative communication researchers, resulting in a large body of work on topics such as the effects of media violence on children. Film theory devoted more of its energy toward issues of cinematic specificity, arguments over aesthetic valuations, and understanding of representation.

Contemporary film theory of the seventies concentrated on issues of meaning and representation and their ideological implications. Some writers

(Christian Metz being the most influential) attempted to arrive at a theory of "pleasure" and "desire." What pleasure does the cinema afford, and what desire motivates our viewing? Linking the Althusserian bent of ideologically based theory with Freudian and Lacanian theories of subject formation, Metz foregrounded identification as the principal emotive effect in film. Many film feminists, including Laura Mulvey, Mary Ann Doane, Linda Williams, and Christine Gledhill, have struggled with the phallocentric assumptions of these Freudian and Lacanian theories, refining but not reconstituting the central concepts of psychoanalysis to address feminine film pleasures in particular.

The concepts of pleasure, displeasure, and desire used in film studies are too broad to provide specific insight into how a particular film makes its emotional appeal at any given moment, however. If the range of emotion in the film theater is reduced to some point on the continuum between pleasure and displeasure, we lose the flavor of individual texts. Similarly, if we claim that all mainstream film viewing emerges from the same scenario of repressed desire, we ignore the diverse motivations driving the spectator's interest and emotion. Recent psychoanalytic theory has attempted revisions to correct its reductive, overly broad approach. It has posited various positions of desire, rather than the former one or two positions. It has also articulated contradictory pleasures in an effort to make discussions of emotion more nuanced and specific. Nevertheless, I believe that although investigations of cinematic pleasure and desire are certainly important, the ambiguity and spaciousness of these concepts, as currently used, compromises their usefulness. These general concepts are a poor basis for a specific theory of emotion, making them a poor foundation for an approach to filmic emotion.

A far better candidate, I believe, for a productive theoretical perspective on emotion is the interdisciplinary mix of psychology and philosophy called "cognitivism." My book can be understood as part of a burgeoning new area of film studies that asks how cognitive research into mental functions can help us better understand the film viewer's task. David Bordwell, Noël Carroll, Gregory Currie, Murray Smith, Joseph Anderson, Edward Branigan, Torben Grodal, and Ed Tan have all produced major works on film theory from a cognitivist perspective,[2] and my work here should be seen as an outgrowth of their efforts. Although my emphasis on embodied emotion leads me away from emphasizing "pure" cognition, it is important at the outset to position my own efforts against the assumption that all these theorists (myself included) share: that a well-founded knowledge of how mental processes work can provide a solid basis for film theory.

I begin my approach to the topic with the seemingly tautological assertion that film emotions are first and foremost emotions. Unfortunately, this assertion is rarely made in critical literature on film. When film academics do address emotion, they generally proceed as if the concept of emotions were clearly and widely understood; therefore the task of the film scholar is to say what is specific about *filmic* emotions. I believe that we have relied too long on commonsense understandings of emotions in such discussions. We need to better understand what emotions are before we discuss any unique qualities of filmic emotions. And so in this book I do not discuss specifically filmic emotions, nor do I examine the specific nature of emotional responses to fiction, which much recent philosophy has investigated. There may be specific responses that the cinema and no other medium is uniquely qualified to elicit, but this book will spend little time examining such questions. Films are objects that are well constructed to elicit a real emotional response from our already existing emotion systems. Given a better understanding of that system, what film structures are well suited to activating that structure?

I lay out both a *theory* of emotion and an *approach* to filmic emotion. In Chapter 2, I survey recent psychological research on emotion and synthesize a theory of how the emotion system is structured. Based on my psychologically rooted theory of emotion, I then formulate an *approach* to analyzing a film's emotional appeals. Following Kristin Thompson's usage, an approach is "a set of assumptions about traits shared by different artworks, about procedures spectators go through in understanding all artworks, and about ways in which artworks relate to society." I am not outlining a method ("a set of procedures employed in the actual analytical process").[3] I share Thompson's concern that preconceived methods tend toward predetermined outcomes, which narrows the analysis. The theory of emotion outlined in this book provides the grounding for the approach's assumptions about emotion, but a theory alone does not show a critic how to analyze particular texts. On the other hand, an approach without a theoretical foundation can provide innovative readings, but it needs to be rooted in a cohesive, systematic whole to be convincing.

What would a good combination theory-approach to analyzing filmic emotion look like? How might someone determine if one approach were better than another? To evaluate the approach to filmic emotions in this book, we should agree on some desiderata for an approach:

1. A good approach to filmic emotions should provide *specific* explanations, not generalizations, for how particular films elicit emotions. A good approach should provide different explanations for how film A and film B elicit emotional responses. If the approach reduces different films to the same mechanisms over and over, then it is reductionist. Such tools lead critics away from specific consideration of individual films, and a good approach should lead them toward the particulars of a film.

2. A good approach to filmic emotions should provide terminology for discussing emotions and how they are evoked. This desideratum is an outgrowth of the previous one. If a theory of the emotions is to be productive, it needs to give us a language to talk about the "messy" world of emotions with specificity and particularity. We need two kinds of terminology: we need to be able to label emotional states with some measure of certainty, and we need terminology to discuss the film structures that encourage these responses.

3. A good approach to filmic emotions should be able to explain emotional phenomena at the global and local levels. A single film can elicit a wide range of emotions and yet still have a kind of emotional unity. We need an explanation for the broader processes of emotion that operate across entire films as well as the more minute processes that govern scenes, and we need a way to describe how these global and local processes cooperate.

4. A good approach to filmic emotions should not only label emotional states but also be able to discuss how they change over time. How does our emotional reaction evolve, progress, wane? How does a film change from one emotion to another? The challenge is for a theory to explain both emotion as stable state and emotion as dynamic process.

5. A good approach to filmic emotions should be able to explain why films are able to elicit such dependable emotional reactions across a broad range of audiences without denying the variations among individual emotional reactions. Again, the problem is dual. Films do get remarkably

similar emotional reactions when shown to a variety of viewing audiences, and this continuity of response needs explanation. Nonetheless, the approach should not endorse a single emotional response as being the only valid one because of the incredible range of reactions among individual viewers. Although no theory can explain every individual's emotional response, it should be able to explain how such a range of responses exists.

6. A good approach to filmic emotions should be able to explain the emotion in a wide range of films. If an approach works for melodrama or contemporary cinema but not for action-adventure or silent films, then it is of limited use value. If an approach is prejudiced toward the kinds of emotional appeals made by the classical Hollywood cinema, for instance, it will tend to reshape other films to fit that mold. Although it may be true that the classical cinema may require a different explanation of emotion than the art cinema, an approach that explains both would clearly be more powerful.

7. Similarly, a good approach to filmic emotions should be able to discuss a wide range of cinematic signification. Films use an enormous set of mechanisms to elicit emotion: lighting, camera, acting, sound, music, mise-en-scène, character, narrative, genre conventions, and so on. If an approach to filmic emotions concentrates too heavily on one of these mechanisms, then the approach is likely to miss much of the other emotion cuing in the film. For instance, many theories emphasize character identification as the pivotal mechanism in filmic emotions. My approach opens up a discussion of the emotional significance of a broader range of cinematic cues, emphasizing the importance of cinematic style in encouraging emotional responses.

8. A good approach to filmic emotions should be able to explain not only why a film succeeds in eliciting emotions but also why another film fails to do so. To show how a film cues emotions is only half the battle. If a theory is to have explanatory power, it must also be able to explain how some films fail to generate emotions. If the approach cannot explain why certain narrative structures are less effective in cuing emotion, then it is too broad to provide specific insight into effective film structure.

9. A good theory of filmic emotions should generate specific research questions for future research. If a theory seems to explain everything so totally

that it precludes further investigation, then the theory is too totalizing to be useful to researchers. A theory that generates a number of interesting, investigatable questions for research is of more use to scholars than a grand theory.

10. Finally, a good approach to filmic emotions should be rooted in a body of theory and empirical research on the emotions. Film studies should take advantage of the explosion of research that has been done on the emotions in recent years. Our conception of filmic emotions should be consistent with the best available models of how the emotions work. In particular, the researchers who are using empirical methodologies (particularly psychology, anthropology, and sociology) have an edge in discovering new insights into the emotions. All too often, discussions of the emotions perpetuate generally held beliefs about the emotions that may or may not be true. Of course, empirical researchers are susceptible to the same self-perpetuating ideas, but at least they have the opportunity to encounter data that refute these ideas. Empirical research is particularly useful in dealing with the emotions to create a solid foundation that is rooted in real-world processes.

Film Structure and the Emotion System proposes to bring to film theory a more nuanced understanding of what emotions are and how they function, based on current research in experimental psychology. Advances in neuropsychology have opened up new and more complicated understandings of the brain's interconnectivity, making it more difficult to separate "reason" from "emotion" in any strong sense. Current researchers in neuropsychology are adding more finely tuned tools to investigate emotion (in addition to those developed by traditional experimental psychology), giving psychology a more precise understanding of the basic nature of emotions. This burst of new attention to emotion in psychology has altered that field's basic understanding of what emotions are. One of the basic assertions of this book is that film studies' understanding of emotions should be consonant with (or at least not directly contradictory to) the best current understanding of emotions in psychology.

There is much that psychology is not well suited to tell us about emotions. For instance, anthropology is more likely to produce work sensitive to cross-cultural differences in concepts of emotion, and sociology is more geared toward examining how socialization shapes people's emotions. The burgeoning research on emotion in these fields should help continuing efforts in film studies to explore the importance of cultural difference in film viewing.

I believe, however, that we should begin this close attention to filmic emotion using the insights that experimental psychology provides. The insights sociology and anthropology provide should not contradict the psychological ones, because culture and socialization shape the individual but do not fundamentally rework the basic structures of the human. Sociocultural experiences help us define what particular emotions are, but the shape of the emotion system itself and the basic mechanisms by which it operates are best articulated by close attention to the individual.

This volume is concerned with this emotion system's structure, rather than with particular emotions themselves. This is not a book about sadness or joy; instead, it deals with the foundational structures that make such emotions possible. Culturally nuanced work on particular emotions certainly needs to be done, but we should make sure that we first understand the basic principles of how the emotion system is constructed. Although the subject of this book may initially seem too all-encompassing, in actuality its aims are humble. I do not attempt to explain all of emotional experience. I do assert, however, that an understanding of the basic nature of the emotion system should provide a firm (if limited) foundation to more fully understand filmic emotions.

Nor do I attempt to provide a particular theory for how each cinematic component evokes emotion. I do not present a theory of music, followed by a theory of facial expression, followed by a separate theory of camera framing, and so on. Instead, I present a theory of how the emotion system is designed to coordinate information from these subsystems. Certainly I believe that more work needs to be done on the specific relationship between emotion and such specific aspects of film. In applying my approach to films in the case studies, I frequently return to music (for example) as an important factor in cuing filmic emotions, thus emphasizing the need for a more systematic approach to film, music, and emotion[4]; a complete theory of the interrelationship among music, film, and emotion is outside the scope of this study, however. I do not believe that we must wait for a complete theory of emotion for each cinematic component before we can make valuable assertions about the nature of filmic emotions.

As the title of this work indicates, this book is about both emotion *and* film structure. Once we have a better understanding of how the emotion system operates, we can then take note of how certain film structures are particularly well designed to manipulate emotions.

The primary research questions addressed by this work are (a) how is the emotion system structured? and (b) what filmic structures seem particularly well suited to take advantage of the properties of this structure?

For the purposes of this work, "film" is assumed to be a highly coordinated visual (and usually audial) medium that has developed a number of conventional strategies (shared by producers and consumers) for storytelling in uninterrupted real time. This book deals only with emotion and the structure of *narrative* film. Admittedly audiences respond to nonnarrative and avant-garde films, and such responses call on the same emotion system in audience members as do narrative films. The structures in avant-garde film are, however, considerably different from those in films trying to tell a story, and so these structures are outside the realm of this work.

A crucial assumption for this book is that film takes place over uninterrupted time. Temporal limits for emotionality are built into the emotion system, and so the temporal unfolding of the filmic stimulus is crucial to the way it appeals to this system. A similar audiovisual medium such as broadcast television in the United States is more interruptive and so is structured differently in the way it tells stories. It deserves separate consideration of how its structures appeal to the emotions.[5]

Also important to this understanding of film is that audiences and producers share a certain set of narrational conventions that allows the story to be told and understood. When I examine film structure in Eisenstein's *Strike* or Vidor's *Stella Dallas,* I assume an "educated viewer," one familiar with the necessary basic conventions for making sense out of the film. This viewer is not necessarily a "spectator" (with all the implications of being ideally "positioned" by the cinema to receive pleasure), nor is the viewer an actual person with specific experiences at the cinema. The "educated viewer" simply has the (not necessarily conscious) knowledge to allow an understanding of the story and an emotional response to it.

Of course not all individuals who view a film may have the required knowledge to understand and respond to the film. I am not trying to specify the emotional responses of every viewer sitting in front of a screen watching

Casablanca. There will necessarily be individual differences in emotional responses, depending on the ways that people's personal experiences have shaped their particular emotion networks. Neither do I want awareness of this variation in people's emotion networks to paralyze film criticism. It is all too easy to conceive of emotions as so messy and individualized that one cannot talk about them with any specificity.

Films do not "make" people feel. A better way to think of filmic emotions is that films extend an invitation to feel in particular ways. Individuals can accept or reject the invitation. Those who accept the invitation can accept in a variety of ways, just as people invited to a party can participate in very different activities. Although there is much variety among what partygoers are doing, there are implicit conventions that set limits on the ways that most people accept the invitation (for instance, showing up at the party with no clothes on would in most situations be considered a violation of convention). One can acknowledge the range of partygoers' responses and simultaneously conceptualize a hypothetical "educated partygoer" who knows the rules for party behavior.

Films offer invitations to feel. Film audiences can accept the invitation and experience some of the range of feelings proffered by the text, or they can reject the film's invitation. To accept the invitation, one must be an "educated viewer" who has the prerequisite skills required to read the emotion cues. Not all "educated viewers" accept the invitation, of course. You can properly recognize how a film is cuing you to feel and still reject the invitation by not feeling those emotions. Film complicates the "invitation" metaphor, because film does not extend a single invitation but a succession of invitations across time. Film continually extends invitations to feel, and we can accept or reject any one of them.

As long as the film critic is dealing with the film text alone (as I am doing in this work), there are limits to the emotion analysis that can be done. I can discuss the range of emotional responses that a film encourages, but I cannot specify a particular emotional response without having access to a particular audience member's reaction. This is a book that examines the ways that particular films cue emotion, not a book about actual human emotional responses. Because my method deals with the text, I can only elucidate the primary invitation that the film offers. In textual analysis, it is also difficult to examine highly complex emotional states (for example, existential angst), at least until more work on the sociocultural bases of higher-level emotions is done. For now, my textual analyses concentrates on relatively less complex emotional states because they can be more dependably discussed, at least until further work by sociologists and anthropologists of emotion allows us to understand these more complicated emotions in more detail.

Such textual study is a necessary prerequisite for a film scholar dealing with emotions. We have much to learn about what emotions are and how films cue emotions before we venture into the significantly more complicated laboratory of the real world. By knowing more about the emotion system, we can better articulate what texts are doing and potentially discuss audience responses in more particularity.

In Chapter 2, I synthesize a range of research from experimental psychology and neuropsychology to create a cohesive, empirically based understanding of the emotion system. In Chapter 3, I discuss the implications of this research on our concept of film structure and demonstrate the basic concepts involved in analyzing a film's emotional appeals using four short case studies (*Raiders of the Lost Ark, Ghostbusters, Local Hero*, and *Stranger than Paradise*). Chapter 3 outlines a basic approach for the critic analyzing a film's emotional appeals, which I call the "mood-cue approach." In Chapter 4, I situate the mood-cue approach in the context of the growing body of literature on film, cognition, and emotion, differentiating my own approach from the assumptions of my predecessors Noël Carroll, Ed Tan, and Torben Grodal.

Chapters 5 through 9 provide more full case studies of how my conception of the emotion system can provide insights into texts. Each case study is designed to test a different capability of the critical approach. Can it explain how one text successfully shifts from one emotional appeal? Can it explain how a film might exhaust the audience's emotion system? Can the mood-cue approach explain how a film's emotional appeal fails? Can it provide a more insightful explanation than previous critics have done of the timeless appeal of a film like *Casablanca*? Can it mine new insights into a film that has been exhaustively studied by psychoanalytic film scholars (*Stella Dallas*)? Chapter 10 then provides a brief conclusion, suggesting future avenues of research open to scholarship. For those interested in such matters, an appendix follows that examines the Freudian assumptions about the nature of emotion that are the underpinnings of psychoanalytic film theory; I argue that these assumptions make Freudian-based theory a poor choice to explain the nature of emotions.

The analytic approach defined here is not prejudiced toward one particular cinematic narrational paradigm in a way that promotes "cookie-cutter criticism." The mood-cue approach demands that the critic pay close attention. The goal of this approach is to help critics to see and articulate the cinematic structures that appeal to audience emotions.

2 The Emotion System and Nonprototypical Emotions

This volume relies on recent research in cognitive psychology and neuropsychology to create a model of the emotion system. The resulting synthesis provides a systematic explanation of emotion, which in the next chapter becomes the basis for our exploration of the emotional appeal of narrative structures in film. Cognitive psychology and neuropsychology provide the basis in an empirical theory of emotion that helps my approach satisfy the desiderata.

This chapter examines several key questions. How do we define the category called "emotion"? What is the relationship between cognition and emotion? How may emotions be elicited? What roles do society and culture play in emotion formation and development? I propose a theoretical framework that provides answers to these central questions. This theory is by no means one with which all cognitive researchers would agree, because cognitive psychology is not without internal squabbles. Nonetheless, this chapter synthesizes recent findings in cognitive psychology and neuropsychology and provides one coherent explanation of the current state of cognitive research on emotion.

Why Cognitive Theory?

On first impression, cognitive theory seems an unlikely choice to provide insight into emotion processes. When cognitive psychology emerged, it announced that it would emphasize human functions that could be modeled using logical linear processing, like that of a computer. Subjective states such as the emotions were not on the early research agenda for cognitivism because they were clearly too messy to be modeled using classical logic. It was conceivable to think of computers as being able to model memory, but it was more difficult for cognitive researchers to conceptualize a computer-based model of emotions.

After discovering that real-world processes do not always follow classical logical structure, cognitivism began exploring less linear modes of reasoning.[1] Researchers have discovered that many real-world tasks (such as determining if an individual is a member of a category) do not depend on classical predicate logic. Trying to determine if an egret is a bird (under ordinary circumstances) involves comparing the individual to a prototype (e.g., a robin). It is much simpler to recognize that there are numerous similarities between the egret and the robin than it is to ascertain if an egret has all the Linnaean factors required to classify it as a bird (Does it have feathers? Does it lay eggs? Is it warm-blooded?). Trying to determine if a film (e.g., *Psycho*) is a horror film or not is a process that, for ordinary viewers, involves a rough comparison with an exemplar of the horror film, not the careful logical consideration of the nature of the "monstrous" that Noël Carroll applies in *The Philosophy of Horror*.[2] Real-world categories (such as emotion) have imprecise boundaries, and we make probabilistic comparisons with our prototypes using decidedly unclassical methods that resemble the mathematics of "fuzzy set logic"[3] more than they resemble the linear logic of computers.

Our minds must make decisions based on limited information, and we do so based on resemblances, probabilities, and temporary fits. We do not rely on a careful system of "if-then" logic to categorize our world. Classical predicate logic provides a clarity of argument that still dominates much philosophical discussion (including discussions of emotion),[4] but this mode of reasoning is a poor model for the complexities of many real-world processes. Such discussions may help us understand what our prototypes of emotion are, but they shed little light on how actual emotions work.

As it becomes apparent that the classical model of thinking describes only a subset of cognition, our understanding of cognition becomes messier, less tied to simple logic, and more tied to low-level processes. This makes the distance between ordinary cognition and emotion seems less daunting because emotions have traditionally been considered "messy," less "logical" states that are obviously deeply imbricated in low-level processes of the body.[5] As we learn more about the interdependence of bodily and cognitive functioning, emotion begins to look less like an exception and more like another example of the highly interconnected human processing.

Psychologists examining human emotions tend toward one of four broad theoretical emphases in their researches. The oldest approach is to emphasize how important the peripheral nervous system is to emotions. This research agenda began in the 1890s with William James, who believed that emotion is the perception of bodily changes. James argued that although the bodily expression of emotion seems to be caused by a mental state (we cry because we are sad), this causal sequence is actually reversed. We are sad, according to James, because we cry. Emotions begin with bodily states, which we then evaluate mentally.

Peripheral theorists, following James, emphasize the feedback that we get from various peripheral systems. In particular, many of these theorists have recognized the unique contribution played by the face. "Facial feedback" theorists, noting the high concentration of nerves in the face and the importance of the face in emotional displays, argue that the information provided by the face is particularly important in determining emotional experience. Elaborating on the folk wisdom that smiling will make you feel happier, these theorists[6] believe that information from facial muscles and nerves can determine emotions, distinguish among various emotions, or modify an emotional state.

Not long after James proposed his peripherally based explanation of emotions, another psychologist proposed an alternative: emotions are based in the central nervous system. Walter Cannon challenged what came to be known as the James-Lange theory, stating that the seat of the emotions was in the thalamic region of the brain. Cannon argued that the emotions underwent much more rapid changes than did the viscera (the periphery), and so the periphery could not be responsible (as James hypothesized) for the emotions. Cannon's attention to the central nervous system has been elaborated by several researchers who take advantage of neuropsychology's increasingly sophisticated understanding of the brain's chemistry.[7]

A third psychological approach emerged as a theoretical outgrowth of Magda Arnold's appraisal theory and an experimental outgrowth of Stanley Schacter and Jerome Singer's 1962 experiment.[8] Schacter and Singer gave subjects an injection of adrenaline, telling them that they were involved in an experiment on the effects of vitamin supplements on vision. The injections caused the subjects to have bodily arousal that they could not explain, and the subjects labeled their feeling states according to the emotion cues provided by their environment. This experiment reinserted the importance of cognitive appraisal of the situation into the psychological study of emotion, and a large body of work followed.

Such appraisal theorists have produced elaborate models of how we process situational cues and respond emotionally based on our assessment of these situations. Arnold examined how we appraise our situation and determine if objects may harm or benefit us, and this appraisal urges us to approach or avoid these objects. Nico Frijda posits a series of "laws" that govern the appraisal of stimuli and that produce action-oriented responses.[9] For a cognitive appraisal theorist, emotion depends on how people characterize objects and how they assess their relationships with those objects.

A fourth psychological perspective accentuates the social nature of the emotions. Social constructivists assert that cultural forces are not merely overlaid onto more essential biological foundations of the emotions, as a modifier might inflect a noun. Instead, they argue that emotions cannot be understood outside of culture and the shaping forces of society. The rules of emotion are learned through socialization, which guides us toward a preferred set of responses. Emotions serve social functions; they help us occupy roles within society overall.[10]

This emphasis on social construction helps this perspective privilege cultural differences in emotion.[11] Language has an important socializing function in shaping how we conceptualize our experiences, and social constructivists study the way language parses our world into different configurations. Social constructivism reverses the individualistic emphasis of the other three perspectives and situates the emotions within a broader context.

Although certain psychologists have created integrative approaches that attempt to synthesize a range of perspectives,[12] most research occurs within one of these perspectives: the peripheral (Jamesian) theories, the central neurophysiological theories, the cognitive appraisal theories, and the social constructivist theories. These four research emphases have produced a rich body of research on the emotions. The task of this chapter is to sift through this research and synthesize the insights provided by these approaches into a broad theory of how the emotions work.

Cognition and Emotion

Conscious thought can deliberate one's course of action, propose and evaluate alternatives, and construct a rational framework for decisionmaking. All this takes time, however, and in many situations we need a speedier method of initiating a course of action. Emotionally assessing a situation determines if such a quick response is needed and then provides a powerful motivation for necessary actions. Viewed in this way, emotions resemble reflexes because they provide simple, quick responses to the environment.

Reflexes, however, respond to the same stimulus in exactly the same manner over and over, and they will not respond at all to other kinds of stimuli. Emotions necessarily must operate more flexibly. We need to be able to label a variety of circumstances as "sad": the death of a loved one, a game one's favorite sports team loses, or a bleak rainy day depicted in a film. Similarly, we need a wider range of responses than can be encompassed in automatic reflexes. Crying may be a prototypical response to sadness, but it is by no means the only one. Emotional expression depends on the social situation and the person's role in that situation. A traditional man in a Western culture may be prone to inhibit any expression of sadness, except in particular situations when certain such expressions are expected of him (funerals of loved ones).[13] Although emotional responses are sometimes romanticized as being uncontrollable, they are in the vast majority of cases subject to social inhibitions.

Emotions therefore resemble thought in that they allow us to act on incomplete situational information and to respond flexibly to a variety of stimuli with a range of appropriate behavior. Emotions resemble reflexes in that they provide an urgency to action that encourages us to act quickly and motivate us to pursue an action more fervently than would be possible with pure rationality. The emotion system is not capable of the higher abstract reasoning of the conscious mind, but it is not necessarily antithetical to that reasoning.

What does cognitive psychology have to say about whether cognition is necessary for emotion? Cognitive psychologists have battled for years concerning this question. Both Lazarus and Zajonc,[14] the two primary combatants on the issue, agree that cognitions can have a mediating effect, but they cannot agree concerning the necessity of cognition in the emotion system. Lazarus asserts that emotions necessarily involve cognition, and Zajonc insists that cognition is not required in emotion processes. Lazarus and Zajonc have waged a war of increasingly clever laboratory experiments to prove their respective cases, but the debate is primarily between two definitions of emotions. The difference between Lazarus's and Zajonc's understandings of emotion is indicative of a central chasm dividing much work on emotion.

Most emotion research emphasizes either emotional experience or emotional expression.[15] Emotional experience is the subjective feeling state consciously perceived by the individual, which is often studied using self-report measures. Researchers concerned with higher levels of cognition[16] (for instance, the social constructivists and appraisal theorists) tend to emphasize this facet of emotion. Those concerned with lower level structures[17] (many peripheral and most central theorists) emphasize emotional expression, the physiological or behavioral response to an emotional stimulus.

The difficulty arises when two theorists (for example, Lazarus and Zajonc) are studying different objects that they both call by the same name ("emotion"). Lazarus is arguing about emotional experience, and Zajonc is arguing primarily about emotional expression. Much of the contention in emotion research comes from misunderstanding which emotional object is being studied.

Emotional experience researchers and emotional expression researchers are equipped to study different portions of the spectrum of phenomena we call "emotion." As researchers examine the development of emotion in children (who cannot articulate their emotional states well) or the possibility of emotions in animals,[18] they need a concept of emotion that is not completely centered on conscious thought. Studies of the complexities of emotions outside the laboratory must take into account a person's awareness of the social situation and the cultural mores defining his or her role in that situation. The theory of emotion that I propose in this chapter accepts both emotional experience and emotional expression as valid and valuable components of an emotion system. Most ordinary emotions involve both facets.

When one examines the broad range of studies on emotional expression, it becomes difficult to maintain that cognitions are necessary for emotion. Cannon noted that emotional behavior may be expressed even when the cerebral cortex has been anesthetized. Normansell and Panksepp report that play behaviors in decorticated animals continue, although they are reduced. Jacobs and Nadel have noted that appropriate cognitions are not required for phobias. Pylyshyn elaborates on the difficulty of eliciting and extinguishing emotions through purely cognitive efforts. My theoretical framework agrees with these central neurophysiological researchers[19] that conscious cognition is not required for emotion.

Because conscious thought is not a necessary part of all emotional functioning, I do not place conscious thought at the center of my explanation of the emotion system. Because conscious cognition does play an important part in most everyday emotions, the challenge for my theory is to give consciousness a powerful, but not a crucial, influence on emotions.

Emotion Prototypes and Nonprototypical Emotions

Let us begin with the important cognitivist notion of prototypes. Prototypes, as described earlier, organize human experience by allowing us to categorize new data. They guide our expectations concerning what members of a category should look like and what they should do. Understanding broadly held intuitions about the nature of the emotion prototypes will help us to gain a better understanding of the emotion system and the way emotions are discussed.

First, emotions are prototypically seen as object-oriented states (as appraisal theorists emphasize). In Brentano's terms, prototypical emotions are intentional, meaning that they are directed toward something (the object of the emotion). We are afraid *of* something instead of merely being afraid. An intentional object is not the same thing as a cause. One's fear can be directed toward something that is not its cause. Fear can be chemically induced, but the resulting fear is not directed toward the actual cause itself (the ingested chemicals) but toward an object (perhaps something in the room). According to the prototype, however, emotions are thought of as having both causes and objects.

Second, the prototypical emotion is an action tendency toward a goal. Emotions tend to urge us into action: fleeing a fearsome object, embracing a loved one, hitting someone in anger. Prototypical emotions are functional, providing a short-term urgency that motivates us toward action to change our situation. The comparison between emotion and reflexes emphasizes the tendency both have toward action.

Folk understandings of emotion tend to consider emotion as a gestalt, a feeling tone that cannot be broken down into component processes. Laura Mulvey relies on this commonsense understanding of emotion when she says that "analyzing pleasure, or beauty, destroys it."[20] To dissect an emotion is to destroy it, according to this assumption. "Feelings simply *are* feelings," most would say. "You can't explain them further." Because emotional experience is considered to be an unanalyzable gestalt, it is frequently considered to be less culturally conditioned than many other human behaviors. If one sees emotions as pure feeling tone, it is easy to assume that emotions are universal.

Some psychologists have argued that all emotions do not fit perfectly within the prototypical understanding of emotions. For example, there are emotions that are not so clearly functional. Frijda[21] suggests that certain emotions "express" the subject's concerns rather than ensure that those concerns are satisfied, and I offer the label "expressive-communicative emotions" for these states. Emotions such as depression do not promote the subject's well-being, but they express the subject's state. Many expressive-communicative emotions could also be considered functional (in the case of an upset infant whose cries summon the caregiver), but this depends on subjects being in an environment where their communicative act can elicit help. A person sitting depressed alone in his or her room is experiencing an expressive-communicative emotion that is no less forceful simply because it is not functional. Although we prototypically think of emotions as functional, they are not necessarily so.

Contrary to expectations based on the prototype of emotions, some actual emotions require neither an object or a goal. Emotion can be elicited by extremely diffuse stimuli, like a dreary day, and can have nondirected expression (like depression). Öhman, Dimberg, and Esteves have shown that fear can be produced by stimuli below the conscious level.[22] If I feel happy because it is a sunny day, my emotion has a cause, but the "object" (everything surrounding me) is too diffuse to be an object in any meaningful sense. If I am so depressed that I am immobile, it is difficult to view such an emotional, self-perpetuating state as being an "action tendency" toward a goal.

To stretch concepts of "goal" or "object" to include such cases would make these concepts extremely thin, perhaps meaningless. My theory asserts that, in spite of our prototypical understanding of what emotions are, actual emotions need not be goal- or action- or object-oriented.

The system outlined in this chapter uses emotion prototypes, but it does not rely solely on them. The flexible emotion network allows us to create a variety of associations with an emotion (a gray rainy day, a slouched posture, a frown, an oboe playing in a minor key) that can cue us to experience and express the emotion. Associations need not be conscious; they can form between a wide range of emotional stimuli and responses. Associations open up the possibility of nonprototypical emotions.

Prototypes fit the majority of cases we experience, and reducing emotional experience to a sort of "majority rule" would make this chapter's model considerably simpler. But we cannot shrink the range of experience to those cases that fit our societal prototypes. Leaving out nonprototypical emotionality would rob this model of some of the complexity that makes the emotion system more responsive. Although emotion prototypes powerfully shape our experiences, associations make it possible to bypass prototypical functioning. This book relies on associations as the foundation of both prototypical and nonprototypical emotions.

The Structure of the Emotion System

Cognitive research has traditionally concentrated on the simpler building blocks of cognition – processes such as memory, object recognition, and categorization that have relatively well-defined inputs and outputs. Visual recognition, for instance, works on information received from one sensory channel (the eyes). Unlike visual recognition, however, the emotion system receives information from several sources of input, of which the eyes are only one. The fact that the emotions are flexible enough to process information from several channels necessarily makes studying emotions more complex, and as we shall see, this distributed processing provides the system with its crucial flexibility.

The theory proposed in this chapter asserts that emotions are what may be called multidimensional response syndromes,[23] meaning that they are groups of responses to several possible eliciting systems. We have already noted that the capacity to produce multiple responses helps differentiate emotions from reflexes. Not only can emotions provoke a range of responses, but the emotion system can also be invoked by several subsystems. The subsystems that have been discussed as being important to eliciting emotions are (a) facial nerves and muscles, (b) vocalization, (c) body posture and skeletal muscles, (d) the autonomic nervous system, (e) conscious cognition, and (f) the nonconscious central nervous system.

Researchers have investigated these six areas in search of the underlying bases of emotions and found that each plays a part in the general concept of emotion. The question is, what is the relationship among these systems? Is any one system alone necessary to produce emotion, or does each system merely have a contributing or mediating effect on emotion? The next pages give an overview of this literature in an attempt to understand how these systems interact to create emotions (with the exception of conscious cognition, which is dealt with earlier in this chapter).

Autonomic Nervous System (ANS). The autonomic nervous system (the motor nerves that regulate involuntary functions of muscles in respiration, the heart, the blood vessels, and the digestive tract) has been associated with emotion theory since William James's[24] day. Research by peripheral theorists[25] has discovered distinctive ANS patterns associated with anger, fear, and disgust. The contributing effect of ANS activity in emotion is in little doubt. But whether ANS activity is essential to emotion is a more difficult question.

Researchers have attempted to determine whether the ANS is necessary for emotion by studying patients with spinal cord lesions. In reviewing this literature, Higgins[26] notes several studies in which neural damage resulted in a lessening of felt emotion. But there are many confounding factors in the study of lesioned patients, so these studies should be only cautiously used. Experimenters were able to isolate the ANS more successfully (although not perfectly) by administering beta-blockers to anxious and angry subjects.[27] In both cases, ANS arousal decreased, but no difference in emotional experience was observed. This casts serious doubt over whether the ANS is necessary for emotion. In Marañon's early study,[28] subjects whose viscera were stimulated by epinephrine reported that, although they did not feel emotional, some felt "as if" they were emoting. This study suggestively indicates that ANS activity almost triggers emotional experience, but something is missing.

The ANS is involved in virtually all ordinary emotional experiences. There is no conclusive evidence that ANS activity is sufficient to cause emotion. Rather, it seems that stimulating the ANS provokes a person almost to the point of experiencing emotion, but such stimuli remain under some important threshold level.

Facial Nerves and Muscles. The face is here treated separately from other skeletal muscles and other components of the ANS because of its particular significance in expressing emotion. Facial feedback theorists[29] argue that the face has a high density of neural representation and a socially unique communicative instrumentality, qualifying it for a unique position in emotion theories. Theorists suggest that nerve responses from the face to the central nervous system (called afferent responses) are the key to emotionality.

The difficulty with much of the facial feedback research is that the subjects, when told to smile and then asked what emotion they felt, could cognitively determine the "right" answer. Some experimenters have found ways to test the facial feedback hypothesis by minimizing this confounding factor, such as Strack et al.'s[30] technique of holding a pen in one's teeth (simulating a smile) or in one's lips (simulating a frown). Ekman and Friesen's[31] Facial Action Coding System instructs the subject to move facial muscle groups one at a time instead of using traditional linguistic labels such as "smile." Such investigations have found evidence that facial positioning can affect processing of emotional stimuli.[32]

As Izard notes, however, "[t]here is no reason to believe that emotion experience is always dependent on, and signaled by, observable expressions."[33] Ekman et al.[34] did find recognizable patterns of ANS activity associated with posed faces, but their subjects did not report emotional experience. Ekman[35] further states that certain emotions (shame and guilt) do not have specific facial expressions associated with them.

Positioning the face can produce a low level of emotional expression or modify emotional experience, but to suggest that the face is crucial to the emotion system would contradict our understanding of emotional flexibility. Although we often conceive of particular facial expressions as part of an emotion's prototype (smiling for happiness, frowning for anger, etc.), there is no evidence that the face is necessary or sufficient to produce emotional experience. Facial expression is merely a contributing (and not a necessary) factor in the emotion system.

Body Posture and Skeletal Muscles. Many theorists acknowledge the potential influence of the nonfacial muscles and overall body posture, but few except Gellhorn[36] have assigned them specifically important roles. Folkman and Lazarus as well as Riskind and Gotay[37] have found that body postures can affect emotional experiences. Pasquarelli and Bull[38] found that subjects could not feel an emotion when their bodies were put in a position suggesting the opposite emotion (using hypnosis).

A mediating effect for body posture and skeletal muscles on emotion seems fairly well accepted, although the dearth of specifically nonfacial research makes it difficult to determine whether body posture is necessary for emotion. Perhaps the diffuseness of this input channel contributes to the difficulty in getting specific research findings on body posture and emotion. Because a strong version of the facial feedback hypothesis has not been confirmed by peripheral theorists, however, it seems unlikely that body posture (having far less density of nerves than in the face) should prove to be necessary.

Vocalization. Vocalization is widely suggested as being significant to emotion, but, like body posture, it has been only infrequently studied. Tomkins postulated more than forty years ago[39] that a distinctive set of vocalizations is associated with distinct emotions, just as has been shown to exist in facial expressions. Researchers have only recently begun to gain the sophisticated digital sound technology that would allow them to follow up on this suggestion.[40]

Preliminary study indicates that there may be some agreement in the vocalized expression of certain core emotions (anger, fear, joy).[41] It is unclear, however, whether particular emotions have specific vocal signatures or whether the observed vocal differences simply reflect the distinction between high and low states of arousal. Some researchers have begun more interpersonal work on voice and affect, because the voice's primary function is communicative.[42] Bloom and others[43] have begun studying the development of affective vocalization to examine how young children integrate affective speech with emotional expression as they develop their cognitive and emotional capacities. Much of the early development work on children, emotion, and language centers on how children are socialized to gain an understanding of emotion categories,[44] not on how they develop affective vocalizations.

Tomkins's suggestion concerning emotion and the voice remains an intuitively forceful idea. Nonetheless, it seems unlikely that vocalization could be considered either necessary or sufficient for emotion, because cultures have such strong norms prescribing vocal affective displays.[45]

Nonconscious Central Nervous System. Central neurophysiological emotion researchers have concentrated their efforts on the limbic system as the common pathway of emotion. The limbic system, a richly interconnected group of forebrain structures around the brain stem, evaluates sensory data and decides whether the emotions should be activated. The system then attaches an emotional "shading" to the information and can instigate appropriate behavior.[46]

The technical details of this system are important to an understanding of emotion structure. At the entrance to the emotion system is a gate (the thalamus). Data from the senses pass through the gate on their primary route to the cortex for conscious processing. A crucial decision must be made at this point. The gatekeeping thalamus must judge whether the data it has just received is emotionally significant. If it decides that the signal requires an emotional response, it relays the signal along a secondary route to the emotional core of the brain (called the amygdala). This emotional core "spices up" the data, adding a "flavor" that gives the information its emotionality. Or, to use another metaphor, it "shades" the data with a particular emotional "coloring." If a threshold of emotional intensity is passed, the emotional core activates the hypothalamus to instigate behavior, provoking a low-level response without involving consciousness.

The emotional core (the amygdala) also is connected to the conscious processing in the cortex. The cortex examines the emotive signal and the sensory data and decides whether the emotional reaction should be increased or inhibited. The cortex then communicates back to the emotional core, commanding it to inhibit or intensify the emotional feeling. Status information from the viscera begins to arrive at the cortex as emotional behavior begins, and this feedback figures into the overall information processing.

Now there are several signals being processed simultaneously and inter-actively: sensory data, the feeling tone (the emotionally "colored" signal), commands from the cortex to inhibit or intensify emotions, commands to instigate and continue behavior, and status information from the viscera.

This emotional core (amygdala) is the crux of the emotion system. It is, as Panksepp describes, a "way station,"[47] a common pathway for the emotions. It receives a variety of signals from different sources and creates the feeling tone for the emotion system. Cannon[48] suggests that lesioning or removing portions of the limbic system leaves the person without affect. I know of no research to contradict this finding. Therefore, I place the limbic system, the only necessary component of emotions, at the center of my emotion system.

The question becomes, what should we do with this synthesis of research? Can we not simply describe the components of the emotion system, their interworkings, and their interconnections as one might describe the work-ings of an automobile engine? Perhaps, but this would leave our emotion theory too tied to the specific components as they are currently understood by researchers, and we simply do not understand the emotions as well as we understand cars. At any point someone may discover that some types of emotion processing are dealt with outside the amygdala, or that the amyg-dala handles a broader range of outputs than previously understood, or that other subsystems are involved in emotion processing. If we put the physical entity known as the amygdala at the center of emotion theory, then the entire theory may be overturned by a few empirical studies.

Recall that the point is for our theory's description of the emotion system to be *consistent* with our best understanding of current research. What we need to do is come up with a *model* of how the emotions work, a theoretical description of the system. This model should fit the research as we know it, but it need not be tied absolutely to the physical details of the system. We are, after all, trying to come up with an approach to understanding the emotional appeals in films. Such an explanation need not rest on whether the amygdala is the absolute crucial component of the emotion system.

Regardless of what neurological research brings in the coming years, we are unlikely to overturn the portrait of complexly interwoven activity that now characterizes our understanding of the emotions. None of the emotive systems except the limbic has been shown to be necessary for emotion, yet all of them contribute to emotion in some way. A simple model of an emotion system is therefore not feasible. To understand the emotion system, we need a model that allows multiple causes without fixed sequencing, because all potential causes except one can be circumvented. No single system has been shown to be sufficient to cause emotion (not even the limbic system) without help from the others, so the model must allow for joint causation.

I propose an associative network model of the emotion system that is consistent with the highly interconnected structure of the limbic system.[49] In my model, the various components of the emotion system are connected by a series of associative links. Emotions (the nodes of the system) are tied to particular thoughts and memories as well as patterns of physiological reactions. Conscious cognitions (memories, social mores, emotion labels, etc.), autonomic and central nervous system patterns, action tendencies, vocalizations, and facial patterns are all interrelated.

For example, a node in the network labeled "fear" might be associated with a childhood memory of falling from a height, a trembling voice, running, increased heart rate, increased right frontal hemispheric activity in the brain, and widened eyes. If only one of these six systems is activated, the chances of the fear node being activated in an associative network is small. If two are activated, the chances of having the emotion increase, perhaps providing an "as if" emotional experience.[50] As more nodes are activated (as more channels of input provide emotion cues), the emotion is more likely to be experienced and expressed. Whether an emotion occurs in a situation depends on how many channels of emotion provide emotion cues and how intense those signals are.[51]

This yields an approximation of a system that is flexible, that is not tied to any particular input channel but can receive emotion cues from any of several sources. There are many possible ways to access the emotion network, because any component can initiate an emotive sequence of events, but no single component (except for the limbic system) is required. Yet the system is not flighty; it does not activate the "fear" node every time one's heart starts beating faster. To experience and express an emotion requires redundant cues, such as those that occur most frequently in the rich environments of real life. This model of the emotion system relies on the redundant cuing of the real world to elicit forceful emotions, but it also explains the lesser emotional phenomena produced with constrained stimuli in laboratory conditions. Such a model, balancing flexibility and dependability, helps my approach explain why films can evoke both remarkably similar responses across audiences and widely varying responses across individuals, which is one of our desiderata for such an approach.

In this proposed model, emotion nodes are not only connected to the multiple input channels, but they also can be connected to other emotion nodes. Accessing one emotion node tends to activate other nodes that are associatively linked. This proposed linkage of emotion nodes gives an explanation for why certain emotions (anger and depression, for example) may often be seen together. A member of the network can potentially be linked to virtually any other network node, opening up the possibility that associative links can be built between such disparate states as pain and happiness to create sadomasochism, for example. Stimuli need not pass a stringent "if-then" test to activate the system.

There probably exists a point after which more node activation does not significantly add to the emotional experience and expression. If five of the six contributing systems are activated, whether the sixth is activated probably makes little difference. The system undoubtedly has certain thresholds, a minimum number of nodes that must be accessed to experience or express emotion. Also there are probably thresholds of cuing intensity, so that insignificant stimuli cannot trigger the emotions. These thresholds may vary according to the individual's particular network construction (making some people more easily prone to emotional expression in general, or more likely to express a particular emotion).

Having several input channels for the emotion system make its function simultaneously more complex and better protected. This distributed system ensures that if any path becomes inoperative, other paths can compensate. A distributed network of interconnections ensures that the emotions can still provide their motivating urgency even if some input channels are not functioning properly. If a threatening stimulus does not gain the attention of one subsystem, there are other systems monitoring the environment that can also instigate an emotional action to deal promptly with the threat.

This model at its center relies on parallel processing. Sensory data are sent to the cortex for conscious processing, while the same data are sent to the emotional center of the brain to gain feeling tone. One process is primarily cognitive, the other primarily emotive, but both begin simultaneously.[52] Once cognition and emotion are separately activated, however, the two processes are almost always yoked together. They begin to interact heavily, changing emotional expression and behavior. Parallel processing of thought and feeling allows a person to react quickly to an emotion system, but the interconnectivity permits us to inhibit or intensify feelings based on social situations.

Importantly, this connection between conscious thought and the core of the emotion system allows our emotion prototypes to affect emotional experience and expression. Prototypes allow us to store a rich set of information about an emotion: what responses are appropriate, what kinds of objects tend to be causes of the emotion, the script of how the emotion tends to change as it progresses. This information is fed into the emotional core, altering the responses it calls for in the autonomic nervous system, the face, and so forth. These subsystems report back their altered functioning to the emotional core, and a cycle is in place that alters emotional experience in light of emotional prototypes.

This model disagrees with the notion that emotional data are neutral, which is an assumption underlying the "classic" experiment that instigated a flurry of psychological research on emotion: Schacter and Singer's study. When Schacter and Singer used adrenaline to simulate emotional arousal, they assumed that emotions depend on an undifferentiated physical arousal (a gestalt) and that higher cognitive facilities labeled and assigned meaning to this tabula rasa based on conscious knowledge of the situation. Emotions are not based on a generalized arousal state that consciousness can evaluate as it sees fit, however. Emotional data are already encoded by lower-level processes by the time they reach consciousness.[53]

This low-level emotional appraisal is the core of what I refer to here as "affect." Affect is a rather broad emotional state with little specificity, usually referred to as being either "positive" and "negative," which guides us to approach or withdraw from an object.[54] Affect provides the "feeling tone" of emotion to the conscious mind. It is the fundamental, atomized component of the emotion system, a developmental antecedent of emotion that exists at birth and that cannot be taught to respond in any other way besides its hardwired response. It is the foundation of the associative network and not an emotion per se. Based on the affect we feel and our conscious understanding of situational cues, we make decisions: to fight or flee, to label our state as "angry" or "afraid."

In summary, I propose an associative network model of emotions with multiple sources of input (facial feedback, autonomic nervous system, conscious cognition, etc.) feeding into a system of emotion "nodes" and interconnections. No one input is required to initiate the emotion, but if several subsystems are initiated, it is likely that the emotion node attached to them will be activated, regardless of logic. This emotion system can be initiated without relying on conscious cognition. Emotional evaluation (creating an action tendency toward approach or withdrawal that is called affect) takes place in parallel to the conscious assessment of stimuli. If the emotion system's signals become strong enough to reach consciousness, emotional experience results. Once both conscious thought and the emotion system are initiated, they tend to interact through a highly interconnected linkage, allowing thought to influence the course of an emotion and vice versa.

Building the Network, Learning the Prototypes

Although cognitions are not necessary to activate the fully constructed associative network, they are required to do the developmental work of building that network. Cognitive and emotional developmental stages mirror each other because cognitive skills are required to build the architecture of the emotions. No emotion can exist until the organism is cognitively advanced enough to create a corresponding emotion node in its network.

The newborn expresses approach and withdrawal responses that guide its behaviors until two months. Developmental researchers[55] have noted a significant behavioral shift at two months, involving the appearance of the social smile and cooing, changes in sleep patterns and visual attentiveness, and increased potential for conditioning. Joy and surprise may be observed at this age level, and Izard et al.[56] also report anger expressions at two months. In Piaget's terms, this represents the transition to stage II of sensorimotor development and involves the coordination of senses. Without the two-month-old's coordination of sensory input, he or she is incapable of the experience and expression of surprise, joy, and anger.

Emde[57] notes another biobehavioral shift at seven to nine months. The child responds fearfully to strangers but not to caregivers and becomes afraid of "visual cliffs."[58] This corresponds to Piaget's stage IV of sensorimotor development with its understanding of means-ends relationships and object permanence, and this cognitive ability to anticipate events has emotional ramifications. Without an understanding that certain events bring about other events, the child could not anticipate danger and therefore would react to a frightening stimulus with shock or surprise, not fear.

Clearly this model does not propose that the cognitions necessary for building the associative network be conscious or high level. It assumes sensory and perceptual processes that are not representational.[59] Higher cognitions do help build the network in the older subject, however. The more "subtle" the emotion (existential fear, for example), the higher the cognitive development required to place it in the network. As Minsky suggests:

infantile emotions are comparatively simple in character and . . . the complexity of adult emotions results from accumulating networks of mutual exploitations. In adults, these networks eventually become indescribably complicated, but no more so than the networks of our adult intellectual structures.[60]

The accumulation of associations simultaneously creates both an intricate cognitive network but also a complex parallel system for emotional response.

This system does not suggest that more subtle, adult emotions are created by combining more "basic" emotions. Emotions are not like colors. Complex emotions are not produced by combining more primary emotions, as one can make purple from the primary colors red and blue. Emotions are all produced through a coordination of cognitive and emotional developments. Some emotions may be considered more "basic" in the same sense that some cognitions are more "basic" because they appear earlier in the individual's development. The sequence of emotional development is universal to the same extent that cognitive stage development is universal.[61]

As people develop, one of their principal tasks is to increase the interconnectedness of their emotion network, just as they must create an ever more complicated network of thought. Individual experiences create unique associations among nodes in the network, and it is through such personal circumstances that each of us creates our distinctive emotion network.

An emotion system develops habits, just as individuals do. We try out particular emotional responses, and if they prove effective, we tend to use these responses over and over, developing a personal emotional style. One individual may tend to respond to a threatening situation angrily, whereas another may respond fearfully. One person may learn to depend more heavily on one source of emotional input, and data from that source may become more heavily weighted in the system's functioning (for example, actors trained to be particularly aware of body posture may find that a characteristic gesture allows them to feel a character's emotions). Individual experience can also alter the emotional makeup systemwide. If people are encouraged not to express or acknowledge emotion, over time their thresholds for activating the emotion system may rise.

The system is not completely malleable; there are undoubtedly limits. It is impossible to raise the system threshold so high that one cannot feel emotion, nor is it probable that one can significantly alter the emotional evaluation that occurs before conscious awareness. Given certain limits, however, the emotion system is remarkably flexible. Associations can link emotions to seemingly unconnected objects (as Freud noted in fetishes), and the emotion system can connect emotions that appear to be opposites. A roller-coaster aficionado can tie enjoyment to the irreducible fear or withdrawal affect activated by falling, and horror film fans can have rollicking fun when their uncontrollable startle reflexes are jolted. Because associations are the basic connective tissue of the emotion system, this provides the network with the necessary flexibility to become well suited to an individual's environment.

Building an emotion network, then, is a lifelong process of adding new associations on top of old ones, creating a more complexly interconnected system capable of more nuanced response as the individual assimilates new experiences.

Emotion and Culture

Emotions are prototypically conceived of as subjective experiences, and so in discussing individual differences it is easy to underemphasize how culturally constructed emotions are. If an emotion network is built through personal experience, then the social framework that allows us to make sense of our experience plays a crucial role in creating an emotion system. All societies, not merely modern industrialized nation-states, have a vested interest in controlling the emotions of their members.[62]

Part of the socializing work of a culture is to provide its members with scripts for expressing and experiencing emotion, prescribing what sorts of circumstances elicit emotions, who should feel, and the boundaries of appropriate feeling and expression. Stein and Trabasso[63] postulate that because emotions are usually goal-oriented states, much cultural variation comes from cultures placing different values on particular goals. Lutz's pioneering work on emotion in South Sea Island natives[64] supports this assertion. She notes that the two forms of anger self-labeled by the Ifaluk are differentiated based on the cause of the anger. One form is a reaction to intentional harm and is considered to be positive; the other is anger without socially justifiable cause.[65] Cultural anthropologists and social constructivists have clearly demonstrated the potential for culture to shape emotional experience,[66] thus challenging the predominant Western conception of the emotions as universal.

Most acknowledge that there may be different culturally specific rules for expressing emotion,[67] but many assume that emotional experience is a feeling that is "natural," beyond the reach of social forces. My theory of emotion agrees in part with this Western folk understanding. There is a portion of the emotion system that is "hardwired" beyond the influence of conscious thought. The development of certain basic emotions seems to transcend culture, just as children around the world learn certain basic cognitive and physical tasks in a particular sequence. By rooting socially constructed prototypes in certain simple materialities, societies are able to justify their prescriptions on emotion as if they were "natural."

In no strong sense do I assert that "emotions are universally felt." Nonetheless, we need to acknowledge that there are basic similarities built into humans. The new psychology's precise attention to the brain and the body provide a better portrait of the "form" of the emotion system. In dealing with the "content" of the emotion system, however, we should turn to the anthropology and sociology of emotions. There are cross-cultural "universals" in the emotion system, but the sociocultural network of emotional associations that individuals have constructed has more bearing on most everyday emotional experiences than any "universals."[68]

Then what is the importance of such universals? Such universals are limited but foundational. Sociocultural influences shape our emotions, but they cannot fundamentally remake the construction of the emotion system. This system, then, places limits on culture's ability to mold emotional experience. Culture and society do not have infinite influence on our emotional makeup. There are neurological boundaries to what culture can ask human structures to do.

By laying out very specifically the unenculturated portions of the emotion system, I wish to nuance the linkage between the emotions and their naturalness. The universal portions of the system structure are constitutionally basic but are less important to everyday emotionality than is the enormous network built by people's attempts to make sense out of their world.

Temporality and Orientation: Emotions as Process

One of the difficulties in studying emotions is that researchers often use the same word "emotion" to label quite different phenomena. As mentioned earlier, much misunderstanding comes from calling emotional expression and emotional experience by the same term. Because so much of emotion terminology also has common usage, emotion researchers need to be specific about what they mean by "generally understood" terms such as emotion and mood. I first distinguish such terms as "emotion" and "mood" from each other based on how long such emotion states last.

The temporality of emotions seems an unproblematic matter, if you consult your memory. According to my memory, I was angry at my department chair for a full day, or I was happy all weekend long. However, memories of emotions are notoriously suspect sources of evidence about actual emotions, although many studies examine such memories and treat them as if they were real emotions. Humans can be remarkably bad at remembering specifics of their own experiences – and for good reason. Instead of storing all the details of our experiences, it is much more efficient to put a condensed version with a clear label into memory. If a prototypical script labeled "jealousy" covers much of our experience during a particular episode, then we can label that memory as a jealous episode, even if that label does not fit all the emotional ups and downs we felt.

Here again the power of emotion prototypes is important. Prototypes and scripts organize not only the way we interpret our surroundings but also the way we store and retrieve information about our experiences. Emotional memories are better sources of evidence concerning what our emotion prototypes are than they are concerning the details of emotional experience. This may be particularly true of the way we remember emotional duration.

More precise attention to emotional experiences and expressions as they occur is giving us a different picture of emotional longevity than the one we remember. We do not remain angry for an entire day. Instead, evidence suggests that emotions are relatively brief states.

The duration of emotions seems to be measured in seconds or minutes rather than hours or days. Researchers with quite different methodologies, from studies of electroencephalographic patterns to observations of marital interactions, have found this to be true.[69] Studies indicate that emotional expression changes frequently during an emotion episode. Ekman[70] observed that most emotional expressions on the face last between half a second and four seconds. Other subcomponents of the emotion system (for instance, the autonomic nervous system) change less rapidly. Heartbeat frequency does not alter as quickly as facial expression, and so emotional expression has different longevity in different subsystems. Emotional longevity may differ from emotion to emotion. For instance, Ricci-Bitti and Scherer[71] suggest that sadness tends to last longer than fear. Although there is variation in emotional longevity among emotions and emotion systems, the overall duration of emotions seems to be relatively brief. In addition, studies have found little variation in emotional duration across European cultures,[72] suggesting that there may be system limits to emotional longevity. When one examines actual emotions in progress rather than self-reports of memories, one discovers that emotions are comparatively fleeting states.

This finding needs some explanation. How can we seem to have a coherent long-lasting emotional attitude toward a situation when we experience a series of short bursts of emotion? The answer lies in an additional faculty of the emotion system. We have discussed how emotions can operate as action tendencies to spur us toward functional activity and how other emotions serve to express the person's internal state. In addition, the emotion network can also orient us toward our environment. Emotions not only provide urgency to a chosen course of action but they also can provide urgency to the way we gather information. Surprise, for instance, is an emotion-related state that quickly prepares an organism for response when that organism is not already in an appropriate preparatory state. After evaluating the stimulus quickly, the orienting state of surprise is immediately followed by the appropriate action-oriented response (fear, joy, etc.).

Orienting emotional states tend to be preparatory. They ready the body and turn the attention toward particular stimuli, thus changing the way we interpret our environment. The orienting function of emotions highlights those portions of our situation that are emotion-congruent. For instance, people in love might interpret the day's weather in relation to their positive feelings, and so the same sunny day shared by an angry or fearful person would be perceived very differently. The orienting function of emotion encourages us to seek out environmental cues that confirm our internal state. It is this crucial orientation that provides a consistent framework for brief emotional experiences.

The primary set of orienting emotion states is mood.[73] A mood is a preparatory state in which one is seeking an opportunity to express a particular emotion or emotion set. Moods are expectancies that we are about to have a particular emotion, that we will encounter cues that will elicit particular emotions. These expectancies orient us toward our situation, encouraging us to evaluate the environment in mood-congruent fashion. A cheerful mood leads one to privilege those portions of one's environment that are consistent with that mood. Moods act as the emotion system's equivalent of attention, focusing us on certain stimuli and not others.

These expectancies are themselves low-level emotional states that tend to be more diffuse and longer lasting than emotions. They are not emotions per se, but they are tendencies toward expressing emotion. A mood, therefore, is a longer-lasting but less forceful emotion state with an orienting function that encourages us to express a particular group of emotions. Although not as intense as emotions, their longevity helps make them a crucial part of the emotion system.

Moods have an inertia. They tend to keep us oriented toward expressing and experiencing the same emotion. They encourage us to revisit the stimulus again and again, each time refreshing the emotional experience with a new burst of emotion. These surges of emotion in turn support the mood, making us more likely to continue to view the world emotionally. A fearful mood puts us on emotional alert, and we patrol our environment searching for frightening objects. Once we see a frightful sight, this bolsters the mood and makes it more likely that we will continue evaluate future stimuli as frightening, thus giving the fearful mood its inertia. This cycle continues as long as there are emotional stimuli present.

A mood requires these brief, stronger doses of emotion to continue. Mood, therefore, is in a partnership with emotion. A mood is a predisposition that makes it more likely that we will experience emotion. Mood supports and encourages the expression of emotion. At the same time, brief bursts of emotion encourage the mood to continue. Without occasional moments of emotion, it would be difficult to sustain a predisposition toward having that emotion.

A combination of mood (emotional orientation) and external circumstances forms a sequence of emotional moments that Nico Frijda calls an emotion episode. An emotion episode[74] is a series of emotions that are perceived to be a structured coherent unit having a beginning, a middle, and an end. When we remember being angry for a significant period of time, we are usually remembering an emotion episode. An emotion episode is an emotional transaction between a person and his or her environment, a transaction composed of several subevents but that is perceived to have an internal consistency.

Thus, emotion episodes more closely resemble our emotion prototypes than do emotions or moods. They require the presence of an object; they are not diffuse as moods and low-level emotions can be. They are usually action tendencies as well as activation states. They can last for long periods of time. The primary difference between our prototypical understanding of emotion and emotion episodes is that emotion episodes are processes, not states. The term *episode* implies a (bounded) narrative sequence of events, emphasizing that emotions change throughout the course of the coherent unit. We tend not to remember the episode's rapid changes because they are smoothed over by the orienting capacity of the emotion system.

An emotion episode lasts as long as the mood and the stimulus are engaged in a transaction.[75] They are dependent on both mood's orienting tendency and the presence of a coherent emotional object. They are usually longer than emotions (measured in seconds or minutes) and mood (which can last for hours, although many last between four and fifteen minutes).[76] Emotion, emotion episode, and mood: this range of temporalities will help my approach discuss how filmic emotions change over time, as specified in the desiderata.

The orienting capacity of the system acknowledges that most situations do not change second by second. Most environments change only incrementally, and therefore a consistent emotional stance toward that environment is required. Brief periods of emotion can provide the urgency and speed needed to deal with sudden changes in the world, but they cannot provide the steady emotional orientation required to deal with a stable environment.

Mood provides that consistency of expectation, which means that we do not constantly have to attend to the variability of our emotional experiences. Mood helps us to select the stimuli that are most likely to be important. It filters out extraneous emotional stimuli and gives occurrences a coherence that usefully simplifies our experiences and our memories. Together these different temporalities help give the emotion system a sophisticated combination of flexibility and efficiency, speed and stability, adaptability and coherence. Mood and emotion give my approach a way to discuss both global and local emotion phenomena, which was one of the desiderata listed in the introduction to this study.

In those desiderata, I suggested that a good approach to filmic emotions should be rooted in a coherent body of empirically based theory, such as the one outlined in this chapter. I argue that if critics want to explain the emotional appeals of certain films, they should pay attention to how long-term mood and brief emotion interact across the film. A good approach to filmic emotions should not rely solely on the prototype of emotions as object-, goal-, and action-oriented. A critic should pay attention to how emotion prototypes shape our experiences of cinematic emotions while simultaneously being sensitive to the many possible cues that can elicit emotions nonprototypically. The emphasis on associations in this chapter reminds us that we should pay attention to the flexible way that emotions can be tied to stimuli and elicited by evoking these associations. The task of the next chapter is to explore how films call upon the structure of the emotion system outlined here.

3   The Mood-Cue Approach to Filmic Emotion

Given the flexibility of the emotion system, it would seem difficult for a mass-media form to elicit emotional responses with
any degree of consistency across a wide range of viewers. If social and cultural differences create diverse emotion scripts and prototypes, then audience members can be using very different prototypes when emotionally
assessing the same stimuli. Even if an audience shares a basic understanding of an emotion, one viewer's emotions may be more easily elicited by
facial positioning or conscious thought, whereas another viewer may favor
a different channel for emotional access. Also, no single emotion channel is
sufficient to create a large level of emotional response without a significant
degree of redundant cuing.

How can films be structured to elicit dependable responses from a wide
variety of audience members, as noted in the desiderata? If emotions are
such brief states, how can a film maintain a consistent emotional appeal
throughout its running time? What part do emotion prototypes play in
film, and how do emotional stimuli that are not part of the prototypes
factor into a film's emotional appeal?

Recognizing the structure of the emotion system will help us see the structures that filmmaking practice has developed to elicit emotional responses
dependably, as I demonstrate in a few short case studies. The emotion system's constraints make certain emotional appeals impossible to succeed (for
instance, emotions cannot be sustained for long periods of time) and give
certain kinds of emotional appeals more chance of success. The approach
outlined here is meant to explain how films are structured to appeal to audience's emotions. While applying this approach to four different films, I have

created neologisms to describe the cinematic structures that this approach uncovers. Naming new narrational structures seems to be a useful by-product of this approach, and our desiderata specifies that an approach should produce such terminology.[1]

The Central Assertion: The Interaction between Mood and Emotion

I argue that the primary emotive effect of film is to create mood. Generating brief, intense emotions often requires an orienting state that asks us to interpret our surroundings in an emotional fashion. If we are in such an emotionally orienting state, we are much more likely to experience such emotion, according to my theory.

Film structures seek to increase the film's chances of evoking emotion by first creating a predisposition toward experiencing emotion: a mood. Films rely on being able to elicit a lower-level emotional state, which can be established with less concentrated cuing than would be required for emotion. The first task for a film is to create such an emotional orientation toward the film.

To sustain a mood, we must experience occasional moments of emotion. Film must therefore provide the viewer with a periodic diet of brief emotional moments if it is to sustain a mood. Therefore, mood and emotion sustain each other. Mood encourages us to experience emotion, and experiencing emotions encourages us to continue in the present mood.

Film structures attempting to elicit mood can take advantage of the various means of access to the emotion system. Because emotions can be evoked using a wide range of stimuli linked in an associative network, films can use the full range of perceptual cues to evoke emotion, as noted in our desiderata. Filmic cues that can provide emotional information include facial expression, figure movement, dialogue, vocal expression and tone, costume, sound, music, lighting, mise-en-scène, set design, editing, camera (angle, distance, movement), depth of field, character qualities and histories, and narrative situation. Each of these cues can play a part in creating a mood orientation or a stronger emotion.

Films, however, cannot dependably rely on using single emotion cues. There is considerable variation among individual viewers' emotion systems, and single cues might be received by some viewers and missed by others.

Films therefore provide a variety of redundant emotive cues, increasing the chance that differing audience members (with their differing preferences of emotional access) will be nudged toward an appropriate emotional orientation.

As a brief and simple example of how film cuing works, let us examine how Alfred Hitchcock coordinated emotion cues in a familiar scene from *Psycho*. When Marion and Norman share a meal in Norman's parlor, redundant cues begin to alert us that something is wrong with this young man and that we should begin to fear for Marion's safety. Dialogue connects Marion (who "eats like a bird") and the birds that Norman stuffed and placed on the wall, suggesting that perhaps Marion might receive the same fate as the birds. The narrative situation places Marion alone in the hotel with Norman, a man whom she only barely knows. Low angles make Norman more menacing, particularly when he is framed with the birds (lit from below to create elongated shadows). His stuttering, given the norm of perfect Hollywood diction, can be seen as a hint of deeper troubles. The close-up of Norman when he bitterly describes a madhouse, along with the orchestral music in a minor key, further alerts us that Norman is a man to be feared. The cues are not so foregrounded that we are certain Norman will do something evil, but they are coordinated enough to signal to the viewer that they should be fearful.

Redundant cues collaborate to indicate to the viewer which emotional mood is called for. The viewer need not focus conscious attention on each of these elements. Some of these cues activate the associative network of the emotions, and this creates a low level of emotion. If a film provides a viewer with several redundant emotive cues,[2] this increases the likelihood of moving the viewer toward a predispositionary mood state.

Once that mood is created, it has a tendency to sustain itself. A mood is not entirely self-perpetuating, however. If we do not find any opportunities to experience these brief emotions, our particular mood will erode and change to another predispositionary state. It requires occasional moments of strong emotion to maintain the mood. A critic should look for these occasional moments of strong cuing that bolster an audience's emotional orientation.

The purpose of this chapter is to outline, elaborate, and demonstrate my approach to analyzing a film's emotional appeals. This approach, rooted in the assumptions of the previous chapter's theory, I call the *mood-cue approach*. The first step for the mood-cue approach is for the critic to pay close attention to the way that emotion cues act together to create mood at the beginning of a film. The approach assumes that the film will use coordinated sets of cues to signal an emotional orientation toward the film as a whole.

Then the critic pays particular attention to later bursts of highly coordinated cuing that can bolster or alter the mood. To satisfy the desideratum that an approach to filmic emotions explain both global and local emotional phenomena, the mood-cue approach emphasizes the interaction between mood and the arrangement of coordinated cues to evoke emotion. By monitoring these subsequent cues as they change or support the initial emotional orientation, the mood-cue approach satisfies the desideratum for an explanation of emotions across time.

As I progress through this chapter, I demonstrate the usefulness of this approach to films ranging from *Raiders of the Lost Ark* to *Stranger than Paradise*. These small case studies flesh out the mood-cue approach, coining new terminology along the way, but throughout this discussion the key is the central relationship between mood and emotion cuing.

Coordinated Cuing: The Emotion Marker

Narrative provides a series of diegetic goals and obstacles, and goal achievements and obstacles frequently provide the necessary mood-reinforcing payoffs. We rejoice when the protagonist achieves a goal or subgoal; we are sad, fearful, or anxious when a goal is frustrated. Goals and obstacles are highly foregrounded in the narrative, and so they create highly marked opportunities for moments that are significant both narratively and emotionally.

Almost every narratively significant moment has the potential to provide some emotional payoff, but not every emotional payoff is narratively significant. The classical Hollywood cinema frequently uses what I call "emotion markers," configurations of highly visible textual cues for the primary purpose of eliciting brief moments of emotion. These markers signal to an audience traveling down the goal-oriented path of a narrative, cuing them to engage in a brief emotional moment.

The emotion marker is not there simply to advance or retard the narrative's progress. Neither is the emotion marker an informative device offering more detail about the story or offering authorial commentary on the diegesis. The primary purpose of an emotion marker is to generate a brief burst of emotion. Often such moments could be excised from a film with little or no impact on the achievement of narrative goals or the state of story information.

These markers do fulfill an important emotive function in the text, however. For the viewer engaged in an appropriate mood, they give a reward that helps maintain that predisposition toward expressing emotion. Few texts can rely only on narratively significant moments to provide mood-sustaining emotion. Most have to provide markers to shore up the mood the text has created, even if the markers have little or no effect on the overt diegetic aim: the character's achievement of a goal.

An example will help illustrate this, and I have selected the opening of a film that densely packs obstacles to the steamrolling forward progress of its action-oriented, protagonist-centered narrative: Steven Spielberg's *Raiders of the Lost Ark*. *Raiders* is an exercise in putting one obstacle after another in front of Indiana Jones's (Harrison Ford) attempt to find the Ark of the Covenant and save the world. These retarding moments endanger the hero, allying the audience with him and providing the audience with traditional adventure serial pleasures such as fear and excitement. Yet even a film with as many exciting hairpin escapes as *Raiders* uses emotion markers to provide even more emotional payoffs.

The opening sequence of the film follows Jones through the jungle and into a booby-trapped cave in search of a golden statue. The mood is suspenseful, apprehensive of the imminent attacks of jungle savages or the swift triggering of hidden death traps. The musical score is an unsettling mix of unusual melodic intervals and percussion; the environment is full of deep shadows, and the camera tracks behind Jones. One of Jones's trail guides tries to shoot him from behind, and Jones saves himself with a quick lash of his whip, establishing his character's skill with the weapon. That whip helps Jones and his remaining guide cross over a deep pit, only to have their support slip, almost plunging the guide to his death. This whip-and-pit obstacle must be crossed again on their way out of the cave. These obstacles use multiple emotion cues (musical stingers, facial close-ups, etc.) to signal emotional expression of fear, both serving important narrative functions (impeding progress toward the goal and providing the setup for future narrative occurrences) and providing emotional payoffs.

Along the way there are moments that are just as emotionally marked without serving such significant goal-oriented narrative function. One of the guides traveling through the thick jungle uncovers a grotesque stone idol and screams, accompanied by the loud flapping of a flock of flushed birds and a musical stinger. Clearly this is a concentrated organization of emotion cues coordinated to prompt a startle reflex in the viewer, yet unlike the previously discussed emotional elicitors, this emotion marker neither hinders nor helps the protagonist's progress toward his goal, nor does it provide new story information. What this moment does do is provide a reliable burst of congruent emotion that helps maintain the sequence's suspenseful mood. This is the primary purpose of the stone idol scare.

It is difficult to argue, given the interconnected nature of narrative, that any moment has absolutely no bearing on goal progress or story information. The stone idol scare may have some minor contribution to the state of story information (letting us know that Jones is near the place where the golden treasure is housed), but clearly the functionality of this narrative incident exceeds its narrative informativeness. The main purpose of the stone idol is to shout "Boo!" at the audience. It is a sort of red herring that marks this moment as fearsome, bolstering the mood's predisposition toward emotion (a necessary function given the structure of the emotion system).

The appearance of tarantulas on Jones's and the guide's backs in the cave is another emotion marker. Here the case is a bit less clear-cut. One could argue that the tarantulas are an obstacle to Jones's progress, but their function as obstacles is minor compared with the emotional effect called for. Jones merely brushes the spiders off, making them an extremely minor obstacle (and the only obstacle that is not reencountered when Jones and the guide race back out of the cave). The tarantulas' primary function is to elicit disgust or fear in the audience, relying on common societal associations with hairy spiders. Their emotional function greatly exceeds their goal-oriented function.

Note that both of these emotion markers are fairly simple and reliable devices. The startle reflex when hearing a loud noise is impossible to suppress, even if one becomes accustomed to hearing artillery fire daily. The disgust reaction at seeing a hairy spider is as widespread and dependable today as it was on my elementary school playground. When choosing emotion markers to buoy the mood, the filmmakers relied on some of the more dependable and simple emotional elicitors. Emotion markers in general tend to be uncomplicated and direct.

Also note that these markers need not elicit exactly the same emotions for them to continue the mood. The stone idol may prompt a fearful startle reflex, and the tarantulas may elicit disgust. What is required is that the emotion markers prompt emotions that are congruent with the suspenseful mood. Emotions are not sharply discrete entities; one cannot argue that a cue must elicit either fear or disgust and not both. Disgust is associated with fear, and when one pathway is activated, the other is often triggered as well. Filmmakers need not be concerned that they elicit precisely the same emotion throughout a sequence. Because of emotional interconnections, related emotions serve to maintain the mood.

Emotion markers do greatly exceed their limited function in providing story information, but I want to differentiate emotion markers from the related concept of "excess" articulated by Kristin Thompson.[3] Like Thompson's excess, emotion markers accentuate the materiality of the signifiers (the screeching of birds and violins) and cannot be reduced to their functioning vis-à-vis the plot. Unlike excess, however, emotion markers are not counter-narrative. They do not encourage the viewer to dwell on them and play with their materiality. Instead they are brief moments of emotion that support the narrative's emotional address just as obstacles and motivations support the ongoing process of narration.

It is useful to consider texts as composed of a series of emotion cues, such as cues of narrative situation, facial and body information, music, sound, mise-en-scène, and lighting, that access the emotion system in prototypical and nonprototypical ways. Films call on emotion prototypes (nodes of association often containing scripts) when asking us to interpret characters' actions, given their narrative situations and their facial expressions. But emotion cues also provide the possibility of nonprototypical access to the emotions, and therefore they tend to be used redundantly so that they may more predictably gain access to the flexible emotion system.

Cues are the smallest unit for analyzing a text's emotional appeals. Emotion cues are the building blocks that are used to create the larger structures such as emotion markers. Mood is sustained by a succession of cues, some of which are organized into larger structures (narrative obstacles, emotion markers), some of which are not.

The basics of the mood-cue approach to analyzing a film's emotional appeal are simple. The critic's task is paying attention to small emotion cues and to how they are coordinated. A basic assumption is that a film will encourage viewers to establish a consistent emotional orientation toward the text (a mood), and so the critic looks for highly coordinated sets of emotion cues that will communicate the proper orientation to the viewer. Once the mood has been established, the mood must be bolstered by occasional bursts of emotion, and so the critic looks for a series of emotionally marked moments that will sustain or alter the basic emotional orientation. Using these basic components allows us to discuss with particularity the differences between the way texts make emotional appeals.

Brief Prototypes: Mixing Genre Microscripts

Genres are composed of narrative and iconographic patterns, but they also specify patterns of emotional address, providing the viewer with scripts to use in interpeting a genre film. How does a particular genre structure its use of emotion cues, mood, and emotion markers?

The most significant genre scripts with relation to emotion are not the broad expectations for the overall shape and form of a film, but genre microscripts, intertextual expectation sets for sequences and scenes. We approach a film with an enormous collection of microscripts we have gathered from real-world experience and from encounters with other genre texts, scripts for feuding lovers, showdowns, fight sequences, romantic reconciliations, chases, and stalkings. These microscripts encourage the viewer to anticipate what will happen next narratively, stylistically, and emotionally. Because emotions tend to be brief microlevel phenomena, smaller generic units tend to be more useful guides for the emotion system.

We do not interpret the mood of the *Raiders of the Lost Ark* opening based solely on its emotion cues. Instead we recognize it as a sequence in which we follow a protagonist into hostile territory. The threat of off-screen savages is rooted in experiences with other jungle adventure movies or with westerns and stalker films. Genre signposts of mise-en-scène (dark jungle), cinematography (tracking camera following the protagonist as he walks), and so forth quickly orient us toward the appropriate emotionally prototypical script to use in this particular narrative situation. The schemata for generic sequences contain information about the kinds of emotion cues usually used in such sequences and how those cues are arranged, and these schemata guide us in making hypotheses concerning what emotional events will soon occur. Emotion cues confirm or question our initial choice of a script, modifying or supporting or escalating our mood.

Such genre microscripts are primarily tools to help us recognize which emotional responses are called for. By themselves, such scripts can serve a purely cognitive function: cuing us to identify an appropriate emotion. Recognizing and labeling an emotion are not the same as experiencing it, but consciously labeling an emotion state is an important factor in shaping most emotional experiences because conscious thought is one of the primary inputs into the emotion system outlined in the previous chapter.

By combining such genre microscripts with coordinated patterns of emotion cuing, however, a film can make an emotional appeal to its audience that exceeds the purely cognitive. Coordinated emotion cues associatively encourage the viewer toward a mood, and when we note genre microscripts that are consonant with our mood, we are encouraged to do more than simply recognize these emotion scripts. We are encouraged to feel, to execute these scripts in our own emotion systems. Again, a text provides only an invitation to feel, not an irresistible prescription. If mishandled, genre microscripts can derail the emotional appeal established by the mood. When used in conjunction with other emotion cuing patterns, however, they can make complicated emotional appeals, as the following case study illustrates.

Sequences do not always use cues that are consonant with traditional genre expectation. A film can leave out cues that we would normally anticipate or use emotion cues that are associated with other genres. In this way filmmakers can play with the emotional possibilities of a genre, sometimes blending components of different genres into a complex emotional mix.

Ivan Reitman's *Ghostbusters* is an example of such a genre blend. *Ghostbusters* is ostensibly a comedy that contains numerous elements from the horror film. Examining sequences from this film illustrates how an individual film makes a unique emotive mix out of our various generic expectations. This short case study is meant to be indicative of how a critic might examine the complex interactions among genre microscripts.

The first scene in *Ghostbusters* is a recognizable one from the horror/ stalker genre. A lone woman is being followed from behind by a dollying

camera. When the camera follows such characters performing ordinary actions (the kind of actions usually elided in narrative film), we are encouraged
to hypothesize that offscreen forces are going to threaten her (otherwise such
insignificant action would not be shown).

And yet this particular tracking shot does not fit perfectly into the genre
prototype. The woman is clearly middle-aged, not young. The lighting in
the library stacks is high key with no menacing shadows (unlike the dark
jungle in the opening of *Raiders*). The nondiegetic music is bouncy and
playful, although the oboe melody maintains some associations with unsettling music generally heard in such sequences (like the music in *Raiders*'s
opening).

In addition, viewers have probably brought some genre expectations for
comedy with them to the film. Publicity, promotion, previews, reviews, and
the star images of Bill Murray, Dan Ackroyd, and Harold Ramis all signal
that an appropriate mood for *Ghostbusters* is a comedic one.

Given this mix of competing genre schemata, it is difficult to decide
which mood is called for. Some emotion cues (cinematography, for example)
point to a tense mood from a horror film. Some cues (lighting and casting)
undermine those expectations, and some cues (music) point simultaneously
toward horror and a lighter mood like the comic. The scene ends with some
poltergeist activity, the woman running toward the camera while screaming,
a quick fade to white, and the loud beginning of the upbeat title music,
providing a coordinated burst of cues to signal the end of the scene with little
definite information on the emotional state appropriate for this sequence.

This scene is followed by a broadly comic scene in which Peter Venkman
(Bill Murray) tries to seduce a young woman during an ESP experiment.
Here the cuing is clear: we are expected to laugh. Once we have this clear
mood information, the parapsychologists are called to the library stacks
we've just seen in the previous sequence to investigate a ghost sighting.

Once again we are shown the stacks, and the difference between this scene
and the previous library stack scene is instructive. The film presents us once
again with the same mix of emotion cues as before – light oboe music, high-
key lighting, camera following characters through the stacks – but a comic
mood has been established, and this influences how we read the scene. In
addition, Venkman makes regular humorous remarks, further reinforcing
the comic mood.

Now that a comic mood is clearly signaled, the text is free to present more strongly marked horror cues than before, knowing that the comic mood strongly predisposes us toward laughter, not fear. Unlike the previous library stack scene, this scene actually shows the ghost (accompanied by a generically expected zither sound). Most importantly, the scene ends with the ladylike ghost suddenly transforming into a death's head that rushes toward the camera. The effect is briefly horrific, inducing a dependable startle reflex, but the predisposition to laugh that has been reinforced many times over the last two scenes reasserts itself. We are cued to laugh over the upbeat music that follows, laughing at ourselves for flinching after someone says "Boo!"

The primary mood is comic, predisposing us to laugh, but this particular film will introduce strongly marked horror cues into the mix. If *Ghostbusters* used a long sequence of horror genre cues, the comic mood would gradually be extinguished, and a more fearful mood might take over. As long as *Ghostbusters* keeps its horror cues fairly brief, the comic mood is not overturned, according to the mood-cue approach. And as the comic mood becomes more firmly established through the course of the film, *Ghostbusters* can use longer and more marked horror cues without fear of changing the predispository state. By the film's climax, the comic mood is so established that the confrontation with the god Gozer can be staged as a fairly straightforward horror scene without changing the mood state. *Ghostbusters* mixes the emotion cues from two differing genre prototypes, but it does so in a way that signals which genre expectations are to remain dominant. Once that hierarchy is founded, the film can more liberally introduce elements from the secondary genre (horror), creating a complex emotional mix. A text therefore can create its own particular framework for emotional interpretation using generic prototypes altered by specific patterns of emotion cues.

Classifying the Appeal: Goal Orientation and Sparse Information

According to the mood-cue approach, an emotional framework sketches the range of possible emotions that a film may elicit. Our first example, *Raiders of the Lost Ark*, establishes early a predisposition toward excitement, danger, and fear. The film also tries to inject humor in the mix, but it does not do so until after the excitement mood is clearly founded. The first action sequences (finding the statue, escaping the natives, a Nepalese barroom brawl) contain no foregrounded laughter cues. They consist almost entirely of fear, disgust, excitement, and endangerment cues. The next action sequence, however, emphasizes its humor. Arabs kidnap Marian (Karen Allen) in a busy marketplace, setting off a chase and fight sequence. For the first time, an action sequence foregrounds its comic moments (Marian hitting her pursuers with a frying pan, Indiana Jones responding to a swordsman's challenge by shooting him). This sequence encourages us to modify our construction of the film's emotional framework to include the comic as a potential emotion that can be elicited later in the film.

We can classify a text's framework as following more or less consistent genre expectations. Only the most standardized genre products maintain strict generic consistency, and a few classical films intermix genres in the way *Ghostbusters* does. Most texts fall somewhere in between.

Film texts can also be classified according to how densely informative they are regarding emotions. A film with dense emotional information attempts to elicit emotions with great frequency and specificity. These texts contain many redundant cues, using them frequently and in a highly foregrounded manner. *Raiders of the Lost Ark* is such a densely informative emotional text, providing us with many cues as to how to respond. For example, *Raiders* strongly marks the introduction of each major Nazi character, using loud musical stingers, low-angle dolly shots, and menacing facial features to mark them clearly as characters to be hated. A film like Bill Forsyth's *Local Hero* would be considered a less densely informative emotional text, having sparser emotion cues. Jim Jarmusch's *Stranger than Paradise* is an even less densely informative emotional text, restricting itself to only a few formal possibilities among the range of cinematic emotion cues.

A film does not maintain a uniform level of emotional informativeness. Instead, its level of emotional information varies. Even a densely informative emotional film like *Raiders* does not provide the same quantity of emotion cues throughout the film. Texts are more densely informative at certain points and less so at others. *Raiders* stages the Nepalese barroom brawl without music, helping to make it a less emotionally marked sequence than the chases and confrontations at the film's climax.

Texts may also vary depending on how strong or weak their goal orientation is. If a film places a protagonist's goal at the center of the narrative, and it shows the character doggedly pursuing that goal, the entire film becomes oriented around this character's success or failure. Such strategies may certainly have narrative payoffs, but they also have impact on a film's emotional appeal. If a narrative shows highly goal-oriented characters performing actions that move them toward a clear series of goals, then this makes for easier comparisons with the scripts in emotion prototypes. Given clear goals, it is easier to label the emotional states of a character like Indiana Jones and to make sense out of other emotion cues. *Ghostbusters* also deals with highly goal-oriented characters (like *Raiders*, the film is about preventing "Judgment Day"), but its protagonist is not so devoted to the central goal. He neither understands nor is interested in the details of how to capture ghosts. Venkman is more interested in seducing women (which is certainly a goal but not the central one established by the film), and his wisecracks undercut the pursuit of the overall narrative goals. None of the characters in *Stranger than Paradise* has a strong goal orientation, which makes the process of labeling emotions more complex. Because goal orientation is an important quality of emotion prototypes, it provides a significant function within the prototypical cuing of emotions in film.

Just as the density of emotional information may vary across a film, so may the level of goal orientation vary throughout a film. *Local Hero* openly lays out a clear narrative goal for its protagonist: purchase a Scottish town to prepare the way for the construction of an oil refinery. McIntyre (Peter Riegert) is designated to bring about the deal, and in the initial stages of the film he pursues that goal in a businesslike fashion. The middle portions of *Local Hero* do not share this strict pursuit of the overt narrative goal, however, making the viewer more dependent on subtler emotion cues, not goal-oriented emotion prototypes. Later the film returns to its earlier strong goal orientation.

In the terms outlined here, *Local Hero* is a less densely informative emotional film with varying degrees of goal orientation. It is a film with relatively few clear generic expectations (perhaps films about quaint magical communities or films about technology encroaching on old value systems are the principal intertextual points of comparison). As such, the film was referred to as a "mood film" or a "slight" or "subtle" film by reviewers.[4] The textual classifications outlined here helps us better specify how such a "mood film" is constructed.

As mentioned earlier, *Local Hero* begins with a clear narrative goal orientation for its characters, communicated through a fairly standard series of scenes. In a board meeting we are given an expository summary of the importance of the refinery and this particular Scottish site. We see McIntyre in his office preparing to leave for Scotland, letting us know through dialogue that he's not particularly excited about his assignment to this job. These scenes are standard instances of character and situation exposition, but each has a slight twist foregrounded in the mise-en-scène. The board meeting is conducted entirely in a whisper, so that Happer (Burt Lancaster) is not awakened. McIntyre discusses his assignment with officemates only a few feet away, but he uses the telephone to communicate. In each situation the actual narrative information is almost overshadowed by an unexpected element emphasized in the mise-en-scène (the sleeping Happer, the telephones and glass walls). *Local Hero* presents straightforward narrative exposition while upstaging this information with comic cues, creating a goal-oriented framework while simultaneously signaling the appropriateness of the comic mood.

McIntyre arrives in Scotland and initiates negotiations with a solicitor to buy the entire village. The solicitor says he will handle the situation and suggests that McIntyre spend some time getting to know the area while the solicitor negotiates. At this point, McIntyre's pursuit of an overt goal grinds to a halt because there are no obstacles. The townspeople are delighted to sell the land, and Knox Oil and Gas is delighted to pay for it. The solicitor stalls so as not to appear too eager, but we are shown that there are no known forces opposing the achievement of the goal. At this point, *Local Hero* becomes a significantly less goal-oriented text.

What we are left with is a series of comic cues and markers. McIntyre and his assistant eat a meal, squirting juice into their eyes as they dine. A loud motorcycle whizzes by, nearly hitting McIntyre and the assistant. We hear overhead the solicitor and his wife giggling during sex play. The early goal-oriented scenes prepared us to expect such comic cues, and when the primary goal pursuit vanishes, this comic mood must be supported by a continuing stream of emotion cues and occasional emotion markers (like the loud motorcycle zooming past). These cues are usually not highly redundant or marked, but in the absence of the clear initial goal they serve as the primary emotional elicitors in this sparsely informative emotional text.

Local Hero does not lose all goal orientation when McIntyre reaches the village, however. Instead, it replaces McIntyre's initial goal (to buy the village) with a much less concrete goal, a more internalized goal that the protagonist doesn't even know he wants, a goal that can be pursued in small increments through this series of sparsely informative cues. The goal during most of the Scottish portion of the film is for yuppie careerist McIntyre to change into a gentler, more easygoing fellow who learns to fit in with the town's slower rhythm. McIntyre's dress becomes progressively more casual; he loses his watch in the ocean; he learns to pause before leaving the hotel to avoid being run over by the motorcyclist. We learn slowly about McIntyre's conversion through a series of accumulating details presented in brief vignettes.

The classical cinema is usually concerned with change in its protagonists. Along the way to achieving the overt narrative goal, classical protagonists must often undergo character change themselves. This internal change makes the achievement of the action-oriented goal possible. In this fashion, overt goal orientation and internal character change are usually linked. In Local Hero, however, character change and the overt narrative goal are separated. When the pursuit of the land deal comes to a halt, McIntyre begins his transformation into a less driven person. This transformation, once isolated from the clear initial narrative goal, becomes a goal in and of itself, but this goal is pursued intermittently in brief comic cues. Instead of character change being organized by the pursuit of an action-oriented narrative goal, Local Hero presents its hints about McIntyre's metamorphosis as part of a relatively unhierarchized series of comic moments. Vignettes giving us details about McIntyre are not marked more pronouncedly than other vignettes primarily concerned with the townspeople. The overt narrative goal established early in the film no longer lends its narrative force to organize the scenes in a strong linear progression toward the goal's achievement. Instead, the progression is intermittent rather than strongly goal centered, episodic rather than simply linear, sporadic rather than steady. This relatively weaker goal orientation during most of the Scottish portion of the film makes labeling filmic emotions less clear-cut.

The mood-cue approach would suggest that if a film does not take advantage of emotion prototypes associated with genre or goals, it must rely on nonprototypically organized emotion cuing. One solution might be to arrange a rapid series of smaller cues that sustain the mood. By shifting to a faster pace of cuing, the film may provide reinforcement for the mood orientation, even if there are few goal or genre expectations to guide our anticipation.

On first impression, *Local Hero* does not seem to be a particularly fast-paced text. On closer examination, one discovers that it presents a remarkably speedy series of emotion cues. These cues are brief (McIntyre's assistant practicing holding his breath underwater, snippets of conversation with bit players) and rarely redundant. These fragmentary cues fit the brevity of the audience's emotional experience and allow the filmmakers to string together a rapid-fire series of emotion cues. The fact that these cues are not highly marked or redundant helps us position *Local Hero* as a "subtle" film.

Local Hero uses music selectively to help convey its "subtle" quality. Highly foregrounded music (such as the music in *Raiders of the Lost Ark*) would too obviously telegraph its emotional appeal, so *Local Hero* almost entirely abandons music when McIntyre arrives in Scotland. Music is used only occasionally in the early Scottish portions of the film, and then it functions as a transition device when the film moves to a very different time and space. Because such music cues are so clearly motivated functionally, they are not foregrounded as highly visible (or rather, audible) emotion cues.

Music is next heard in the film as a clearly marked diegetic source while people dance. Only after the community dance scene does *Local Hero* use Mark Knopfler's highly foregrounded, nondiegetic music. Not coincidentally, the appearance of nondiegetic music occurs when *Local Hero*'s protagonist resumes his initial goal pursuit. Immediately after the community dance scene, the solicitor discovers that the beach is really owned by an old man who refuses to sell. This is the first obstacle to the initial goal's achievement, and we encounter it three-fourths of the way through the film. The final quarter of the film is goal-oriented and uses highly foregrounded nondiegetic music. *Local Hero*, which early on uses few redundant emotion cues, relies on more and more redundancy later in the film.

This progression allows us to label *Local Hero*'s emotional appeal as "subtle" (unlike that of *Raiders*) and yet takes advantage of the emotional power provided by this later redundant cuing. Initially a film establishes not only an expectation for what kinds of emotion cues we will see and hear but also how quickly we can anticipate receiving those cues. The early lack of redundancy sets our expectation for relatively sparse emotion cuing, and the gradual progression toward more and more redundant emotion cues near the film's climax provides a significant emotional payoff.

This exercise in analyzing a subtle "mood film" emphasizes the fact that such textual qualities as density of emotional information and level of goal orientation are comparative terms. We can only say that one text is more densely emotionally informative than another. We cannot point to these qualities in the texts without using intertextual comparisons. For example, *Raiders of the Lost Ark*, a much more densely informative emotional text than *Local Hero*, uses a similar progression of gradually more foregrounded music to that of Knopfler. After the initial whiz-bang find-the-treasure-and-escape scenes, *Raiders* becomes relatively silent musically, using music only as a transition device. The next action sequence, the Nepalese barroom brawl, is done without music at all. When Indiana and Marian enter the marketplace, we hear exoticized Eastern music motivated by the diegesis. Only after this diegetic music does *Raiders* return to a relatively dense use of musical cues.

This pattern of no music–music as transition–diegetic music–nondiegetic music is the same as Knopfler uses in *Local Hero* to make "subtle" emotional statements. Very different kinds of texts, then, can use similar patternings of emotion cues. John Williams's score for *Raiders* has a subtle progression of its own, but his foregrounded redundant cues (e.g., stingers introducing Nazis) help make the film a more emotionally informative text.

Stranger than Raiders

Audiences can perceive differences between more and less emotionally informative texts, although they may not be consciously aware of how the text's emotion cues are structured. This perceived difference can form a basis for audience tastes, with some viewers preferring highly informative texts that clearly dictate a text's emotional appeal and others favoring less densely informative texts that seem less emotionally prescriptive. Although the density of emotional information varies across a text, texts usually establish fairly stable sets of expectations concerning the level (and types) of emotion cuing a film will provide. We label a less emotionally informative film like *Local Hero* as a "modest" or "slight" film, and we tend to retain that label even when the last quarter of the film becomes significantly more densely informative.

Certain audiences seek slighter, less overtly prescriptive texts, texts with subtle appeals that seem to call upon the interpretive skills of discriminating, actively engaged audiences. To appeal to those audiences, a text must establish a sparsely informative framework. Jim Jarmusch has a vested interest in audiences' labeling *Stranger than Paradise* as a "hip," "alternative" text that does not strongly try to dictate audience emotional response in the way that *Raiders* does. Once this emotional framework is established and we have labeled the film as making some sort of "minimalist" appeal, *Stranger than Paradise* is free to provide more densely informative cues at crucial narrative moments, as Hollywood cinema typically does.

The point here is not to elide the considerable differences between *Raiders of the Lost Ark* and *Stranger than Paradise*. Both texts prescribe emotional responses to their audience, but it is not the case that *Stranger than Paradise* uses entirely different tactics than *Raiders*, thus requiring a different approach to analyzing their emotional appeals. The point is to show that even a sparse work like Jarmusch's can be productively analyzed using the terminology developed here, revealing how its minimalist emotional appeal is structured.

Stranger than Paradise restricts itself to few of cinema's expressive properties. The film eschews most of editing's potential by always using a single uninterrupted shot for each scene of continuous space and time. Scenes are shot from a single camera setup; the camera only occasionally moves to reframe moving characters. This strategy restricts the range of angle, shot scale, and compositions available. Characters are seen mostly in medium-long to long shots, providing little detailed information on facial expressions. Eva's (Eszter Balint) hair and Willie's (John Lurie) and Eddie's (Richard Edson) ever-present hats frequently hide portions of their faces, particularly because many of the interior group scenes are shot from a slight high angle. In fact, many scenes are shot with the protagonists facing away from the camera so we cannot receive any facial information whatsoever. The black-and-white lighting is flat with almost no sculpted effects to convey no more specific emotional states than a rather diffuse and bleak mood. The interior locations have almost no decorations (unlike the more detailed art direction of modern Hollywood), providing virtually a tabula rasa against which the actors are positioned. The film uses only occasional bits of diegetic and nondiegetic music, and there are often long pauses between lines, giving the film a sense of being starkly muted.

Neither does the film provide us with clear character goals that would help us label the characters' emotions. The characters are idlers, drifters whose primary goals are geographical: getting to Cleveland or Florida. When they actually arrive at a destination (Cleveland, for example), they do little but sit around watching television and playing cards. In the film's first act ("The New World"), there is not even a progression toward a geographical goal. Instead the first act is concerned with waiting, as Eva must spend ten days in Willie's apartment. *Stranger than Paradise* hints at some personal goals (perhaps Eddie or Willie is enamored of Eva), but they are never directly addressed. Primarily the characters' actions seem motivated by boredom more than the pursuit of any goal.

Nor are there strong genre cues to guide our interpretation. At times *Stranger than Paradise* seems like a road film (except for those lengthy sections when the characters are going nowhere at all). At other times it is reminiscent of absurdist comedy. The film defies traditional genre categorization and therefore does not take advantage of the set of emotional expectations that genre prototypes bring.

As the mood-cue approach suggests, it is the set of genre microscripts we carry that are most useful in reading a text's emotion cues, not the broad scripts we have for a genre text's overall construction. These microscripts can be invoked quickly and simply, often with a line or two of dialogue. In this way, *Stranger than Paradise* can elicit emotional responses without depending on more obvious strategies such as a recognizable genre form, maintaining its strong differentiation from Hollywood product while taking advantage of the small narrative scripts we have accumulated through countless encounters with Hollywood products.

For example, when Eva leaves for Cleveland after a stormy ten days with Willie, their farewell moments are shaped by our labeling the scenes as a wistful good-bye between people who care (romantically?) about each other. We have seen them arguing over trivia in several preceding scenes, and our experiences with countless romantic comedies show us that argumentative banter can be read as an expression of romantic interest. On the other hand, perhaps they are truly arguing with each other. The text nudges us toward the former interpretation when Willie gives Eva a dress (which she promptly pronounces to be ugly). The mise-en-scène privileges Willie's face as he watches her pack, encouraging us to watch him for further hints of his sadness at her leaving.

Given this preparation, we are encouraged to interpret their halting good-bye in terms of a genre microscript: a couple parting without ever acknowledging their feelings for each other. The farewell is sad, wistful, and poignant, almost signaling pathos (at least in relation to the minimal emotional expectations that have been established). The moment is sad largely because of the genre microscript that has been evoked, as opposed to having densely informative emotion cuing at that moment, which would be too blatant in comparison with the film's sparse framework.

When Eddie says that he has a good feeling about going to the dog track and betting money, this invokes a standard Hollywood genre microscript. If film characters say they feel lucky when they go to gamble, this sets up a time-honored expectation (particularly in comedy) that they will lose their shirts (which Eddie of course does). We anticipate the comic payoff when Willie and Eddie return from the track having lost almost all the money. Such moments create brief narrative hypotheses that can be quickly and comically confirmed.

Stranger than Paradise seems to be a more "open" text (in Eco's[5] terms), calling upon active contributions from the reader or viewer to fill in the narrative hinted at by the "subtle" text. Such texts do not seem to prescribe reader or viewer responses in the way that "closed" texts like *Raiders of the Lost Ark* do. Instead, they feel as if more of the work is done by the reader or viewer, not by the text leading its reader or viewer by the nose. All films, however, call upon readers to make interpretive contributions based on their previous encounters with movies. The differences between the use of genre scripts by *Raiders* and *Stranger than Paradise* are primarily ones of scale and frequency, not a radical disjunction between the mechanisms of "open" and "closed" texts.[6] *Raiders of the Lost Ark* uses both large genre prototypes (the adventure serial) and genre microscripts to signal its appeal. *Stranger than Paradise* almost exclusively uses smaller-scale narrative scripts to guide our emotional hypothesis formation.

Many of *Stranger than Paradise*'s comic effects depend not only on our expectations of what certain kinds of texts or characters will do in particular narrative situations, but also on our understanding of what Hollywood narratives agree to show and not show us. Some of the laughs are evoked rather traditionally through character banter (e.g., arguing over football or TV dinners), but other laughs occur as we cut away from a scene, long after dialogue has stopped. In these cases the joke is often a joke at the expense of traditional Hollywood narration.

Classical Hollywood cinema elides moments in which there is no dramatic action, and traditional Hollywood practice tends to cut away from scenes while dramatic tension is still present, not after it has dissipated. *Stranger than Paradise*, on the other hand, sometimes cuts after long pauses that are narratively extraneous. It shows us scenes with no apparent impact on the plot's unfolding, mundane scenes that would probably be elided in the classical cinema (e.g., dully watching television). The humor comes from our surprise at the filmmaker including such scenes or such pauses at all. Some audiences find this "joke" more frustrating than amusing, but both audiences recognize the violation of our assumptions concerning what a film will and will not show us.[7] The emotion (anger or humor) depends on our overall prototype of how film narration presents a story.

Once our expectations are established, Jarmusch can vary slightly from these emotion cuing norms, creating emotional peaks in relation to its minimalist standards. Once we have learned not to expect dense emotion cuing, an increase in the cuing density marks that moment as a relative high point, even though such moments are themselves far less densely informative than much of *Raiders of the Lost Ark*.

For example, the nondiegetic solo string leitmotif that we hear at irregular intervals becomes much more frequent around Eva and Willie's farewell. The early occurrences of this leitmotif alert us that this text, from time to time, will use a brief repeated nondiegetic music cue to bridge the gap between scenes. In the first act this cue is heard infrequently, just often enough so that its appearance will not be totally surprising to the audience. So when we hear this leitmotif at the end of the scene in which Eva spurns Willie's gift, we are prepared for the occurrence of such cuing. Then we hear the same music cue again at the end of the next scene (Eva packing for Cleveland). Never before has the text used the music cue in consecutive scenes. Next comes the farewell scene (without music), followed by a scene in which Eva removes the dress Willie gave her, a scene once again marked by the string solo. Within the miminalist context of the film, this is rather rapid cuing in addition to the emotional appeal of the farewell genre microscript (noted earlier). These factors mark the farewell section as a peak emotional moment in the film, a moment that verges on (relative) pathos.

Note, however, that we do not hear the repeated music cue in the farewell scene itself. Having too many cues coincide (genre microscripts and music) might threaten to make this scene too markedly different from the modest emotional appeal already established. The coincidence of a sad music motif with a traditionally sad narrative incident might too overtly convey the emotion cuing, making the viewer conscious of the "heavy-handedness." So Jarmusch chooses not to use the music cue at the dramatic moment's peak, and instead uses it before and after the peak to mark the incident's significance more subtly. In this way *Stranger than Paradise* preserves its carefully constructed framework of minimal emotions while subtly calling for stronger emotions for an individual moment.

Again and again in this study, we will return to the way music functions at the microlevel of style to associate one scene with another. As I argued with genre microscripts, the importance of music in the mood-cue approach seems to be in its function as a local structure. Because emotions are brief, the brevity of music cues help make them an ideal way of appealing to the emotion system at particular moments.

Stranger than Paradise finds other ways to communicate its emotion cues without their being called to our attention. This film makes many obvious choices to limit the cinema's emotional expressiveness (single camera se-tups, long shots, long takes, etc.). However, the film uses rather dense cuing in an expressive register that is not usually privileged in our spectatorial consciousness: sound effects. The filmmakers choose to mike the diegetic sounds very closely instead of matching the sound perspective to the dis-tanced visual perspective. We hear the crisp sounds of cigarette packs being unwrapped, the sounds of chairs scraping the floor, and so on. Because the scenes frequently feature long pauses in the dialogue, such proximate sound effects become more pronounced, more important.

This sound proximity gives the diegesis a quality of "nearness" that balances the visual distanciation strategies. Consider how remote the ap-peal of the diegesis would seem if Jarmusch chose to duplicate the visual distanciation techniques in the audio register. The resulting film would be even more detached. Choosing to remain visually distant from but aurally close to the characters takes advantage of the fact that we generally consider the visual to be dominant in the cinema, and therefore visual strategies tend to be more easily noticeable, particularly to the cinema aesthete. We are trained as spectators to pay relatively less conscious attention to the audio track (other than dialogue and highly foregrounded music such as Screaming Jay Hawkins's "I Put a Spell on You"), so Jarmusch can use denser cuing in his sound effects track with little risk of disturbing the film's consciously minimalist framework.

The film also becomes significantly more goal oriented in its third act after having previously established itself as a static or (at best) a broadly wandering narrative. In the act titled "Paradise" Willie, Eddie, and Eva travel to Florida to try to win a lot of money gambling. For the first time in the film, the characters actually go somewhere and *do* something when they get there, allowing us to label their emotional states more precisely. We understand their excitement when they reach Florida, and we fathom Eva's and Willie's anger when Eddie loses the money at the dog track. In this act *Stranger than Paradise* operates much more like classical narrative cinema (within the formally restrictive parameters of its mise-en-scène) with comic twists on losing the money, gaining it back, and losing it again. Here the film's plot owes much to the tradition of cinematic comedies about gambling (ranging from *Guys and Dolls* to *Lost in America*).

This increased goal orientation gives the final act a more straightforward emotional appeal, encouraging the viewer to respond more strongly at the film's climax. If the film had revealed this kind of character goal orientation at its outset, we would be encouraged to label the film as a much more traditional narrative structure with some visual quirks. Instead Jarmusch begins with the least goal-oriented act, calling on the viewer to create more modest emotion cuing expectations, which are exceeded in the comic "big finish."

In this way *Stranger than Paradise* resembles *Local Hero*, another film that works hard to establish its subtle emotional framework, only to turn to a more goal-oriented narrative in its final sections. This allows such films to provide their audiences with emotionally satisfying payoffs without seeming too coarsely or overtly prescriptive. Having labeled the films as sparsely informative, we are asked to read the films' climaxes as more emotionally marked. As long as the films do not continue too long in this more densely informative mode, we tend not to revise our framework, and so we leave the theater after a highly marked emotional moment while still maintaining our conception of the film as a subtle work.

This short study of *Stranger than Paradise* points out the difficulties of labeling such a film in terms of the overall interpretive framework called for in the film itself. If we simply consider *Stranger than Paradise* to be a minimalist film (or an "open" text), we can overlook the considerable variation in type and density of cuing that occurs over the course of the film. Instead I argue that we should examine how the film works to create its emotional appeal moment by moment. Using the structural vocabulary developed in this chapter in such specific and limited instances, we can see how a film asks a viewer to respond emotionally, and we can examine how cinematic emotional appeals are both related and relatively different.

I began this chapter with an admission of how the flexibility of the emotion system would seem to make it difficult to evoke emotion consistently across audiences. Given this system, it seems easy to explain the fact that emotions can vary widely among individual viewers, which was part of our desiderata. This chapter provides an explanation for the contrasting part of that desideratum: the fact that a film can provoke remarkably similar responses across audiences. Films rely on broadly held prototypes of emotion and widely shared genre microscripts to invite consistent responses. But these tools are not enough. According to the mood-cue approach, films also coordinate nonprototypical emotion cues into structures (such as the emotion marker) that can dependably evoke emotion in audiences.

This chapter addresses other of our desiderata. The flexibility and variety of inputs to the emotion system encourage us to look at a broad range of film cuing, which is one of the desiderata. The brevity of emotions emphasizes the need for brief local structures (for instance, genre microscripts and musical motifs) to signal those emotional moments. The need for redundant cuing to sustain a mood leads us to examine the many ways films structure their cues into clusters to appeal to the emotion system, including new concepts such as emotion markers and densely informative emotion cuing.

The mini case studies in this chapter are intended as an initial demonstration of how the mood-cue approach can satisfy our desiderata. For more comprehensive demonstrations, I refer the reader to Part Two of this book (Chapters 5–9), which addresses specific desiderata using full-length case studies.

4 Other Cognitivisms

The mood-cue approach is not the first attempt to explain filmic emotion from a cognitivist perspective. This chapter situates my work in relation to my predecessors: Noël Carroll, Ed Tan, and Torben Grodal. Carroll, Tan, Grodal, and I inherit the strengths and weaknesses of our respective disciplines, which shape our understandings of emotion. Cognitivism is an interdisciplinary approach that has taken root most firmly in two disciplines: philosophy and psychology. It is by no means a monolithic enterprise. Although cognitive philosophers and cognitive psychologists share certain key assumptions, they explore the nature of cognition and emotion using the different methodologies that they have inherited from their disciplines. Cognitive film scholars, while sampling ideas across disciplines, also rely primarily on either the philosophy or the psychology of emotions.

In this chapter, I articulate primary assumptions that Carroll, Tan, and Grodal make concerning filmic emotions. I share a great deal with these fellow cognitivists, but in this chapter I concentrate on the differences between their approaches and my own. I argue that one primary advantage of the mood-cue approach is that it does not rely on person- or character-centered concepts (such as identification or allegiance) as being crucial to filmic emotional response. Although the other cognitive approaches certainly acknowledge the possibility for stylistic emotion cuing, they give it a subordinate role to the dominant schemas of motive, action, and goals.

Noël Carroll: The Philosophy of Objects

The foremost figure in the philosophy of filmic emotions is Noël Carroll. He has applied insights from cognitive philosophy to a broad range of film topics, including point of view, the power of movies, music, suspense, humor, and horror (the topic he has examined most closely). Although Carroll clearly is proceeding in a "piecemeal" fashion that eschews grand overarching theories explaining everything about film,[1] he returns again and again to central questions of how films evoke emotions across broad audiences.

Much of this effort has been centered on Hollywood genres. Because genres such as suspense and horror are defined in terms of the emotional appeals they make, Carroll has concentrated on how these genres are constructed. In *The Philosophy of Horror*,[2] his largest work on genre, Carroll says that narrative horror forms depend on the presence of the monster in the diegesis. The monster blurs the distinctions between social categories: between human and insect in *The Fly*, between living and dead in zombie films. The monster evokes a mixture of fear and disgust at its unknowable and incredible concept-blurring formal properties. Our desire to know the unknown and the unbelievable makes us willing to endure the disgust the monster evokes. *The Philosophy of Horror* not only provides a definition of a film genre but also discusses the nature of this genre's emotional appeal.

Carroll and I agree that "prototypical emotions" have objects. That is, they are directed toward something in the external world. Carroll's approach and my own differ in what we make of the prototypical concept of emotional objects. The mood-cue approach says that non-object-oriented emotional states exist and that they are nonprototypical emotional states. For Carroll, however, a state that is not directed toward an object is not only nonprototypical but also is not an emotion, and this distinction is crucial. By definition Carroll says that such "sheer bodily states" cannot be emotions; they must necessarily involve a cognition of some object: "You can't be angry, unless there is someone or something that serves as the object of your anger."[3] Carroll tends to think of nonprototypical emotional states as localized phenomena with little long-term ramification on our emotion system. For instance, he admits that "[u]ndeniably, there are some occasions where a loud noise, say a firecracker, makes us frightened and where upon reflection we say 'I guess that really frightened me.' But this is not paradigmatic of garden variety emotional states."[4] Although acknowledging the contributions of such factors, he also minimizes them in relation to more prototypical emotion states.

Whether one considers non-object-oriented states to be "sheer bodily states" and therefore not "emotion proper" or whether one considers them to be "nonprototypical emotion states" is a matter of definition. Definitions cannot be proved or disproved, but they can be compared in terms of rightness of fit. I believe that it makes more sense to include non-object-oriented emotional states in the category "emotion" because both non-object-oriented and object-oriented data are processed by the amygdala, the emotion center of the brain. This encourages me to consider them both to be emotional states and not entirely separate phenomena.

The distinction between Carroll's and my definitions comes from the faith we have in different kinds of evidence. Instead of empirical experiments, a philosopher like Carroll is prone to use "thought experiments." For example, in one of his discussions Carroll engages in a bit of what he calls "science fiction," imagining a drug that can simulate the physiological effects of an emotional state. What might the experience of this drug be like, Carroll ponders, given that someone who took it would have no object for an emotion and no cognitions related to emotion? For the philosopher, this "experiment" is a mental exercise that can lead the reader to thinking more clearly about the nature of emotions. I base my definition on continuities discovered through psychological and neurological research. Carroll relies on the philosophical tradition of the thought experiment to test his definitional distinctions.[5]

Choosing one definition over another has consequences for conceptualizing emotions. Bracketing off non-object-oriented states as being not "emotions proper" allows Carroll to reduce his attentions primarily to what he considers to be the most important component: cognition. If emotions differ from each other primarily through their cognitive components, then a critic wishing to explain distinctions among emotions can deal primarily with cognitions about the emotional object. If emotions by definition require an object, then one can concentrate on that object and how it is perceived.

Horror, then, is a matter of determining that an object is "monstrous," that is, it violates our conceptual categories. This experience triggers certain physical responses, certainly, but the key to understanding horror is to understand our cognitions about the emotion-causing object: the monster. "Sheer bodily states" are an important part of emotional experience, but they are not causally significant. According to Carroll, "[e]motions require cognitions as causes and bodily states as effects."[6] Such a belief further orients the philosopher Carroll toward our cognitions of the diegetic object that cues emotion.

This necessarily leads Carroll to an emphasis on the diegesis, particularly on dramatic characters and their characteristics. He defines horror not in terms of the text's narrational strategies but according to the characteristics of a diegetic entity: the monster. Nonmonstrous characters are also crucial to horror. They model how we should respond to the monster, encouraging us also to be terrified and disgusted. Similarly, he defines suspense in terms of characters and our allegiances with them. Suspense depends on the probability of a negative action happening to a character we favor. Without this assumption of allegiances with characters, his concept of suspense loses its primary explanatory value. Suspense and horror depend on our formal appraisals of and emotional alliances with diegetic characters.

Carroll carefully distances his theory from the concept of identification. According to him, we do not necessarily have to "identify" with the protagonist in any strong sense to experience emotion at the cinema. Just because we and the protagonist are screaming at the same monster does not mean that we are identifying with the protagonist. We can both evaluate the villain as "monstrous" and experience parallel emotions. Although Carroll does not embrace the notion of identification,[7] his system still remains quite character centered, depending on our alliances with protagonists and on the protagonists' reactions to guide our own responses.

Because Carroll emphasizes emotional objects, he does not pay enough attention to the contributions of non-object-oriented cues. Thus, he tends to reduce the key factors in horror or suspense to character actions, goals, motivations, and characteristics. Although Carroll acknowledges that such subtler non-object-oriented cuing is possible, his basic definition of what constitutes an emotion proper leads him away from such matters.[8] What counts most, according to Carroll, is evaluating the emotional object using formal criteria.

However, it is not consistently clear where these "formal criteria" reside. Are these criteria, for Carroll, located within viewers, or are they criteria for critics to use to classify films? At times Carroll refers to the criteria that viewers use to make sense out of the film and to experience emotion in response to the film. Horror viewers respond with fear and disgust because they recognize the monster's category violations. At other times, however, Carroll's use of formal criteria slides into genre criticism, in which he uses these criteria to define a genre corpus. The monstrous becomes the defining characteristic of art-horror, and so Carroll the genre critic can construct a body of films that fit that criterion. He compares films to that standard and determines if they fall within the category he has just defined. Therefore, *The Blob*'s indeterminate monster makes it a horror film, but *Psycho*'s psychologically determined villain is not a monster, excluding *Psycho* from the horror film.

The fact that Carroll can excise what many people consider to be a pivotal horror film recognizes that Carroll's formal criteria act primarily as genre constructs, not descriptions of viewer processes. The two are not unrelated, of course,[9] but the critic's process of creating an internally consistent genre corpus and the viewer's process of labeling emotion cues are very different. Carroll desires to create a category with clear rules for including and excluding films from the horror genre, a perfectly appropriate activity for a genre critic. Viewers proceed using fuzzier logic. Based on the cues they perceive, viewers make a rough fit between the film they are watching and their own formal criteria for a horror film. Many viewers classify *Psycho* as a horror film because it matches much of their prototype for what a horror film is. They do not make the same careful logical comparison to the monstrous that Carroll does.

Carroll acknowledges that there are many features that lead viewers to classify *Psycho* as a horror film. He mentions the imagery of the dark house and the skeleton, the shock tactics (particularly sudden movements and Bernard Herrmann's score), and the narrative buildup to a final appearance of the creature. For Carroll, however, the primary question about *Psycho* is whether Norman Bates is a monster. Carroll argues that Bates cannot be a monster because Bates has schizophrenia, a personality aberration that is accepted within the categorizing scheme of modern scientific psychology. The concept of a person with schizophrenia does not destabilize our categories in the way that a vampire's combination of dead and undead does. Carroll's horror classification does not on the viewer's process of identifying horror characteristics in the narration, soundtrack, and visual style of the film, but these are just the factors that would be crucial to the mood-cue approach to reading *Psycho* (along with Bates's characteristics). An important advantage of the mood-cue approach over Carroll's is that it can provide explanations of filmic emotion without relying solely on character-oriented cues.

As genre criticism, Carroll's work on horror is admirable (one has to admire the chutzpah of anyone who argues that *Psycho* is not a horror film). As a description of the overall shape of viewer processes, it has much to commend it. Viewers do make "formal" comparisons based on their generic prototypes. However, the messier process of comparing films to prototypes has little to do with the careful logical consideration that Carroll demonstrates.

The cognitive philosophy of filmic emotions can be the source of striking insights. (For example, Carroll's work gives a sharp picture of what the prototype for "horror" or "suspense" might look like.) However, I believe that the nonempirical nature of the philosopher's investigations makes it difficult for the philosophy of emotions to consider the possibility of non-prototypical emotions. If investigators are limited to thought experiments about emotion, they tend to explore commonly held understandings (prototypes) of emotion rather than actual emotional data. This is not to say that philosophical methodologies cannot produce original reconceptions. Instead, I argue that the primary value of the philosophy of the emotions (and it is a considerable one) to the mood-cue approach is to articulate further the prototypes of emotion.

Ed Tan: The Psychology of Interest and Action

The mood-cue approach places most of its faith in the work done in the other cognitivist camp: cognitive psychology. Ed Tan in *Emotion and the Structure of Narrative Film: Film as an Emotion Machine*[10] shares my faith in the empirical work of cognitive psychologists. Instead of attempting to synthesize a range of psychological research into emotion, however, he chooses the work of a single psychologist (Nico Frijda) as the basis of his account of filmic emotions. One can hardly fault Tan for his choice of theorists. Frijda's work synthesizes much other emotion research and is comprehensive enough to cover a wide range of emotional experience. His theories generate "laws" of how emotions work, which can be usefully used to produce specific hypotheses. Frijda takes a more "humanistic" approach to the psychology of emotion, emphasizing larger cognitive structures and processes over the minute workings of subprocesses, making his work more straightforwardly applicable to the humanities. The danger of relying so heavily on one theorist, even one as integrative as Frijda's, is that one can leave out significant factors that are better dealt with by other researchers.

Tan asserts that the central emotional mechanism in film viewing is "interest." Interest induces us to investigate the film and discover more about the diegetic world it presents. It encourages us to anticipate possible future events in the narrative, which engages us more strongly in the story. Interest fluctuates over the course of a film; it is a temporal phenomenon. A canonical narrative film promises to reward our interest with narrative payoffs, such as the resolution of open plot questions. For Tan, interest guides both our cognitive and emotion processing of narrative information.

Although Tan's system emphasizes the importance of interest, my system emphasizes mood. At first glance, these concepts seem to be similar. Both mood and interest provide an overall emotional orientation toward the text and encourage the viewer to peruse the text and search for further emotion cues. Both mood and interest are structures that provide unity for the emotional experience. In fact, Tan even points out that mood in film helps produce this unity of emotional response.[11] But for Tan mood is a mere by-product of the more central process of interest. To understand the distinction, we need to examine Tan's definition of the emotions.

Tan follows Frijda in asserting that emotions are action tendencies, and so for Tan, interest encourages us to perform certain actions: it leads us to examine the text closely and to anticipate what will happen next. In the movie theater, we engage in the actions that are appropriate to interest; we do not act in ways inspired by the emotions we feel concerning characters. Pity or anger at characters only create virtual action tendencies. We do not attempt physical harm on film characters when they make us angry, and so these emotions are not given full expression. But we do fully engage in the actions called for by the emotion of interest.[12] We do investigate the film and scrutinize it for further emotional data. If action tendencies are crucial to the definition of emotion (as they are for Tan and Frijda), then actual action tendencies (such as those caused by interest in the film) are more important than virtual ones. This is why Tan emphasizes interest as the primary filmic emotion.

This distinction between Tan's understanding of emotion and my own is crucial. Because emotions for Tan are necessarily action tendencies, he can confine his analysis to those filmic elements that best fit this conception: characters and narratively significant actions.

According to Tan, the two elements that largely determine the way a particular film shapes our interest are action or plot structures (which he calls thematic structures) and character structures (including empathy, sympathy, admiration, and compassion). "Themes" are scenarios that guide our expectations concerning character actions, motivations, and possible narrative outcomes. Common themes include betrayal, self-sacrifice, and deceit. *Psycho*'s shower scene, for instance, activates the theme of "punishment"[13] by doing violence to an embezzler on the run from the law. A "retaliation" thematic structure would involve a malicious act that causes a loss, prompting a character to retaliate by committing a vicious act in return. The script for such themes is composed of smaller plot units, which are the major plot landmarks, such as successes, losses, and malicious acts.

Tan's detailed analysis of the structure of plot episodes allows him to model how viewers take in narrative information one piece at a time and assemble this into cohesive emotional scenarios. For instance, in the Danish short feature *Straf* (*Punishment*), we see a girl maliciously destroy her father's beloved violin, and then the father discovers the wreckage. These plot events summon the retaliation scenario, which then leads us to expect that the father will punish the girl. Tan breaks down the short film *Straf* into elementary events that are the components of the plot. Events include "Marjan goes into her father's room and destroys his violin," "Marjan and Robbie sit down to play the piano," and "Marjan waits in suspense in the kitchen." Tan tested subjects who had seen the film to determine that the "retaliation" theme was conveyed to the audience. Guided by their feedback concerning which scenes were most salient, Tan plotted the course of rising and falling interest over the course of the film. In this way, Tan was able to differentiate between scenes that contributed to interest in the film's "foreground" (the story of retaliation between Marjan and her father) and those that primarily contributed to the "background." Tan parses through films, tracing the ebb and flow of viewer interest based on the diegetic events in the films, noticing how certain plot events raise and confirm viewer hypotheses about what will happen next.

Although Tan notes the possibility of nonempathetic emotions, his account of the viewer's emotional experience centers on our empathy with the characters. Differences in our understandings of characters become key for Tan because they yield differences in our emotional responses. For example, empathy toward a weak character creates compassion; empathy toward a strong character creates admiration. Depending on whether we consider Lila or Marion or Norman to be strong or weak has significant bearing on the quality of our empathy with them and the emotional experiences we have in watching *Psycho*.

If Tan were to apply his system to *Psycho*, he would examine the film using a very different approach from Carroll's. He would organize the film into "themes" that provide a cohesive structure for interpreting character actions as emotion episodes. He would pay attention to how our changing knowledge about characters' motivations affects our allegiances with them and our interpretations of their actions. Much of *Psycho* revolves around a central theme of fear of discovery. Will Marion be caught for embezzlement, and will Norman's mother's crimes be discovered? What changes during the course of the film is which character is the potential discoverer and which character is on the verge of exposure. Tan would note that *Psycho*'s first order of business is to establish a sympathetic motivation for Marion's behavior. She needs the money so that she can marry Sam and become respectable. Establishing a relatively acceptable motivation for her embezzlement inflects our fears of her imminent capture; she has entered a life of crime for somewhat respectable reasons.

On the other hand, when the film organizes itself around the question of whether Norman and his mother will be captured and exposed, it denies us knowledge of a similarly benign motivation for their actions. Norman's mother (we are told) seems to kill Marion out of jealousy for her son's affections or out of an overprotective urge to keep him from loose women. Although the film pursues the same theme (fear of discovery), it does so from very different emotional perspectives.

Tan might also note how the information we have on the various investigators alters the emotional equation. When Arbogast investigates Marion's disappearance at the Bates Motel, his actions appear to be motivated by a desire for a paycheck. When Lila, Marion's sister, takes over the investigation, her more personal motivations lend a special urgency to the process of discovery. The narrative information we are made privvy to concerning the various characters' motivations changes our emotional alliances within the theme that remains primary throughout the film.

Tan's system yields hypotheses that are specific enough to be tested on actual viewers, and this is a significant achievement in understanding how the emotional appeals operate. Nonetheless, although his structural analysis gives us specific ways to talk about character goals, motivations, and plot events, it provides no guidance concerning how to talk about emotion cues that are not character oriented. In addition, "interest" may be a convincing explanation for the overall appeal of the cinema, but as an explanatory device for the emotional appeal of particular film texts, the central concept of interest does not encourage the critic to examine nonprototypical cues.

Relying on a single researcher's theories gives Tan's account of cinematic emotions more internal coherence than mine. Frijda is not overly concerned with the new research in the neuropsychology of emotions, and this allows him to provide an explanation that is highly systematic. For instance, Frijda (and Tan) assert the functionality of emotions, and this helps lend their account strong coherence; but this finding is not borne out in lower-level empirical research. When one examines the full range of recent psychological research on emotion, Frijda's explanation seems to be an articulation of emotion prototypes.

Frijda is the cognitive psychologist who has provided perhaps the most innovative articulation of higher-level emotion processes. He posits numerous "laws" that emotions have to follow, and these "laws" are extraordinarily useful in producing verifiable experimental hypotheses. But Frijda's explanation of emotions (although among the most comprehensive) has a "top-down" flavor that makes me uncomfortable. As cognitive psychology takes up the question of the emotions, an emphasis on the "bottom-up" microprocesses being examined by neuropsychology keeps us from relying too heavily on our own preconceived notions of what "laws" emotions should follow. My account of the emotion system is significantly "messier" than Tan's. Synthesizing a broader range of research forces me to use a complex model of emotional functioning (the associative network), but I believe that this produces a more subtle description of the emotion system.

Tan's methodology is strongest where mine is weakest. Because he is dealing with actual subjects, he can confidently label emotion states elicited by films because he has empirical data from real viewers. He need not wonder about whether a film's emotional appeal is primarily "fearsome" or "suspenseful" because he can easily ascertain which label his subjects use to describe the cinematic emotion. His approach goes further toward satisfying the desideratum concerning specific emotion terminology than my textually based approach possibly can. Tan's methodology is weakest where mine is strongest, however. His functionalist system remains tied to evaluating character-oriented behaviors (ascertaining character motivation, etc.), and it is less helpful in discussing the microprocesses of film narration. As Hollywood blockbusters continue to accentuate spectacular special effects and intricate soundtracks over nuanced characterization and classical well-made narrative organization, film criticism should not embrace an understanding of emotion that is rooted solely in character and plot.

Torben Grodal: The Psychology of Flow

The film scholar who has most recently proposed an explanation of filmic emotions based on cognitive psychology research is Torben Grodal. Grodal's book *Moving Pictures: A New Theory of Film Genres, Feelings, and Cognitions*[14] begins by investigating an enormous issue: the status of fictional representation itself. He provides a striking explanation for the philosophical conundrum of how we can respond emotionally to representations that are not "true" or "real" in a strict sense. Using cognitive research on brain architecture, Grodal argues that judging reality depends on the modularity of the mind, on the potential for parallel processing by separate function centers in the brain. He posits two systems: a more global system for evaluating the reality-status of phenomena and labeling them as "real" or "fictional," and a more local system for processing perceptions and activating responses. Mental representations of a fictional or a real object have the same "local reality" in the mind, but the global module that judges reality-status prevents us from mistaking the fictional for the real and also allows us to experience emotions evoked by the local simulations.[15]

Grodal provides a convincing model for the interrelationship between fiction, reality, and emotion, a broader issue than the ones explored in this book. Much more than Tan, he believes that the understanding of emotion used in film analysis should be congruent with current neuropsychological research into emotion. Grodal relies on studies of central and autonomic nervous system structure as key sources of insight into the emotion system structure. He emphasizes parallel processing and the interaction among separate mental modules as important principles for understanding emotional functioning.

In particular, Grodal asserts the importance of associations in the emotion system. For Grodal (and the mood-cue approach), words and images summon a host of sensations, ideas, motor simulations, and memories, opening up the possibility that film style can evoke emotion. Instead of simply "throwing away" stylistic information as we, the spectators, process a film's plot, these stylistic data remain in our enormous visual memory, where it can be worked on by the associative network. Based on a similar neurologically based conception of emotions, Grodal's system contains the seeds of a radical approach to analyzing film emotions – one that depends on stylistic cues of all kinds, not simply a person-oriented understanding of emotion.

Grodal does not create such a stylistically based approach, however. Because of certain other assumptions he makes, his system becomes very character oriented. Grodal turns away from the more radical potential of his emotion system because he believes in the primacy of identification.

Through the interaction of identification and empathy, the viewer "tries to construct the preferences, plans, and goals" of the character and "to assess the means and possibilities of implementing these plans and goals."[16] By simulating a character's state through identification, we activate cognitive scripts concerning the character's motivations toward goal achievement. If we then empathize with that character, this activates the emotional experiences that correspond to the cognitive script.

How these characters pursue their goals is crucial to Grodal's typology of emotional modes of experience, and this typology is a primary product of his system. If the narration focuses on a goal-driven character who has active control of the fictional world, then we experience a mode of affect that Grodal calls "tense." Blocking those goals leads to a modality he calls "saturation," in which tension accumulates because it cannot be transformed into an action or motor tendency. Such saturation can occur when we are identified with the passive protagonist of the melodrama who is paralyzed into inaction. The difference between active and passive protagonists is critical in Grodal's classification of our filmic emotions, because this distinction leads to active or passive emotional simulation among viewers. As characters find blockages in their diegetic paths, we viewers also experience blockages in what Grodal calls the "downstream" processing of narrational "flow."

The key to Grodal's system is this model of "flow." According to Grodal, narrational flow normally progresses in a "downstream" manner from simpler to more complex processes, beginning with the encounter with the images themselves. Patterns of color, contrast, intensity, and so forth can create simple emotional responses such as surprise. Abstract avant-garde films do not provide representations for the flow model to process, and so in these films the viewer's emotional experience is blocked from progressing to the next more complex level, leaving the viewer to respond purely to the image patterning. In more representational media, the viewer moves downstream to the next level of the flow model, in which the viewer is encouraged to work over the associative linkages with the images. A lyrical nonnarrative music video may remain at this level, but traditional narrative films ask us to attain the next level: appraising actions and organizing them into narrational schemes, such as characters, motivations, and goals. In conjunction with identification, these narrational patterns create larger emotional reactions. The downstream direction of this flow model pushes the viewer toward these larger emotional responses, unless this flow is interrupted by blockages.

These blockages are not limited to diegetic obstacles. For instance, if a film shifts into slow motion, this postpones goal achievement and shifts us toward a more affectively charged perception of the images' sensations, which Grodal calls "lyrical." Whenever goals are blocked for the character through diegetic or nondiegetic means, the viewer's emotional experience flows into a different modal quality.

Grodal's system depends on a metaphor of fluidity. Whenever the downstream flow of the emotion process is blocked, the flow shifts toward another mode of emotional experience. For instance, because *Double Indemnity* begins by showing us the protagonist near death, the normal forward-looking (telic) love-crime narration is blocked. We already know what the outcome of the events will be (in all likelihood), thus short-circuiting the goal-oriented emphasis of its canonical narration. According to Grodal's hydraulic system of flow, this blockage redirects our emotional experience "upstream" toward saturation and lyricism and away from tension and suspense. Grodal's classification of films and their resulting emotional experiences depends on various kinds of blockages to the normal downstream flow processing.

Grodal's use of the terms "flow" and "blockage" gets a bit slippery. By using identification as one of his foundational concepts, he makes it easier for him to elide the differences between blocking a character's goal in the diegesis and a block within the viewer's own emotion system. Because of identification, blocking a character's goal necessarily blocks the normal processing flow of emotions in the viewer. These two "blockages" (one in the diegesis, one in the viewer) are not equivalent, although sharing the same label helps them seem interchangeable.

In *Psycho*, for instance, Grodal would be interested in the shift in identificatory characters and the blockages that occur in accordance with these identifications. The film carefully positions us to empathize with Marion, and while her actions control the film (i.e, when she decides to steal the money), *Psycho* would be labeled "tense." Almost immediately fears of being caught enter Marion's mind, causing her to become less an active shaper of the story than a passive character dreading her imminent capture. Grodal would suggest that this would be a shift toward saturation mode, because the character's progress is being blocked. Then, surprisingly, our locus of identification is removed when Marion is killed. This is the most overwhelming of blockages; we can no longer identify with Marion as she lies cold on the bathroom floor. Grodal correctly notes that her death creates a "vacuum" in our identification, and there is only one person onstage to step into that vacuum: Norman Bates, a seemingly perverse choice for our empathy.[17] The viewer is encouraged to identify with Norman as he carefully cleans the bloody bathroom. His unrestricted effectivity in the world again returns us to a tense modality, but then the film returns to saturation as blockages begin to occur in Norman's life. As Arbogast, Sam, and Lila close in on Norman and his mother, Norman's actions become constricted and nervous. Soon the film presents more morally acceptable figures for our identification; first, the detective Arbogast, and when he is killed, Marion's sister Lila. As they begin to tighten the noose around Norman, we identify with these characters who gain active control of the fictional world. Grodal's system is as character oriented as Carroll's or Tan's. Of the three, however, his is the system most closely linked to identification.

The primary advantage of this system of flow and blockages is that it helps Grodal to produce an array of labels for various emotional experiences, providing the terminology called for in the desiderata. Blockages of different types create the need for labels for the resulting emotional experiences, and Grodal creates a dizzying array of terms, for example, telic and paratelic enaction, tensities, and proximal and distal foci of attention. He attempts to provide a terminological system broad enough to describe the full range of filmic emotional experiences. In some sense, he is trying to provide an emotional equivalent to Metz's *grand syntagmatique,* providing a comprehensive model of emotional response. He creates a top-down classificatory system and then proceeds to carve up the corpus of film into genres and modalities.

The advantage of this system over the mood-cue approach is that it provides a more comprehensive set of terms to describe filmic emotions, as opposed to the bottom-up approach that I advocate in this book. A bottom-up approach may provide a less comprehensive picture of filmic emotions, but it has the advantage of remaining close to the surface of particular films. As the mood-cue approach encounters more and more films, it adds terminology rooted in the specific structures of particular films. Grodal's system of classification is better suited to describing film categories than individual films.

Grodal's emphasis on identification leads him to neglect the possibilities of the associative network. The associative stage of his flow model is placed at a rather low level of processing, a level that in most mainstream film viewing is quickly superseded by larger identificatory processes. Blocking the downstream goal-oriented process (as in melodrama or lyricism) can occasionally cause us to revert back to an emphasis on associations, but once the blockage is removed, the downstream pull of the system moves us toward larger emotion processes. Although Grodal ostensibly shares my emphasis on the power of associations in the emotion system, his person-oriented understanding of filmic emotions shifts his true emphasis onto character-oriented film analysis.

Briefly considered, the mood-cue approach to *Psycho* would emphasize some of the same emotional factors that Grodal's, Tan's, and Carroll's systems do, but it would also foreground other crucial factors neglected by the others. Like Grodal's system, the mood-cue approach would be interested in explaining the switching of audience sympathies from Marion to Norman to

Arbogast to Lila, but the approach would explore both character traits and stylistic means of establishing these allegiances. In the first scene, Marion is given a somewhat acceptable motivation for her behavior that will help ease audiences into identifying with her. The same scene is characterized by fairly standard conversational editing, except for one notable long take in which the moving camera follows Marion down to the bed and then up again as she moves through the cheap hotel room. This viscerally involving camera movement following the character moving through space is an important stylistic marker of her centrality to the narrative.

This device is particularly important because it is rarely used in *Psycho* and marks each switch of identificatory character in the film. When the film switches its locus of identification to Bates, it does so (as Grodal argues) because there is no one else to identify with. It also marks the switch by an extraordinarily mundane sequence of action. After the shower scene, we see a drawn-out series of scenes of the details of Norman cleaning up the mess. He washes his hands, mops the tub inside and out, towels the walls and floor, repacks the car, opens the trunk, wraps the corpse in the shower curtain, and places it in the trunk. Following Bates as he moves through the hotel room marks him as the new locus of identification. Similarly, we follow Arbogast with a moving camera as he searches through the Bates Motel, and later we do the same for Lila as she snoops around the motel and the Bates home. The mood-cue approach suggests that early moments in a film alert us to crucial patterns in shaping our emotional response, and those patterns can be character oriented or stylistic (such as the moving-camera long take in the film's initial scene).

Like Tan, the mood-cue approach would be interested in explaining how emotion episodes are established, labeled, and sustained in *Psycho*. My approach would not place its sole emphasis on an understanding of character motivations and goals, although these are important. The mood-cue approach looks for a series of mood-congruent cues to establish and sustain a Hitchcockian level of suspense. The film's dialogue interrogations (both real and imagined) are just as crucial in cuing a "fear of exposure" reaction as are the characters' motivations and goals.

After Marion steals the money, the film encourages us to worry with her by giving us repeated access to her own paranoid thought processes. While driving, she imagines an involved series of conversations in which her office coworkers and family members discover that she has taken the money. We see her jumpy behavior as she is stopped by a policeman. He grills her, and we wince as she acts suspiciously nervous throughout this interrogation. We watch him shadow her, worried that her suspicious activities will result in her arrest. This repeated process of concentrated dialogue (imagined and real) uncovering the facts contributes to our fears for Marion as much as any other factor.

We see this same stylistic technique at work when Arbogast pumps Bates for information. We wince as Bates is caught again and again in self-contradictory answers and suspiciously nervous behaviors. He initially re-fuses to look at the picture of Marion; he then says he never saw her but later admits to seeing her; he says no one has been at the hotel for weeks but then blurts out that a couple was there last week; he says that he doesn't use the ho-tel register but Marion's handwriting has been recently entered. These inter-rogations are crucial for establishing and sustaining a tense fear that Norman will be found out. These repeated emotion cues are just as important in evok-ing emotion as the broader structures of character, motivation, and goals.

Any theorist inherits certain assumptions about emotions from the re-search, theories, and methodologies they favor. Carroll, Tan, and Grodal all chose concepts of emotion that are rooted in human agents, which preju-dices them toward character-oriented explanations of filmic emotions. But by paying as close attention to style as it does to character, the mood-cue ap-proach is much more capable of satisfying the desideratum for an approach that analyzes the full range of cinematic signification than Carroll's, Tan's, or Grodal's models.

PART TWO

ANALYZING EMOTIONAL APPEALS IN FILM

5 "Couldn't You Read between Those Pitiful Lines?"

Feeling for *Stella Dallas*

K ing Vidor's *Stella Dallas* (1937) provoked one of psychoanalytic feminist film criticism's most extensive dialogues. Considering how strong an emotional appeal this melodrama makes, it is remarkable that emotions are rarely mentioned in the two key articles in this exchange: E. Ann Kaplan's "The Case of the Missing Mother: Maternal Issues in Vidor's *Stella Dallas*" and Linda Williams's "'Something Else Besides a Mother:' *Stella Dallas* and the Maternal Melodrama."[1] Kaplan says little about emotion except that the "cinema spectator feels a certain sadness in Stella's position."[2] Situating her reading both in psychoanalytic theory and genre criticism, Williams merely notes *Stella Dallas*'s mixed emotional messages ("of joy in pain, of pleasure in sacrifice")[3] as characteristic of the maternal melodrama. Although psychoanalytic film theory is often considered to be an important way to describe filmic emotions, these psychoanalytic essays are more concerned with what position the spectator occupies than with the specific emotional appeals the film makes to her once she occupies that position.

This chapter applies my model of filmic emotions to *Stella Dallas* to demonstrate that the mood-cue approach can yield new insights about emotions in even the most closely examined texts in psychoanalytic film literature. (Those interested in the details about how Freud's assumptions about emotions make psychoanalysis a poor choice of theory to explain filmic emotions should refer to the Appendix.)

Establishing the Mood

Stella Dallas begins with a relatively sparsely informative concentration of emotion cues. After the opening credits that introduce the main musical theme, the initial scenes are primarily concerned with setting up relationships between characters and establishing Stella as the protagonist. We observe the teasing, combative relationship between Stella and her brother Charlie through watching them fight in the front yard and in the kitchen, and we recognize that this could be interpreted through one of two possible genre microscripts. Either there is an important conflict between them or this is a case of siblings who squabble on the surface but love each other deeply.

In addition to establishing the relationship between Stella and Charlie, the film gives us necessary exposition concerning Stephen's tragic past and lonely present by showing us a newspaper clipping. We recognize both Stella's infatuation with Stephen and her class inferiority to him through dialogue, his snubbing her, and the overt codes of poverty marking Stella's home. The film ensures that we see Stella as a woman whose ambitions are supported by careful planning. The camera lingers on her face reflected in a mirror as she gets the idea to meet Stephen "accidentally" by taking Charlie's lunch to his work. Through dialogue we learn that she accepts credit for cooking the lunch, although we know that she simply bought it at a delicatessen.

Although she is capable of such little white lies to seduce Stephen, the film carefully makes sure that we do not miscast her as a golddigger. Telling us that Stella is taking a business course to improve herself gives us evidence that allows us to cast her as a woman who is working hard to better herself. The camera shows us detail by detail that this woman is genuinely attracted to Stephen (not faking her affection for monetary gain) because she exhibits evidence of her attraction even when he cannot see her. While Stephen's back is turned, we see her eyes looking up and down his body. When he leaves the room briefly, we see Stella stroke his coat.

In this way the film not only communicates important character information about Stella, but it also prepares us for a narrational pattern that marks the entire film. We will be given visual access to faces that are hidden from other characters. Because these faces are not trying to hide their expressions from other characters, we can read their "true feelings" through conventional interpretation of their unguarded expressions, gaining emotional information that is withheld from certain characters.

Through camera placement, costuming, dialogue, lighting, scenic design, and acting, these early scenes show us the class-based, familial, and romantic interrelationships among the characters, setting the scene for the rest of the film. Although these scenes show Stella to be attracted to Stephen, they also portray Stella as an attractive woman. After having seen the array of spectacularly hideous clothing Stella wears throughout the film, it is easy to forget in retrospect that Stella is made conventionally pretty in the lunch scene with Stephen. Her silky dress and hat and the back lighting would be read as traditional Hollywood cues to indicate her beauty. Stephen's boss comments on how pretty she is, and Stephen concurs. The early scenes are primarily concerned with establishing Stella as an attractive, ambitious, effective woman.

Stella gets her heart's desire: she goes to the movies with Stephen, and they take a moonlit walk arm in arm. Up to this point the narration has been concerned with characterological matters, providing relatively sparsely informative emotion cues to signal what mood would be appropriate. Of course, not all such cues are provided by the text itself. Film audiences could be acting on extradiegetic cues from advertising, trailers, the source novel, or the previous film adaptation of the story (Henry King's 1925 version). At the very least, a basic genre knowledge would tell film viewers that this was a woman's film, leading them to expect the narrational-emotion scripts associated with that genre.

But what kind of woman's film is it? Up to the first time we see them together, it is quite unclear how to categorize the specific genre of the film. The foregrounding of class boundaries is just as much a hallmark of the love story as it is the maternal melodrama. Such class differences can easily form the conflict that drives the plot of the love story and that could be resolved happily ever after. *Stella Dallas* is so widely considered to be a prototypical example of the maternal melodrama that it is difficult to recognize that these early scenes set up no specific emotion cues that would indicate to us that this is not a love story.[4]

The film must establish a dominant emotional orientation toward the diegesis, showing us that the feeling tones associated with maternal melodrama are appropriate, not the ones associated with the love story, and it must do this even though Stella is not yet a mother. During the moonlit walk scene we are given the densest configuration of genre clues that hint at the source of tensions that will come between the couple. Most of these cues are dialogue lines revealing the difference between Stella's and Stephen's perspectives on class mobility. Stella gushes, "I want to be like all the people you've been around. Educated, you know, and speaking nice. . . . No, I don't want to be like me. Not like the people in this place, but like the people in the movie. You know, doing everything well bred and refined." Stephen reveals his prejudices against cross-class masquerade by commenting, "It isn't really well bred to act the way you aren't." This scene clearly establishes the tension between Stephen's attitude (that class is a matter of breeding, not of ambition) and Stella's ambition.

Until this scene there are no strong clues concerning who would provide the narrative's dramatic tension. Would the families perhaps oppose the cross-class union, as is typical in such love stories? During the moonlit walk scene, Stephen reveals for the first time his disdain toward such class impersonation, allowing the audience to anticipate tension between the couple (instead of conflict placed on them by outsiders). Based on our other experiences with such films, we understand that these cues are being given to us so that we might orient ourselves toward the narrative. We know to examine the behavior and dialogue looking for this conflict to surface in a more overtly hostile fashion. We begin to execute a genre microscript of class tension between a romantic couple, a genre microscript that is associated (although not exclusively) with the melodrama.

Of course the seeds of this conflict have been revealed earlier, but what marks this scene as pivotal is the concentration of cues that foreground the tension. Earlier scenes have given brief moments that hint at these attitudes (e.g., Stella's expressed scorn at "millhands"), but they have been isolated narrative threads at moments when the overall narrative, genre, and emotional pattern was not clear. Observant viewers well versed in the conventions of the woman's film might have picked up on these isolated hints, causing them to select the appropriate narrative-emotion script, but Hollywood's mass appeal depends on more dense patterns of cuing. The moonlit walk scene provides the viewer with a barrage of narratively significant dialogue lines (as quoted earlier) alerting us that this is crucial information we need to make narrative-emotional sense out of the rest of the text. The relatively high concentration of these relationally significant lines of dialogue ensures that most viewers will give proper attention to them. This scene provides the basis for the viewer's initial emotional orientation toward the text.

In the case of *Stella Dallas*'s moonlit scene, this particular set of cues trains us to feel *for* the characters because they do not have the full set of narrative information to feel appropriately for themselves. This scene alerts us to a pattern that the film will use again and again to make its emotional appeal: *Stella Dallas* frequently gives the viewer emotional information that is denied to one or more of the characters, giving the viewer a kind of "emotional omniscience." If the characters knew the information, they would be expected to feel a particular way. That information is hidden from them, and this opens up a space for the viewer (who knows the full information) to feel *for* them, to feel what the character cannot feel herself because of her ignorance.

For example, Stella in the moonlit scene is prattling on excitedly about wanting to change. "I could learn to talk like you and act like you," she says. Her delivery is rapid and excited, alerting us that she either misses or disregards Stephen's veiled disapproval. Because the scene is staged with Stella and Stephen walking arm in arm with their eyes straight ahead, both characters have restricted access to the other's facial expressions. The audience, on the other hand, is given superior position to either of the characters in interpreting facial expressions. Stella does not appear to pay attention to the significant information Stephen is conveying, nor does Stephen's face convey any hint that he is strongly alarmed by the sentiments she is expressing. Both appear oblivious to the significant conflict that the genre-trained viewer can spot in this dense set of cues.

Knowing what we know about Stella's ambitions, it is likely that she would stop gushing about changing herself if she recognized Stephen's disapproval as we do. We might appropriately expect that Stella should be embarrassed in this situation if she fully knew what was happening. She doesn't, and this opens up the opportunity for the viewer to feel *for* her, to feel what she would likely feel if she had the audience's full knowledge. This moment of feeling *for*, strongly marked by highly concentrated cues, indicates the dominant mood called for by the text: embarrassment for Stella (who seems oblivious to subtle social disapproval) and anticipation of impending class-based catastrophe.

Feeling *for* a character differs from feeling *with* a character. If a character is being held prisoner at gunpoint, we can feel fear *with* the character because we both understand the danger. If we see that a character (unbeknownst to him or her) is in the crosshairs of a telescopic rifle scope, we can feel fear *for* the character. The difference depends on the state of narrational knowledge. Feeling *with* a character depends on the audience having roughly the same knowledge of the emotional situation. If we have knowledge denied to a character, and if that character could be reasonably predicted to feel a certain way if he or she knew that information, then the text establishes a possibility for us to feel *for* the character.[5] In feeling with, the character exemplifies what the viewer's appropriate reaction should be. In feeling for, viewers can rely more on their own own understanding of appropriate emotional reaction, based on microscripts from other films, socialization, and so forth.[6] The viewer can reject the invitation afforded by *Stella Dallas* to feel for the character, as a viewer who is unappreciative of the woman's film might be prone to do. But the moonlit walk scene provides us with a relatively densely informative configuration of narratively significant cues to encourage us to feel embarrassment for Stella.

In addition to the foregrounded dialogue lines, this scene is also notable because of a formal quality that has been deemphasized in the psychoanalytic discussion on *Stella Dallas*: Alfred Newman's music. Although melodrama has been historically linked with music ("melos") from its origins, the discussion of *Stella Dallas* has emphasized the visual devices in the text. Kaplan, Williams, et al. discuss diegetic action and the structuring of looks that provide various perspectives on the story, but there is no mention of how music is used to appeal to the spectator.

One might think that a film trying to establish a mood early on would take advantage of music as a general signal for the appropriate emotional orientation, yet the early scenes of *Stella Dallas* are almost completely without music. The primary musical theme is introduced during the opening credits:

The music continues briefly into the first scene (a common practice in classical Hollywood cinema to bridge the transition from credits to diegesis)

and then halts when Stephen makes his first appearance. The subsequent scenes in Stella's working-class home and Stephen's workplace have no music whatsoever.

Why not? Part of the answer may be that the absence of music makes these working-class settings seem more austere, less hospitable. But also recall that these early scenes could easily fit within the paradigm of the star-crossed love story. By providing musical cues before the appropriate genre framework is clear, the narration could reinforce the wrong genre hypothesis (that this is a love story, not a melodrama). Musical accompaniment during Stella's attempt to lure Stephen in his office would accentuate the possibility that this is a love story.[7] By withholding music from such scenes, the narration keeps the question open: what is the appropriate script to use to understand *Stella Dallas*?

The scene in the movie theater reintroduces music after a long absence. Piano accompaniment to the silent film Stella and Stephen watch together reminds us that many films (unlike *Stella Dallas* up to this point) use music to cue our emotional understanding. Then, at long last, in the scene immediately after the movie theater, we hear nondiegetic music. At first a flute and then a string section accompanies Stella and Stephen as they walk in the moonlight. Viewers familiar with Hollywood conventions would expect lush strings for a moonlit walk, but this music serves more than just a generic purpose. We have not heard nondiegetic music since the film's opening, so this scene is marked in comparison with the relatively quiet preceding scenes. The denser configuration of cues (both in the music and the dialogue) foreground the information provided by this scene.

The romantic musical theme does not provide specific genre information to the audience. Musical connotation is rarely specific enough to allow audiences to distinguish between a love story and a maternal melodrama, but the presence of nondiegetic music (in contrast to its preceding absence) signals the relative importance of this scene both narratively and emotionally. By withholding nondiegetic music until the narrative conflict and emotional address (asking us to feel for characters) is more clearly introduced, the narration helps the viewer to avoid mistakenly choosing an inappropriate orientation.

A violin solo (with string background) reintroduces us to the primary musical theme we last heard during the opening credits. *Stella Dallas* follows a fairly classical pattern of using musical themes as leitmotifs associated with characters, locales, or broad emotional orientations.[8] When signaling the initial emotional orientation, *Stella Dallas* associatively links a musical theme with the feeling tone. By doing so, the film gains a powerful tool to bolster mood. Repeating this theme in later moments reevokes the emotional tone (feeling embarrassment for Stella and dread of upcoming relationship conflicts) that the moonlit scene carefully creates, thus refreshing the initial mood.

The main theme eventually gains more specific associations as it becomes linked through repetition with the eponymous character. Such a specific connection to Stella helps music gain a specific narrational function (for instance, eventually this leitmotif becomes so tied to Stella that the narration can use a brief snippet of this theme to reveal that a character is thinking about her[9]). And yet the leitmotif never loses its initial function as a signifier of a particular feeling tone. Through their repetitive associative power, leitmotifs and musical themes are valuable tools in evoking and reevoking mood, but they do not depend solely on using the vague cultural connotations of Romantic music. The specific main musical theme gains particularity through coordination with other narrational and emotion cues, enabling the musical theme to make more specific emotion-evoking appeals.

Superior Knowledge

As *Stella Dallas* progresses, it uses variations on the same patterns of emotion cuing on display in the moonlit walk scene. The film's emotional power depends on the film giving superior emotional knowledge to the audience and limited knowledge to individual characters. One of the most important ways this is done is through the staging of the action. For example, Laurel and Stella face the same direction while chopping in the kitchen, allowing us (and not Laurel) to read Stella's jealous expression as Laurel rhapsodizes about Mrs. Morrison being like a goddess or a flower. Mirrors are sometimes used to show us facial expressions that are not seen by certain characters, such as the scene in which Stella puts on cold cream while Laurel continues to jabber about Mrs. Morrison. The most elaborate example of this use of mirrors is the soda shop scene in which the large wall mirror lets us see the gang of upperclass youths snickering at Stella while she shops, unaware of their cruelty.

Usually this staging is done in a way that emphasizes one character's deliberately hiding of some vital emotional information from another. For others' presumed good, characters in Stella Dallas lie about their own feelings, but the staging shows the audience the true expression behind the mask. Characters frequently face the same direction in a "two-shot west" that allows audiences access to the facial expressions of characters concealing their reactions to each other. After Laurel has learned that her upper-class friends at the hotel have been making fun of her mother, she begins packing for home. This action helps justify her facing away from her mother as she hides her expression from the puzzled Stella ("This morning you'd never been so happy") while she displays her painful sacrifice to the audience.

Stella Dallas calls upon a range of techniques commonly used both in theater and in film to stage such melodramatic emotional encounters. For instance, characters in Stella Dallas sometimes embrace in such a way that simultaneously hides the characters' faces from each other and allows the audience privileged access to their "unguarded" expression. For example, when Laurel returns to her mother after the first unsuccessful attempt to have her live with her father, she puts her head on Stella's chest and hugs her. Only the audience can see Stella's pained expression as Laurel says, "Good times, they aren't what make you belong. It's other kinda times. It's when you've cried together and been through things together. That's when you seem to love the most." In Stella Dallas, even an embrace can help hide emotions from other characters as much as it reveals emotions.

The film's staging provides constant reminders that the characters are playacting, making sure that the audience is given privileged "backstage" access to their real feelings after their performances are over. When pretending for Laurel's sake to be a pleasure-seeking woman who wants to be "something else besides a mother," Stella cleans the room and fluffs pillows while stealing occasional hidden glances at Laurel to see if she is believing her act. She maintains the posturing until Laurel leaves the room, and then Stella collapses, showing us the emotional effort she had just expended.

The most elaborate example of Stella Dallas's staging to allow audiences superior access to facial expression (while characters hide their expressions from each other) takes place in the railroad sleeper car scene in which both Stella and Laurel overhear young women gossipping about Stella's scandalous appearance. Laurel in the upper bunk cannot see her mother and fears that Stella is not yet asleep, allowing Stella to overhear. We see both Laurel's panic and Stella's painful realization as the film intercuts between the two bunks. When Laurel peeks to see if her mother is asleep, Stella feigns sleep to hide her new awareness from her daughter. After Laurel climbs into bed with Stella and closes her eyes, Stella opens hers, allowing the audience one last look into her eyes.

I would argue that this is the primary moment in which *Stella Dallas* asks us to switch from feeling *for* Stella to feeling *with* her. At last Stella realizes what Laurel has learned and what we have known for awhile: Stella's gaudy appearance hampers not only her own upward mobility but also Laurel's. At last she has the knowledge that would enable her to feel embarrassed for herself, sad for Laurel's thwarted dreams, touched by Laurel's sacrifice (in choosing to leave the hotel). Stella's pained expression provides an overdetermined space on which these narratively specified emotion scripts may play. In all Stella–Laurel interactions from this moment on, the audience shares roughly the same narrative-emotional information that Stella has, and Laurel's awareness becomes restricted (Laurel can't "read between those pitiful lines" in Stella's farewell letter as we and Helen Morrison Dallas can). Stella's final sacrifices make a different emotional appeal to the viewer because they are performed by a character whose awareness of the emotional interrelationships roughly duplicates our own. If the film's emotional address asked us to feel *for* Stella as she makes her most spectacular acts of sacrifice, the viewer could easily refuse to do so, distancing her actions as socially outrageous. By making a shift to feeling *with* Stella, the film implicates its viewers more strongly in these moments of sacrifice.

I do not argue that this is the first time that we have felt *with* Stella. Just as the state of knowledge varies across a film's narration, so does our opportunity to feel with and for certain characters. Later in this chapter, I examine just such a moment (at Laurel's birthday party). After the sleeper car scene, however, the viewer and Stella continue to share the same knowledge of the emotional situation in subsequent scenes, making this a more permanent and important shift. Even in this instance, it can be argued that the shift to feeling *with* Stella is not total. Do we feel *with* Stella during the brief scenes in which Helen Morrison Dallas prepares Laurel and the house for the wedding (i.e., do we know that Stella shares the knowledge we have)? Perhaps these scenes are a brief respite from feeling *with* Stella, preparing us for the ending tearjerker. Because of the constantly shifting nature of film narration knowledge and communicativeness, it is difficult for almost any film to elicit feeling *with* or *for* for an indeterminate period of time. Perhaps this shift in emotional appeal is what Ann Kaplan refers to when she describes the power of the film's appeal to her personally:

I was talking about a very specific female spectator: i.e. myself, who despite feminist consciousness and critical awarenessess, is with each viewing "seduced" by the film's mechanisms. I am always brought to tears by the sight of Stella standing alone in the rain, yearning to be with her daughter but convinced that she is doing the right thing. My tears tell me that I assent to Stella's loss. I experience the beauty of its pathos and return home more reconciled to the sacrifices of my own life. I have been made to participate in the patriarchal construction of the mother-daughter relationship.[10]

At the heart of the "seduction" that viewers like Kaplan are "made to participate in" is the shift to feeling *with* Stella at the moment of her greatest sacrifice.[11]

This feeling *with* is complicated by several factors in the final portions of *Stella Dallas*. By having several distinct overlapping emotional genre microscripts evoked at the same time (Stella yearning to be with her daughter but convinced that she is doing the right thing), the powerful ending is emotionally overdetermined. Stella may be understood as simultaneously embarrassed about her lower-class status, loving to her daughter, proud that Laurel has achieved social status, sad over her own loss, and happy that she made the right choice. The ending is overlaid with various emotion scripts that the narrative has accumulated throughout its progression, making this moment the most emotionally complex of the film.

Kaplan's unitary reading of this complicated ending attempts to account for the emotionally forceful way that the film encourages the audience to assent to Stella's sacrifice. Williams's concept of multiple identifications tries to acknowledge the conflicted nature of the emotional appeal made in the ending. An understanding of the ending's emotional appeal based on knowledge, feeling with, and emotion scripts captures the flavor of both these readings.

The ending forcefully allies us with Stella because of the recent shift from feeling *for* her to feeling *with*. The text asks us largely to side with Stella (and not Laurel or Stephen) through its manipulation of narrative knowledge and through the visual strategies Kaplan identifies (e.g., placing the camera with Stella outside the window). Yet to describe this ending in terms of multiple identifications does injustice to the text's devices to make the audience feel *with* Stella at this moment. The emotional appeal of this moment is not unitary, however, and cannot be entirely assumed under a purely patriarchal reading strategy, as Kaplan suggests. The emotions elicited here are multiple because there are overlapping emotion scripts that can be applied to the ending (sadness, pride, happiness, love, shame).

An understanding of the complex network of emotion scripts can do more precisely what Williams was trying to do in her argument: to open up *Stella Dallas*'s ending to multiple reading strategies, allowing various historical subjects to interpret the film from progressive or patriarchal positions. Film viewers may accept only one of the proferred emotional appeals, or they may embrace many emotion scripts simultaneously. A viewer emphasizing Stella's beaming face as she walks away may interpret *Stella Dallas*'s ending as "happy," but others may privilege the pain of such an enormous sacrifice. A progressive antipatriarchal reading emphasizing Stella's sorrow at being forced into this sacrifice is not reading against the grain, as Kaplan suggests. Such a nuanced reading is not based on material hidden in the text for later generations of feminists to uncover and use against the text's patriarchal machinations. Instead, these emotion scripts for sorrow, pride, happiness, and shame (in various configurations) are clearly called upon by the complex ending.

Most of *Stella Dallas* is not so overwritten with multiple emotion scripts as the ending is. The film usually offers a much more limited range of emotion scripts for the audience to actualize, as would be expected in a film with mass appeal. A film that called on a large number of overlapping emotion scripts throughout the entire film would sacrifice the clarity of emotional appeal that characterizes the classical Hollywood cinema. Significantly, *Stella Dallas* provides its most emotionally complicated moment at the end of the film, suggesting that it might be hard to recoup a more straightforward emotional appeal after such a highly foregrounded moment of emotional complexity.[12]

Details in the Diegesis

Throughout the film, feeling with or for Stella is made more complicated by the film's encouraging us to judge her harshly. Kaplan emphasizes how the camera privileges the disapproving looks from Stephen and other upper-class bystanders, thus calling upon the viewer to see Stella's excessive femininity from their perspective. The looks we see from socialites tell us that Stella's outfits are gaudy and inappropriate. We judge Stella's class-crossing debacle based on the perspectives we are given from upper-class diegetic characters.

This emphasis on character gazes (characteristic of much psychoanalytic film criticism) hides the fact that the viewer is more frequently asked to judge Stella's inappropriate dress and behavior without any disapproving intermediaries in the diegesis. We do not simply rely on the disapproval exhibited by diegetic characters. Because of the outlandish tangle of signifiers used in Stella's costuming, we the audience evaluate Stella from the shared perspective of our socially acquired knowledge of dress codes.

Stella Dallas works hard to clothe Stella in spectacularly inappropriate outfits. For the abortive birthday party, she wears an enormous corsage that extends from shoulder to waist over a dress with a large flowered print. On the train, she wears a clashing plaid coat over that same flowered dress. When offered more subtle alternatives (dresses with smaller floral prints) by an offscreen clerk, she rejects them and asks for lace to be added to her dress. Each of these ensembles blatantly violates the norms of tasteful Hollywood fashion in which many female viewers would be well schooled.

The scenes that most emphasize Stella's dress and that call on the viewer to judge her garments as gaudy are the scenes at the hotel where Stella makes her first public appearance in Laurel's posh circle. Our first perception of the scene in which Stella prepares for her appearance is the loud clanking we hear as the camera fades in on Stella adding more and more bracelets to her arms. This highly accentuated sound effect alerts us to the importance of paying attention to her costume in the upcoming scene. The film plays with our anticipation as Stella pauses repeatedly in front of the mirror. Just as we think that she can't possibly make her outfit (including a black hat to clash with her floral dress) more ostentatious, she adds more bracelets. She pauses, then liberally doses herself with perfume. She almost walks out the door, but she stops to check her appearance once more in a mirror before she decides to add a white fur boa.

If her violations had been subtle (such as wearing a "cheap imitation necklace" with her formal gown to the River Club), many viewers might have missed her error, particularly because costume tends to play a subservient role in the action-driven hierarchy of classical Hollywood narration. The filmmakers made sure that Stella's dress egregiously violates the norms of Hollywood dress, and they privileged these violations by showing her adding accessories one at a time. It would be difficult for even the most fashion-impaired Hollywood viewer to overlook her spectacular violations of dress norms, calling on us to judge her clothing as embarrassing.

Hollywood narration tends to supply us with considerable redundancy of narratively and emotionally important information, and this is no less true of the embarrassing fashions in *Stella Dallas*. Just in case we didn't note Stella's highly foregrounded fashion atrocities, the text provides an array of disapproving looks by Stephen and the clientele of various upper-class establishments. It also provides numerous cues in the dialogue to call attention to Stella's cluttered style (e.g., when Stella attempts to put additional frou-frou on Laurel's birthday dress, Laurel refuses, preferring her dress "plain" just like her father's upper-class taste). Kaplan is correct to point to the function of such textual devices. They are perhaps most significant when the film introduces the notion of Stella's out-of-place style and when her style threatens Laurel's future in upper-class society. During the River Club scene, the film uses considerable redundancy of cuing (particularly disapproving looks) to make certain that audiences do not miss the first instance of upper-class criticism of her style. During the hotel scenes, the film again uses dense cuing (many comments in the dialogue, joking impersonations of Stella) to provide emotion markers encouraging us to feel embarrassment for Stella.

But most of the other scenes besides these two rely on *our* disapproval of her style, not on others' criticism. This makes us complicit with the same class forces that shut Stella out of upper-class society. If our embarrassment depended on recognizing that other diegetic characters disapprove of Stella's clothing without her knowledge, we could blame those characters (and the patriarchal system behind them) for the harm they bring about in Stella's life. The emotional situation becomes more complicated when we the viewers also judge Stella's dress harshly. Our attitude, based on accumulated knowledge of Hollywood style, convicts Stella of high fashion crime as much as the attitudes of the upper-class characters do.

Different viewers bring different competencies to a film, and female viewers associated with melodrama could be reasonably expected to be particularly cognizant of codes of dress. The ability to spot details in the mise-en-scène and the narrative and to assign them appropriate significance is central to the understanding of the melodrama and the woman's film. As Peter Brooks notes, the melodramatic imagination depends on the ability to read details in the mise-en-scène as signifying data:

significant things and gestures are necessarily metaphoric in nature because they must refer to and speak of something else. Everything appears to bear the stamp of meaning, which can be expressed, pressed out, from it. . . . social signification is only the merest starting point for an immense construction of connotation.[13]

To make sense of the woman's film (with its relative lack of emphasis on physical action), viewers must use a social network of meanings to interpret objects, actions, and speech in the diegesis. This network of meanings enables the woman's film viewers to form hypotheses concerning what will happen next in the narrative.

Stella Dallas's reliance on the viewer's ability to interpret Stella's attire is only a highly foregrounded example of a more general principle needed to make emotional sense out of the text. Stella herself models the kind of attention to detail that the film asks from its viewers when she covertly notices Stephen shining a drinking glass when they first meet. Using the knowledge she has gained through observation of details, she wins his attention by shining glasses just as he did earlier. Stella consistently notes details in the mise-en-scène and makes character-oriented observations about them (for instance, noting that the infant Laurel wipes up her tray just as her fastidious father might do). From its earliest scenes *Stella Dallas* demonstrates how important attention to such character detail can be to the successful character relationships. The viewer must similarly attend to such details if she is to engage successfully with the film's emotional appeal. Such details are the triggers that call genre microscripts into play. Once the viewer has gained an initial emotional orientation to the text, she looks for data congruent with that orientation. In the woman's film such data are usually provided by details in the mise-en-scène and dialogue, which must be interpreted by the viewer to guess what will happen next.

This anticipation becomes crucial in the case of feeling *for* a character. If the viewer is called upon to feel *with* a character, the character herself models an appropriate reaction to the narrative information we share. Her facial expressions, gestures, words, and so on provide additional cues to the viewer concerning how we might feel about the diegetic situation. In feeling *for*, however, we do not have such cues, because the character does not have the appropriate narrative information to feel for themselves. To feel *for* a character, the viewer should be particularly vigilant in interpreting the clues provided by the diegetic world because the character(s) cannot be depended on to do so for themselves.

When Laurel's teacher and a distinguished-looking mother recognize Stella as she frolics with a man obviously not her husband, the woman comments, "Why, Mary Ann's been asked to her party." This line calls on the woman's film viewer to access a genre microscript concerning what might happen once the parents of Laurel's refined friends learn of Stella's lack of propriety, setting up an anticipation of a humiliating, disappointing party. Stella does not have the knowledge to anticipate disaster, so the viewer does it for her.

Not every significant detail anticipates an upcoming plot occurrence, but the film encourages us to engage in this process of emotional hypothesis formation, even when certain evoked microscripts are not confirmed. For instance, the film drops numerous hints that Ed Munn's familiarity with Laurel may be on the verge of crossing the boundaries of the licit. When Stella invites Ed into the room although Laurel is dressed only in a slip, Laurel vehemently protests, "He shouldn't see me like this." Stella replies, "For heaven's sakes, Ed's known you since you were knee high and seen you with hardly anything on." Ed chimes in, "Yes, and even less than that. Now what have you got to hide from your Uncle Ed?" and chases her around the room. In a later scene, a drunken Ed pins Laurel against a wall trying to use mistletoe to extort a kiss from her. The possibility that Stella's laxness may be sexually endangering her child is the strongest accusation that the film raises against Stella's motherhood. By showing us these details, the film calls on us to read them according to a particularly damaging genre microscript, and the competent viewer anticipates that these initial actions could progress into more damaging behaviors. Although these potential actions do not materialize, the mere fact that this frightening possibility has been raised bolsters the overall orientation of dread and anticipation of domestic catastrophe.

If the film raised too many of these possibilities without providing a payoff for the viewer, this would endanger the continuation of the viewer's anticipatory orientation. An occasional unrewarded possibility allows the film to raise the specter of more frightening (and censorable) problems without making them a central part of the explicit plot.

Interestingly, this woman's film shows us a man (Stephen) trying to read details for their proper signification and clearly failing to come to the right conclusion. When Stephen enters his home after a long absence, the film shifts to show us the scene from his perspective. He sees empty whiskey glasses and cigars in his baby's bowl and hears barrelhouse piano playing, boisterous shouting, and his baby crying. Based on this information, he makes a logical interpretation: that his child is being raised in an atmosphere more resembling a saloon than a dignified home. We the audience have superior information, having been told through dialogue that this impromptu party is an unusual and harmless occurrence.

Stephen has done exactly what the film asks its viewers to do: to examine domestic details that are foregrounded as significant and, based on his cultural knowledge, to make assumptions about the narrative situation. The difference is that the viewer is given complete knowledge to make the correct assumption, as opposed to individual characters who may have only limited knowledge. The process that Stephen engages is not invalid, but this process can lead one to misrecognitions if one's knowledge is incomplete. The concept of misrecognition (crucial to so many melodramas) depends mainly on restricting a character's knowledge, thus setting up the possibility of viewers feeling *for* the misguided character.

Music

The competent viewer proceeds through *Stella Dallas* under the orientation of mood, alert for details needed to create anticipatory hypotheses. According to the model, this is not enough to sustain the mood. Occasionally the text must coordinate its emotion cues into denser configurations, giving a burst of emotion that will bolster the general emotional orientation toward the text.

After the initial orientation provided by the moonlit walk scene, *Stella Dallas* provides a string of scenes with highly coordinated cues seeking to elicit emotional responses from its audience and to assure them that their emotional orientation is an appropriate one. These scenes of dense emotion cuing include the River Club dance, the impromtu party that Stephen mis-recognizes, the abortive birthday party, Laurel's first visit to the Morrison's, the Christmas fiasco, Stella's humiliation at the posh hotel, and the reve-lation in the railroad sleeper car. *Stella Dallas* often uses dense configura-tions of emotion cues to mark scenes in which characters make important *recognitions*, instead of highlighting scenes in which they make narratively important *decisions*. For instance, the River Club scene (which foregrounds Stephen's recognition of his wife's tasteless behavior) is much more densely packed with cues than the subsequent scene of crucial decisionmaking (in which Stephen announces he wants to go to New York and Stella refuses to accompany him). It could be argued that this decision is one of the most narratively significant points, changing the course of action for the entire film, and yet this scene is not so clearly marked as emotionally significant. This shows that the degree of narrative significance and emotional signifi-cance, although frequently coincident, are not always linked. *Stella Dallas*'s tendency to separate emotional recognitions from narrative decisions may be an extension of melodrama's overall emphasis on recognition and its relative deemphasis on overt action.

After the film shifts from feeling *for* Stella to feeling *with* her, the frequency of scenes with dense emotion cuing increases, with almost every major scene up to the wedding being heavily cued. The cues relied on in these moments are primarily dialogue, mise-en-scène detail, and music. As noted earlier, the music in *Stella Dallas* follows a classically motivic structure, but Alfred Newman's music does not merely associate musical themes with characters or moods. These motifs interact with other narrative cues to shape the film's particular emotional appeal.

Kaplan, Williams, et al. do not examine this interaction, which is crucial to understanding emotions called for by the text. Following the visually oriented thrust of much psychoanalytic film theory,[14] these critics emphasize the gazes of the camera and the characters, to the detriment of the musical score. To demonstrate how the music interacts with narrative cues to create a complex, nuanced emotional appeal, I examine in some detail one of the most notable sequences of highly coordinated emotion cuing: Laurel's abortive birthday party.

Recall that the viewer trained to anticipate cues of potential social disaster has already been alerted to the possibility that the party might fail ("Why, Mary Ann's been asked to her party"). The sequence begins with Gladys decorating the birthday cake and the nondiegetic music playing "Happy Birthday to You." As Stella enters, the music changes to the main theme now associated both with Stella and with our primary mood orientation toward the film. The viewer is encouraged to read her floral print dress and a massive shoulder-to-waist corsage as outlandish. Laurel comments on how beautiful Stella looks, however, and the camera close-up accentuates Stella's beaming reaction to the compliment. This reiterates the pattern established earlier that the viewer has superior knowledge to that of the characters, encouraging us to anticipate what might happen when the guests see Stella's outfit.

Light strings accompany the scene as we hear the first door buzzer. As Gladys answers the door offscreen, the camera shows us an expectant Laurel and Stella. The alert viewer is expectant, too, but awaits bad news. As we overhear Gladys interacting with a messenger, the string music remains light and in a major key, reflecting Laurel and Stella's anticipation more than ours. As they read the note from Laurel's teacher declining their invitation, we hear first the strings playing a simple minor interval:

A clarinet repeats this interval immediately afterward.

The music subtly emphasizes the shift in knowledge as Stella and Laurel slowly understand what we already anticipate: that the party will be a disaster. The music stays bright until Stella and Laurel actually read the note saying that the teacher will not come to the party. Newman could have chosen to signal the disappointment earlier by playing the minor interval when the door buzzer sounded, but the text calls for us to feel *for* Laurel and Stella, and the music emphasizes their bright expectation and not our gloomy one. Slowly Laurel and Stella will come to share our knowledge. As their knowledge shifts to become more like ours, the use of musical motifs changes as well.

Once Laurel and Stella decide to overcome their disappointment, the nondiegetic music returns to a bright string version of the main theme as they sit and wait. This time the music does not wait (as it did before) until Laurel and Stella actually receive the bad news to play the minor interval again. As soon as the phone rings, we hear the interval first on clarinet and then immediately on cello, signaling to us that our expectations will be confirmed and that another guest will not attend.

Then the main theme is played, not in tempo on light strings but slower by an oboe lead, calling on the darker cultural connotations associated with that instrument. As they wait after the second cancellation, there is dissonance we have not heard before in the main theme. As their knowledge grows to match our own, the text asks us to shift temporarily from feeling *for* to feeling *with* them. Stella and Laurel now anticipate disaster just as we do, and broad musical associations (with minor intervals and slower versions of the main theme played on darker, lower-pitched instruments) signal that we all now share this knowledge.

Once it is clear that the text has shifted briefly to a mode of feeling *for*, the music once again shifts function. When the narration compresses time by showing us the party table being emptied of its place settings, we hear "Happy Birthday" again. This time, however, the tune is played on the oboe in a minor key (followed by a bassoon repetition of the minor interval). This minor version of "Happy Birthday" makes a nondiegetic ironic commentary on the action, a function that *Stella Dallas*'s music frequently performs. This commentary depends on a split between the cultural associations of the musical "content" and the connotations of its particular signifier. This song (and birthday parties in general) should be by definition "happy," but this minor oboe version (and this particular party) are mournful in comparison to the norm. This split between "content" and form makes this use of "Happy Birthday to You" have the flavor of both counterpoint and what Noël Carroll calls "modifying music."[15] The broader connotations of a minor oboe tune is sad, making the music consonant with the emotional appeal of the scene at this moment. And yet the discrepancy between this version of the song and the happier version we heard earlier give this repetition the sense of an external commentary on the action.

Stella Dallas similarly uses a well-known melody to comment ironically on the Dallases' unhappy Christmas. Snippets of "Silent Night" (particularly during the scene in which Stephen takes Laurel away from Stella's Christmas celebration) and "Happy Birthday" function in some ways like what Michel Chion calls "anempathetic music." Anempathetic music shows "a conspicuous indifference to the situation, by progressing in a steady, undaunted, and ineluctable manner . . . reinforc[ing] the individual emotion of the character and the spectator, even as the music pretends not to notice them."[16] Playing "Silent Night" seems appropriate based on the broad understanding of the scene (taking place at Christmastime), but such a peaceful tune is simultaneously inappropriate juxtaposed against the emotional spectacle of a child leaving her mother at Christmas, as if the narration were indifferent to the characters' suffering. Claudia Gorbman points out that such music can almost "sadistically" comment on the dramatic situation by "rubbing it in,"[17] emphasizing that although birthdays and Christmas may be happy for most, they are decidedly unhappy for the Dallases.

Only after the film has asked us to feel *with* Stella and Laurel does the music briefly take on the function of this ironically distanciating commentary. After Stella and Laurel have come to share our expectation that the birthday party will fail, after their emotional knowledge of the situation resembles our own, the film's music shifts to a distanciating mode, inserting a note of irony just as it asks viewers to ally their emotions with Stella and Laurel. *Stella Dallas* only uses anempathetic music after it has manipulated the state of our emotional knowledge to engage our empathy.

This moment is almost an aside, because the "Happy Birthday" motif is only a musical fragment, but this underlines how subtly film music can shift among various emotional functions during a complex moment of dense emotion cuing. Once the text asks us to feel briefly *with* Stella and Laurel, it problematizes that feeling with a hint of irony, asking us to reserve our emotions for the more complete switch to feeling *with* Stella near the film's heartbreaking ending.

Just as we relied on the widely held understanding of the meaning of the song "Happy Birthday to You," we also rely on the associations we have accumulated with a particular musical motif as it is used and reused in a film. As musical themes are repeated in different narrational contexts, they become overdetermined, encouraging the viewer to engage in a strong emotional response while leaving much of the specificity of that response to other narrational cues. When Laurel openly admits that no one is coming to her birthday party, we hear an orchestral version of the main theme with a violin lead as they walk into the party room together.

The music itself cannot specify the particular configuration of emotion microscripts that can be elicited by this narrative situation (embarrassment, sadness, self-sacrifice, bravery, etc.) except in the most general possible terms. Emotion cues provided by other local narrational devices detail the appropriate microscripts with specificity that a repeated musical theme cannot. The repeated theme, however, gives an emotional force to the moment that the local cues associated with this particular situation cannot provide. The associative links that the film has developed allow us to link this moment to earlier dense configurations of emotion cues, bolstering our emotional orientation by providing a significantly marked emotional burst.

This brief analysis of one of *Stella Dallas*'s densely cued emotional sequences shows what a complicated role music can play in eliciting emotion. It can be used to convey rather simple emotional states (for example, the sad three-note minor interval). It can remind us of who has emotional knowledge and who does not, as is done in the scenes in which Laurel and Stella slowly discover that no one is coming to the party. It can help prompt the expectations on which a text's emotional appeal may rely. It can ironically comment on the action itself. It can link one moment to others, lending an accumulative emotional force to a specific situation. Musical repetitions serve both specific, local purposes in a scene and more global functions in the narration. Close attention to the patterns of cuing alert the critic to the ways a specific text weaves music together with other emotion cues to create and sustain a mood throughout a film.

In examining these complex interactions, I have used Kaplan's and Williams's discussions of *Stella Dallas* as useful data concerning two possible readings of the film's emotional appeal (as patriarchal or progressive). The shift from feeling *for* to feeling *with* helps explain the forceful way that viewers may be made to ally themselves with Stella's patriarchal self-sacrifice (as Kaplan describes). The multiple microscripts at work during the ending create a multiplicity of emotional appeals, creating the possibility of a more nuanced response (as Williams notes). My analysis of *Stella Dallas* provides an explanation for both these critic's responses by revisiting the narrational interactions in this film.

It would seem that a text that has been as thoroughly examined by psychoanalytic film critics as *Stella Dallas* would provide little new material to discuss concerning emotion, but because psychoanalytic film criticism does not encourage film critics to scrutinize emotional appeals closely (see Appendix), there remained much to be discussed.

6 *Strike*-ing Out

The Partial Success of Early Eisenstein's Emotional Appeal

As I noted in the desiderata in the introduction to this book, an approach to analyzing the emotional appeals of film narration should be able to explain not only how certain texts such as *Stella Dallas* successfully evoke emotion in audiences but also why certain texts are less successful in their emotional appeal. A useful methodology must not be blatantly prescriptive, emphasizing certain modes of narration and trying to fit alternative modes into that norm. Nonetheless, the fact remains that some texts (or portions of texts) are not particularly well structured to appeal to the emotions. They make demands on the viewer that are counter to the basic structure of the emotion system as outlined here, making it less likely that audiences (regardless of their preferences for *Raiders of the Lost Ark* or *Stranger than Paradise*) will experience emotional responses.

Of course it is impossible to say that a portion of a text is utterly without emotional appeal, given the range of individual variation in viewer's emotional makeup. One may respond to a work based on highly idiosyncratic, personal associations made with a text (e.g., because the film was shot in one's childhood neighborhood). But it is possible to say that the narration's appeal is more or less well structured to appeal to an audience that has the appropriate cinematic knowledge of genre schemas, narrative norms, and so forth.

There is always a danger when critics say a text has a lesser emotional appeal that they are denying the possible pleasures of others; critics must tread sensitively here to try to keep open a space for others to discuss their pleasures. Saying that a text has a less effective emotional appeal is necessarily a provisional statement, subject to revision by other voices articulating their pleasures where previously none were found. Yet to say that it is impossible to determine if a text's narration has a lesser emotional appeal is to slip back into the conception of emotions as too messy to be dealt with.

This case study examines Sergei Eisenstein's *Strike*[1] (1925) to provide an explanation for how certain portions of the text successfully appeal to the emotions, whereas others are less effectively structured. Eisenstein himself came to view *Strike* as a mixture of forceful and weaker sequences. On one hand, Eisenstein used *Strike*'s finale as the very definition of "emotional dynamisation."[2] On the other, he denigrated the film as a "treatise"[3] preparing the way for his later, more proficient work. He compared some of *Strike*'s sequences with those in *Potemkin* and always found *Strike* lacking somewhat in its formal qualities but primarily in its relatively ill-organized emotional appeal. And yet he was vague in his criticisms of the film's lesser appeal, blaming this on its lack of "psychologism,"[4] among other qualities. This case study provides a more useful structural explanation of the film's narrational successes and failures to elicit emotion than the explanation Eisenstein provided. Simultaneously, this case study demonstrates a useful function of the mood-cue approach. As this consideration of *Strike* shows, the approach can help us explore and articulate the ways that a film's emotional appeal can fail.

Stylistic, Not Emotional, Orientation

Strike has the distinction of being the Eisenstein film that uses the greatest range of cinematic devices. Never again would he use superimpositions, flashy graphic wipes, and animated intertitles as he did in this film, choosing instead to rely on composition and cutting as his primary filmic tools. One might reasonably expect that for a theorist such as Eisenstein who believed that audiences respond emotionally to film style, such a plethora of stylistic devices might result in his most broadly emotional film. Yet Eisenstein's dissatisfaction with the film emphasizes that the key to filmic emotion is understanding how style is to be coordinated with narration. Portions of *Strike* fail to make an effective emotional appeal because the film does not initially set up a consistent, well-marked emotional orientation toward the material.

To establish a mood, the first part of *Strike* would have to present at least one concentrated burst of emotion cues to orient the viewer's emotions.

As noted, the film has no shortage of stylistic innovations that could help mark the orienting moments. In the earliest moment of highly marked style, letters in an intertitle become animated. An intertitle telling us that "All is quiet at the factory" is followed by an intertitle with letters (*HO*, Russian for "but") that move until they overlap in a figure that graphically echoes the circular movement of a machine in the next shot. Also during the first part, we see a secret meeting shown in a reflection in a puddle of water in a shot that is even more stylistically marked because it is in reverse motion. The shot begins with a splash in the puddle, which then changes to a clear reflective surface on which we see conspirators gather (walking in reverse motion) to chat. An intertitle announcing the "spreading ripple" of information through the factory's network of spies is wiped away by the spreading ripple of a slow corner wipe to reveal the spies. The first part of *Strike* contains more elaborately showy graphic devices than does any of the five remaining parts. It would seem, then, that this first part would be well equipped to do exactly what the mood-cue approach calls for: use highly marked cues to highlight an initial emotional orientation.[5]

To establish a mood, however, a film needs to present a highly coordinated burst of cues, something that this initial portion of *Strike*, for the most part, does not do. The film uses several distinctive stylistic devices that are highly foregrounded for the viewer to notice, but it shows us these moments one by one without linking them together in a sequence that would alert the viewer that an emotional orientation was being signaled.

Part of the reason Eisenstein's notable style is not coordinated into tight sequences has to do with the nature of silent historical-materialist narration (in David Bordwell's terms). The omniscience of such narration[6] allows it to move at will from one diegetic space to another, and the first part of *Strike* certainly does this. We shift rapidly among various workstations around the factory, managerial offices, and domestic settings where we meet spies. Many films travel widely in their diegetic worlds, but historical-materialist films flaunt this ability to move between vastly different spaces. Instead of tying such knowledge to a character's perspective, Soviet montage films freely juxtapose vastly different spaces to make a rhetorical connection.

This is not to argue that historical-materialist narration tends to have a lesser emotional effect because its wide-ranging narration tends to scatter its cues instead of localizing them in a single diegetic space. A high concentration of emotion cues does not necessarily depend on spatially continuous segments. Nonetheless, when historical-materialist narration (such as that in the first part of *Strike*) flaunts its spatial manipulations, it eliminates one of the primary means to signal to an audience that these cues should be considered as a unit (i.e., the classical sequence of continuous diegetic time and space). Such narration can still coordinate its cues to nudge the viewer toward an emotional orientation, but it usually must find other ways to signal that its marked stylistic instances should be considered together, not merely individually.[7]

In one segment of *Strike*'s first part, Eisenstein did coordinate his style into a highly concentrated, cohesive sequence: the introduction of the various agents and spies. An intertitle introduces the agents (with names such as "The Owl," "Bulldog," and "The Quiet One"), and we see seemingly still pictures of the agents in a book. They miraculously come alive and begin to change clothes within the book's picture frames (one of them hanging his hat outside the frame) before they leave the frames. Then we see a series of "Preparations" in which we are visually introduced to the spies through juxtaposed intertitles, shots of an animal, and close-ups of the characters grotesquely demonstrating their resemblance to that animal. We see a shot of a pulsating owl dissolve to a close-up of a blinking man, whom an intertitle introduces to us as "The Owl." A panting bulldog dissolves to a man exaggeratedly panting, and an intertitle officially introduces us to "The Bulldog."

In these sequences Eisenstein relied on his familiarity with caricature and with constructivist modes of exaggerated acting in the theater to create images of these spies that would be instantly read as grotesque by his audience. These distorted facial expressions graphically connected to animal imagery provide cues that are both emotionally and formally interesting. In addition, this sequence is peppered with a broad range of elaborate wipes (diagonals, horizontal, circular, a vertical wipe to the center, diamond) that further highlights this segment formally. The interconnections of this rapid series of cues encourages the audience to label this as a sequence of highly marked, densely concentrated narrational cuing, which I argue is necessary for a film to establish an emotional orientation.

So why is the "agent introduction" segment ineffective at creating a mood? Let us examine this sequence's structure in more detail. The "Preparations" sequence begins with a shot of a monkey, which was the first animal name in the intertitle list of police agents. A long shot reveals that the monkey is in a shop, and a man with glasses and a dark hat enters. By cutting from the monkey to the man entering the pet shop, *Strike* seems to introduce this man as the police agent called The Monkey. Every other introduction proceeds in the way outlined in the previous paragraph: animal, grotesque figure, intertitle. Although the man in the shop has not been introduced to us in exactly the same way as the others, the sequence clearly uses associative editing to cue us to label the first mysterious man in the shop as "The Monkey."

At the end of each introduction, the film returns to the shop for a brief shot of the man, the monkey, and the shopkeeper. After introducing The Fox and The Owl, the film then introduces us to The Monkey, showing us a monkey drinking from a bottle and dissolving to a graphic match of a man drinking. After the man broadly licks his lips, the intertitle confirms that this is indeed The Monkey. Unexpectedly, this is not the man we were previously led to believe was The Monkey. We then return to the man in the shop with the monkey, who is then revealed (through the now-familiar pattern of animal-figure-intertitle) to be The Bulldog.

This sequence intentionally misleads the viewer into thinking that the man in the shop is The Monkey. Instead of introducing the agents in a consistent manner, *Strike* plays a "bait and switch" game with the viewer. When the man is unmistakably revealed to be The Bulldog, we must revise our earlier hypothesis concerning his identity, aware that we have been set up by the narration. Although Bordwell notes that historical-materialist narration has a tendency toward being overly communicative of narrative information,[8] in this instance *Strike* is intentionally (although briefly) *mis*communicative. The primary purpose served by this highly marked sequence is to signal to the viewer that the narration is not always straightforwardly trustworthy.

Of course the narration does not actually "lie" to the viewer (à la *Stage Fright*). The man in the shop is not mislabeled as The Monkey by an intertitle, only to have that label altered later. Instead, we are led to make a straightforward connection between the man and the monkey because they are linked by editing. They are not, significantly, linked by the exact editing pattern that defines the other police agents, which means that it could be argued that the viewer simply has not been paying attention to the narrational pattern and has made a mistaken connection. But the film encourages us to make that mistaken connection by linking the man and the monkey *before* the formal animal-figure-intertitle editing pattern has been established. Only *after* the fact can we see that the initial connection between man and monkey does not fit the triad pattern. This is a "white" lie and a brief one, but this temporary destabilizing of our trust in the narration coupled with dense cuing makes this sequence an important one in establishing the viewer's orientation toward the text.

The introduction sequence encourages particularly close attention to the text's formal patterns. One could say that if we had been paying utterly close attention to the text's signifiers, we would have recognized that the man-monkey introduction did not fit the pattern of the other introductions, causing us not to be fooled by our first impression. This sequence encourages spectators to be vigilant, not to relax their attention and blindly trust the narration. The film has prepared us for this orientation by giving us brief signals early on that the style is not always what it initially seems. Splashed puddles can become reflections of skyscapes, which can become backgrounds for worker meetings. Simple words in the intertitles (*HO*/"but") can make patterns that form graphic matches. Just as I argue that a strong burst of cues can cement an emotional orientation that has been signaled earlier by brief isolated cues, a strong coordination of distinctive stylistic devices can cement a *formal* orientation toward the film, affirming the earlier isolated formal cues and guiding our later expectations concerning the film's style.

The introduction sequence in *Strike*'s first part does just that: it provides a highly marked message instructing the viewer to pay attention to the film's style. This is one of the primary qualities Eisenstein sought in an audience: sensitivity (conscious or otherwise) to formal parameters. This is also congruent with the positions taken by the Russian formalists that have become a major tenet of contemporary film neoformalism: that an individual film teaches us how to watch it, that it instructs us on what kind of features are most important in this particular text.[9] The first part of *Strike* instructs us on how to orient ourselves toward the formal qualities of the text, but it does little to provide a well-coordinated emotional orientation to the film.

Why not? If audiences respond based on the rhythms of a film's style (as Eisenstein believed), why is an effective formal sequence not by definition an effective emotional sequence? The sequence provides us with a cognitive game of pattern recognition concerning the identities of the various police agents, encouraging us to distrust the film narration and to view it with close formal attention, both of which are primarily *cognitive* concerns. One could argue that there is an emotional response that is likely to be elicited by this miscommunicative narration, a kind of unease triggered by the violation of trust. Even if one considers "unease" to be an emotion, this unease is only temporarily elicited and is not bolstered by further instances in the text that would continue this emotional state. The "lie" is brief and unlikely to inspire viewer outrage, unlike the protracted lie of *Stage Fright*. I do not wish to set up a strict dichotomy between the cognitive and the emotional (or the formal and the emotional), but in this instance the greater response called for is one that can be described in purely cognitive terms (encouraging strict attention to the style). The film contains a collection of cues (including the slapstick action instance in which the foreman is knocked down by a wheel; the repulsive faces of grotesquely exaggerated actors) that could potentially have been coordinated into a highly effective signal to elicit an audience's emotional orientation, but these moments remain isolated and singular. The first part of the film affects principally narrational processes (provoking temporary distrust) and characterological processes (providing a repulsive first impression of the police agents) more than it does clearly emotional processes.

This provides a potential explanation for why Eisenstein said that the workers' gatherings in the early portions of *Strike* are not "especially memorable."[10] If the film had triggered an emotional orientation in the viewer, that viewer would be interpreting the chain of diegetic events in light of that mood, giving emotional weight to those scenes.[11] This lack of initial mood orientation, suggests the mood-cue approach, is responsible for the nonemotional nature of these early segments, demonstrating how this approach can explain the failure of a film's emotional appeal (one of the desiderata).

Eisenstein described *Strike* as a materialist investigation of the process of a revolutionary strike, as the discovery of its "manufacturing logic" and "the exposition of the technique of the methods of struggle."[12] And yet the film spends much more time detailing the processes by which capital represses labor than it does the resistant activities of the proletariat. More than anything else, *Strike* is a film about surveillance.

The first part of the film gains its structural unity by following a piece of information as it proceeds through the elaborate communication network established by the factory management. Eisenstein shifted into a highly marked style relying on flashy graphic devices when he is detailing the process of surveillance. He used shots of reflections (the puddle reflection in part one, an inverted reflection in a spherical glass lamp in part four) and highly foregrounded wipes (such as the rectangular wipe out-wipe in to denote a picture being taken from a miniature camera) most frequently when showing the spies at work, and he relies on considerably less flashy devices (editing and composition) for showing the workers. By alerting us early on to the importance of graphic style and by associating highly foregrounded style with the act of spying, Eisenstein underlined the significance of surveillance in the narrative. In a diegetic world in which spying is the central activity, such vigilance seems useful for both characters and viewers.

A response to slaughtered crowds (at the end of the film) is emotionally clear-cut, but a response to surveillance is less so. Surveillance may provoke a vague sense of unease in an audience, but in *Strike* this emphasis (in combination with the film's formal play) works more to create a cognitive awareness of style than an effective emotional orientation toward the film. The beginning of the film's second part, on the other hand, provides a clear emotional direction through a segment with densely coordinated cues and clearly activated genre scripts. The second part begins when we see Vanov Stronghin's micrometer stolen. Through a matte inserted over Stronghin's worksite, we watch the thief escape. After furiously searching for the missing instrument, Stronghin reports the theft to his superiors, who laugh at him (directly facing the camera) and accuse him of the theft. The angry worker returns to his workplace, where he commits suicide offscreen, triggering the factorywide strike.

By making certain that we know that Stronghin is wrongly accused, the narration encourages us toward outrage and anger at his mistreatment and horror at his death. This segment contains many of the stylistic devices characteristic of Soviet historical-materialist cinema (direct address, noncontinuity editing), but the narration makes a cohesive emotional appeal based around a central diegetic incident. Temporarily limiting the narration to one person's story, *Strike* borrows some of the power of the protagonist-driven classical cinema to suggest a clear emotional reaction to the viewer.

I am not suggesting that historical-materialist cinema must necessarily resort to a more "classical" narration to evoke emotions; however, *Strike* shows that historical-materialist cinema can vary from the narration usually associated with that mode (omnicient, didactic, overly communicative narration concerned with mass heroes) to a narrational mode generally restricted to an individual protagonist in recognizable genre situations. Bordwell also recognizes that Soviet montage cinema sometimes relies on single protagonists, correctly noting that such characters (Stronghin included) are rarely given the individual psychological motivations typical of the classical cinema.[13] But, theorists and practitioners of the Soviet montage cinema, in their zeal to differentiate this cinema from the dominant classical paradigm, often neglect the fact that Soviet narration can occasionally shift in a more "classical" direction, making the films more a mixture of narrational modes than a singular oppositional form. This is true even of a film such as *Strike* that clearly embodies the "mass hero" emphasis of Soviet montage cinema. In restricting its narration temporarily to the plight of Vanov Stronghin, *Strike* uses one of the various narrational means available to the Soviet filmmaker of the 1920s as a way of creating a cohesive emotional orientation.[14]

Moments that we see after *Strike* has established a consistent emotional appeal provide more of a payoff. The acrobatic fight between a striking worker and the man guarding the factory whistle (staged on a seesawing board positioned on another man's back) benefits from its position immediately after the workers have begun to strike (incited by Stronghin's wrongful death). Now that *Strike* has mobilized an emotional orientation of anger and outrage, this fight becomes more exciting than if it were placed in the first part of the film. Contrast this sequence to the one in the film's first part in which workers cleverly manipulate machinery to knock down a management lackey with a wheel. Although the wheel sequence actually is more stylistically notable (because Eisenstein depicts the blow with the force of disjunctive noncontinuity editing), it is merely one incident that remains only loosely connected to the contiguous segments. The later conflict on the seesaw is more likely to be emotionally significant because of the forward momentum provided by the strike.

This distinction helps explain Eisenstein's vague comparison between certain of *Strike*'s sequences and those in *Potemkin*. *Potemkin* uses the attractions of *Strike* in combination with a "new psychologism," according to

Eisenstein. Raiding bourgeois art, Eisenstein uses "doubt, tears, sentiment, lyricism, psychologism, maternal feelings, etc." in *Potemkin* to engage the viewer's emotions in addition to providing "*formal* juxtapositions" (emphasis in original). Of course Eisenstein did not use these emotional elements in a purely classical manner. He "dismembered and reassembled" the elements into a new process. But between *Strike* and *Potemkin*, he recognized the importance of having a clear emotional orientation organizing the attractions. A mere montage using conflict-centered editing to show bodies engaged in spectacularly athletic activities is not enough. Discussing a later sequence in *Strike*, Eisenstein suggested that a dose of "emotionalism" must energize the formal material:

The difference is colossal with due regard for the technician of public sentiment – ascertaining what was the basic emotion of the mass that was just making heroic progress with *construction* – the hosing sequence is elaborated as illustration, logically, as a technical analysis of the combination of bodies and rushing water. On the whole, that is how *The Strike* (or more accurately "an illustration of the strike") was constructed. The "Odessa Steps" sequence appeared at the time of an emerging flood of emotionalism. . . . The continuity from *The Strike* to *Potemkin* lies in the development of a pathos emerging dialectically in *The Strike* that is based on the principle of abstraction and logical technicism.[15]

Certain sequences in *Strike* depict spectacular actions with formal proficiency, but Eisenstein suggested that without the impetus provided by emotional material before these sequences, the segments will remain technically interesting without engaging the emotions. He overstated his case by characterizing *Strike* as being constructed "on the whole" in this manner. In the film's second part, Eisenstein borrowed from bourgeois art to find a narrational mode that would clearly provide the "emotionalism" to energize subsequent stylistic choices.

Kittens, Griffith, and the Child at Play

The emotional payoffs that *Strike*'s segments provide depend on several different cuing strategies. Some of these strategies owe more to the classical and preclassical cinema (particularly that of D. W. Griffith) than one might expect, given the explicitly anticlassical bent of much of Eisenstein's rhetoric.

As noted earlier, the historical-materialist narration in *Strike* calls upon a range of different materials (both radically socialist and retrogressively bourgeois) to organize its segments into coherent emotional wholes.

One of the primary emotional experiences that *Strike* offers is the excitement of a massive crowd running, surging, moving. Eisenstein chose to make *Strike* first (instead of one of the other films in a proposed series on the Revolution) because the material lent itself so well to the concept of a mass hero, and he wanted this early film to announce the distinctness of Soviet montage style from individualist bourgeois cinema. He noted that "[t]he mass approach produces in addition the maximum intensification of the emotional seizure [*zakhvat*] of the audience which, for art in general and revolutionary art in particular, is decisive."[16] Coordinating a massive crowd moving onscreen provides the maximum opportunity to provoke an emotional response in the individuals in his mass audience. So *Strike* is full of dynamic editing of crowds rushing about, dashing through the factory, running from soldiers.

Strike's sequences also provide scenes in which emotion relies on the same genre scripts that a classical film might use. After the strike has continued for a long time, a hungry worker piles up household belongings to sell at the market to support his family. His wife tries to sneak a particular cloth (an heirloom, perhaps) out of the pile, and they argue, accompanied by their child's hysterical crying. Finally the wife gives in and touchingly offers her husband her earrings to sell as well. In another vignette, we see a wife violently arguing with her indolent striking husband before she leaves him. We follow these temporary protagonists briefly for only a short sequence, and the style of these domestic scenes are cut with the fast-paced editing associated with Soviet montage cinema, so they could never be mistaken for classical narration. But when *Strike* wants to evoke our sympathies for the hungry strikers, it turns to scenes that call on a straightforward emotion script that relies on the audience's encounters with traditional melodrama.

In addition to the appeals provided by movement and by genre scripts, *Strike* also relies on images of objects that could reliably be expected to evoke emotion because they call on sentimental cultural commonplaces. Eisenstein uses certain images that would be instantly readable emotionally because of their ability to cue disgust or affection. The broad animistic acting style of the police agents calls on the exaggerated conventions of caricature to create repulsive figures. The dancing dwarves performing for the wealthy signify a kind of decadence that uses grotesque figures as entertainment. By using such instantly readable emotional imagery, Eisenstein calls on the network of socially conditioned imagery that he can reliably expect his audience to possess.

When signaling the audience to feel a peaceful, warm affection toward diegetic circumstances, Eisenstein turns to the most overtly appealing cultural imagery: cute animals. To convey the comparative bliss of the worker's lives immediately after the strike, he shows us shots of domesticated baby animals: chicks waddling beside a lake, piglets hovering near their mother, geese walking accompanied by a child. The shot of kittens frolicking would not seem out of place as a means of signaling affection toward the Gish sisters in a Griffith film.

Of course Eisenstein made clear his respect for Griffith, but in his writing he asserted that he admired Griffith primarily for his technique. Although he called Griffith a master of tempo, he asserted that the Soviet montage cinema has advanced to deal with more complex matters. Soviets can look to Griffith for purely "professional-technical" expertise, but the American master remains too bound in culture to provide guidance in more complex "ideological-intellectual" matters.[17] Yet when Eisenstein wanted to convey a sense of warm affection toward the revolutionary workers, he could find no more efficient means than using imagery of frolicking animals already timeworn from their use by Griffith and his Victorian predecessors.

Perhaps foremost among the cultural commonplaces Eisenstein used to trigger emotional responses in his audience is his reliance on images of innocent children. The section conveying the beatific life of striking workers initially depends on imagery of cute animals, but the majority of this section's emotion-evoking imagery involves children. A child playfully wakes up a sleeping father at 10:30 in the morning. Another child in a bonnet wrestles with his parents as they try to bathe him. A gang of children mimic the way their parents publicly humiliated the factory management, parading around a scapegoat (literally) in a wheelbarrow to substitute for the factory foremen. But when Eisenstein wishes to create a truly strong moment of emotional appeal, he relies on endangered children. The climactic sixth part of *Strike* begins as a worker's child wanders underneath the mounted soldiers who have come to discipline the strikers. The mother discovers that the child is missing, sees him playing unaware beneath the menacing soldiers' horses, and rushes to save him, only to be lashed repeatedly with a whip. The mother's cry for help from her comrades instigates the physical confrontation between troops and workers. As they struggle, the film returns to the child twice more, his cries unheard in the conflict. When the conflict moves into the workers' quarters, Eisenstein once again foregrounds physical violence toward children as the touchstone of his emotional appeal. Early in the scene we see two children imitating the "game" they see below them, using doll riders and kitten "horses." Then to convey "savagery," the film shows one the soldiers traversing the walkways on horseback dangling a child off the edge of a walkway high above the ground. To confirm our worst fears, we see the soldier drop the child to his death, and the film shows us the bloody corpse.

These sequences are anchored by the emotional spectacle of a child in danger, thus providing the unifying emotion in a way that other sequences in *Strike* lack. When Eisenstein described the scene of the crowd being blasted with water from a hose as a "technical analysis of the combination of bodies and rushing water," he noted that this sequence lacks what he called the "new psychologism" that injects the material with "emotionalism."[18] He compared the hosing sequence to the "Odessa Steps" sequence in *Potemkin*, which he argued is an example of the new psychologism. He did not, however, discuss a point of comparison that seems both too obvious to miss and too bourgeois for him to note: that portions of the "Odessa Steps" crowd sequence are organized around endangered children, whereas there is no similar emotional mini story to provide an emotional anchor for *Strike*'s story of crowds being buffeted by pressured water. This new psychologism that differentiates *Strike*'s hosing sequence and *Potemkin*'s "Odessa Steps" sequence depends on the conventionally Griffithian spectacle of endangered innocence.

These sequences are crucial in preparing the audience for Eisenstein's strongest emotional appeal at the end of the film: the segment comparing the soldier's slaughter of the workers with a butcher's slaughter of a bull. It is this sequence to which Eisenstein made the most complimentary reference, discussing it as a paradigmatic example of the montage of attractions and of the emotional dynamization of associational montage.[19] He suggested that "[t]his extremely powerful effect – 'pulling no punches' – is responsible for 50 per cent of the opposition to the film."[20]

There is a tendency in Eisenstein's writing to reduce *Strike* to its most spectacular sequence, deemphasizing the importance of the preceding material that paves the way for this horrifying montage of attractions. Because this montage exemplifies the didactic use of editing to create highly charged "metaphoric" comparisons that distinguish Soviet montage cinema, it claims a higher profile in accounts of the Soviet cinema. Using such cultural commonplaces is not the distinguishing factor of Soviet montage cinema, so there is a tendency to overlook such instances. Close attention to the emotional appeal in *Strike* reveals Eisenstein using a variety of imagery to prepare the viewer for the final horror, however, and the importance of those attractions that are not specifically historical-materialist needs to be reaffirmed in the discussion of this film.

Being able to explain how sequences in films fail to appeal to the emotions is as useful as being able to detail how a film successfully elicits emotion. I explore other key questions in subsequent chapters, but I return to this important notion of how certain films (*The Lower Depths*, *The Joy Luck Club*) may not be well structured to appeal to the emotion system. The ability to provide grounded explanations for a film's failures as well as its successes is a great advantage of the mood-cue approach.

7   **Lyricism and Unevenness**

Emotional Transitions in Renoir's *A Day in the Country* and *The Lower Depths*

E motions display a kind of inertia. When people are fearful or angry or joyous, they tend to remain in that state because the emotion system sets up a processing loop. Our mood encourages us to revisit the emotional stimulus repeatedly, each time gaining a fresh dose of mood-sustaining emotion. This looping tends to continue until it becomes "worn out" (overly familiarized) or until the stimulus is fundamentally reevaluated or removed. Even when we have worked to eliminate the stimulus (running away from a fearful object or violently removing an object that makes us angry), the emotional state still remains for a while because of bodily arousal. The emotions usually involve the body, and the body cannot change arousal states as quickly as the mind can change thoughts. To change from one emotional state to a radically different one requires time for the body to alter its orientation.

Film narration relies on this inertia to sustain its emotional appeal. The mood-cue approach is continuity-based because of the systematic tendency of emotions to maintain a consistent orientation. Does this mean that only films that maintain a unitary tone can successfully appeal to the emotions? Our desiderata specify that an approach to filmic emotion should be able to explain how such emotions change over time. What about films that make an abrupt shift in their emotional appeals? Can the mood-cue approach explain how a film might make such a switch? To explore these questions, I examine two films directed by Jean Renoir: *A Day in the Country* (*Une Partie de Campagne*) and *The Lower Depths* (*Les Bas-Fonds*). The choice of these two films (one a recognized classic, the other a lesser known Renoir work) may seem unusual, but examining these two films together provides a distinctive opportunity for this critical approach.

Both these films contain striking shifts in their emotional appeals. Yet *A Day in the Country* has been praised as "one of the two or three greatest short-story films ever made – a lyric tragedy that ranks with [Renoir's] finest work," whereas *The Lower Depths* has been called "the most uneven Renoir film of the 1930s."[1] What could explain the differences in how successfully these films shift their emotional appeals? Loosely borrowing a strategy from more quantitative methodologies, I choose to hold "constant" several variables that might explain these differences. Both films are made by the same filmmaker, and both are shot at virtually the same point in Renoir's career (in fact, Renoir left the set of *A Day in the Country* in 1936 to begin shooting *The Lower Depths*). This minimizes the argument that Renoir's cinema "evolved" from one film to another. Also both films are adaptations of literary works (a short story by Guy de Maupassant, a play by Maxim Gorki).

Others such as André Bazin have explained differences in Renoir's work by resorting to broad humanist assertions (such as "lyricism"). This case study examines these two films as a way to demonstrate how the mood-cue approach can provide a more specific understanding of how different film texts may make abrupt shifts in their emotional appeals. Specifically, how do these two films, made by the same filmmaker in the same year, differ in the way they shift their emotional tone? How does *A Day in the Country* change from romance to melancholy in a way that may be read as "lyrical," and what strategies does *The Lower Depths* use to attempt to overcome emotional inertia?

The Brewing Storm

A Day in the Country details events around the Dufours family's Sunday picnic at a country inn. Local boatmen Rodolphe (Jacques Borel) and Henri (Georges Darnoux) explore the amorous possibilities presented by Parisians Henriette (Sylvia Bataille) and her mother Juliette (Jeanne Marken), luring them from a doltish fiancé (Paul Temps) and husband (Gabriello). The film announces its emotional appeal in its first shot, showing us the dictionary definition of love: "tender and passionate affection for one of the opposite sex, also an instance of love, a love affair." This highly self-conscious device immediately cues viewers toward the most likely set of relevant genre expectations: the love story.

This dictionary definition, in conjunction with the character interactions we observe soon thereafter, is enough to enable the viewer to reject other possible genres as less likely genre frames. Although this information makes possible a purely rational probabilistic choice of viewer expectations, according to the mood-cue approach a film must do more to appeal emotionally to a wide variety of viewers. It is not enough for a viewer to be able to classify the film intellectually into an appropriate genre. The film must present a highly coordinated burst of narrational and stylistic cues to encourage viewers to have an emotional experience.

The film presents just such a set of densely coordinated cues soon after the Dufours family arrives at the inn. As Rodolphe and Henri sit at a table inside the inn, Rodolphe opens the window shutters, naturally framing Henriette and Juliette on the swings outside. Rodolphe notices the young Henriette, and as his attention becomes centered on her, the camera follows his lead, emphasizing the spectacle of her beauty using the film's most distinctive camera setup. The camera is positioned on Henriette's swing in motion, pointed upward at her as she stands in the swing. She floats vertiginously, outlined against the sky and seemingly unhindered by gravity's bindings. We return to this spectacular shot several times as Rodolphe and Henri discuss the Parisians. We hear the women's rapturous giggling, and Joseph Kosma's nondiegetic music comes into the aural foreground of this complicated sound mix, further marking this notable sequence.

The camera further allies us with Rodolphe's romantic inclinations toward Henriette, giving us the vantage point that would fulfill his lascivious wishes. Henri notes, "But you can't see a thing," meaning no glimpse of her flesh. Rodolphe replies, "Because she's standing. . . . If she sat, it would be more interesting." Henriette, far out of range of their conversation, seemingly responds immediately to his wishes and sits down in the swing. The camera then is positioned on the ground beneath her swing, giving us the daring vista of her legs that Rodolphe wished for. The camera position and figure blocking create a highly coordinated moment of shared voyeurism that makes a spectacle of Henriette's body and establishes the romantic trajectory involving the boatmen, the women, and us, the viewers. In *Strike* Eisenstein used formal devices primarily to establish a cognitive orientation, training the audience to pay attention to the formal play of signifiers. In *A Day in the Country*, camera, staging, and music all coordinate to evoke the appropriate emotional orientation to the text, that of lighthearted romance.

The swing sequence also includes some of the film's most densely packed character exposition, revealed through Henri and Rodolphe's concise conversation. In this sequence, we learn the crucial difference between Henri's and Rodolphe's philosophies of love as they discuss the romantic prospects these women present. Rodolphe reveals himself as a rake in pursuit of lusty, temporary "adventures," ignoring the consequences and denying deeper emotions: "A fine thing, if people couldn't have fun anymore without over-populating the world." By contrast, Henri is uninterested in such "adventures." "At heart I'm a family man," Henri says. "Sophisticated women bore me, the rest scare me." Rodolphe asks, "Scared of the usual thing, eh?" Henri replies, "No, of responsibilities." Rodolphe's hedonism and Henri's fear of responsibilities are the core personality traits that differentiate them as characters and that motivate their behavior in the narrative. Renoir situates this important character information in one of the most highly marked sequences of the film, underlining its importance in establishing an initial orientation toward the film.

This sequence also shows how Renoir trains his audience early in the film to look ahead and anticipate events to come. For instance, Rodolphe's expressed wish for a better view of Henriette's swinging legs is gratified soon after he voices his desire. Characters in the opening scenes of *A Day in the Country* predict what will happen in the narrative, and the narration swiftly proves their predictions to be accurate. Soon after Rodolphe notes that Parisians always eat on the grass, Juliette asks her husband if they will do just that. He replies, "We didn't come to shut ourselves in!" The locals spurn the innkeeper's offer of fish, suggesting that the Parisians should be fed the despised fish. Later Juliette excitedly requests fried fish from the innkeeper.

In addition to these localized predictions, the narration also trains our expectations by making us privy to Rodolphe and Henri's strategic planning concerning the seduction of the women. They discuss whether they should proceed separately or together. They argue over which one of them should approach which woman. They plan a charade of good manners as a way of ingratiating themselves with the Dufours, and we watch them execute their plan: taking the family's picnic spot and then returning it to them in an overly gracious display of courtesy. The narration presents a carefully orchestrated sequence of predictions, plans, and payoffs that instructs the viewer to look ahead and promises that expectations will likely be fulfilled.

This presentation of an internally consistent and predictable diegetic world helps boost our confidence in the initial emotional orientation of lighthearted romance provided by the sequence at the swings. Renoir encourages us to look forward in the narrative to find evidence of what we expect will happen based on our genre microscripts: the boatmen and the women will have a romantic rendezvous. In a world proven to be consistently predictable, a mood can be sustained through a regular progression of emotion-congruent events.

Of course Renoir's film cannot progress in an entirely predictable fashion without losing the viewer's curiosity and interest, but the "surprises" presented are within the realm of broad genre expectations for the love story. Although initially Rodolphe expresses strong desire for Henriette and the diffident Henri agrees to spend time with the older Juliette, the romantic pairings soon switch. Henry becomes enamored of Henriette, and Rodolphe is paired with Juliette. Our previous genre experience lets us know that Cupid's arrow does not always go where it is aimed in such narratives. Our genre microscripts teach us that characters who seem closed down to romance (such as Henri) are often the ones who fall in love.[2]

Once the film establishes major character traits, a genre framework, a consistent emotional orientation, and a sense of predictable progression, Renoir turns his attention toward establishing a base of primarily thematic material. Subsequent conversations affirm nature as a primary concern of the characters. Monsieur Dufours and Anatole, Henriette's fiancé, have a fisherman's discussion concerning carnivorous fish, and they marvel at nature's strangeness: "Nature is a closed book to Man," Dufours says. In the next conversation Henriette wonders about the pleasures and pains of the tiny living things under a blade of grass. She asks Juliette if she ever felt "a kind of tenderness for everything. . . . For the grass, the water, the trees, a kind of vague longing that catches you here and almost makes you want to cry," and Juliette confesses to feeling the same sympathy for nature.

This pair of conversations foreground the theme of nature, and this thematic emphasis has helped critics to connect this film with impressionism.[3]

The connections are several. Jean Renoir shot the film in the Loing region near Montigny where his famous father painted numerous impressionist paintings. The film depicts some of the most frequent subjects treated by the impressionists, such as picnics and couples rowing. Renoir himself downplayed the significance of the connection between impressionism and *A Day in the Country*:

if certain landscapes, certain costumes [in *A Day in the Country*], bring to mind my father's paintings, it's for two reasons: first, because it takes place during the period and in a place where my father worked a great deal in his youth. Second, it's because I'm my father's son, and one is inevitably influenced by one's parents. If I were the son of a nursery gardener, I would probably know a great deal about trees, and I would have an extraordinary taste for gardens.[4]

Rather than further emphasize this connection between the son's film and the father's painting, I wish to assert the functional significance of this thematic material in the overall narrational scheme. These foregrounded conversations about nature call on the viewer to pay attention to Renoir's shots of the natural surroundings. As Rodolphe and Henri relax on the grass, the camera pans upward to the darkening sky. "The wind's shifting west . . . some heavy clouds, too. . . . And the flies are annoying. . . . A storm's brewing. . . . It'll cool us off." After the Dufours finish their picnic, Renoir again shows the gathering clouds.

Renoir also uses the storm to demarcate the switch in emotional appeal from light romance to a melancholy depiction of marital demise. Henri takes Henriette ashore to his "private den," a forest enclosure where they listen to a nightingale. Henri makes advances that Henriette initially rejects, but then she returns his passionate kisses. The film then dissolves to the couple lying side by side, looking away. *A Day in the Country* then presents a remarkable series of picturesque shots of the storm on the river, accompanied by program music. Trees and river grasses bend in the wind, outlined against the sky, and strings play quarter notes an octave apart (low-high-low), a pattern that is commonly used to connote a ticking clock. We see dark clouds moving, and the strings repeat a rapidly descending and ascending musical figure as the rain begins. We track away from the river as the rain disturbs its surface, and the strings begin an ascending series of trills as we move away and the image slowly fades to black.

This is the storm that we have been expecting for some time, a storm that is lent emotional force by the climactic tryst that preceded it. Inertia encourages the emotional orientation cued by Henri and Henriette's passionate and long-delayed embrace to continue through the spectacular presentation of the storm. At the same time, this storm takes on narrational function, relying on cultural commonplaces to signal that a change in emotional appeal is about to occur. The emphasis on the storm alerts the experienced film viewer of a possible emotional "storm" on the horizon.

Rain is widely used in cinema to mark a sad turn of events. Countless breakups have been shown against rain-spattered windows; dreary rain routinely accompanies onscreen funerals; rain-drenched streets are a recognized part of the film noir landscape. Although rain is not always a harbinger of sad times in film, it accompanies sad moments frequently enough to be a recognizable dramatic convention. Add to this the cultural knowledge that relational difficulties are often compared with inclement weather, as in a "stormy" relationship. A violent storm can externalize the upheaval that has been "brewing" among characters, as in the climax of Tennessee Williams's *Cat on a Hot Tin Roof*. When experienced film viewers, trained by the film to notice the foregrounded mentions of nature, hear Rodolphe say that "A storm's brewing," our genre microscripts alert us to the likely possibility that this storm will have dramatic significance.

This storm marks the emotional turning point in the film. Thereafter, the mood is somber, melancholy. An intertitle tersely informs us that "[y]ears have passed. Henriette is married to Anatole. The Sundays are now as sad as the Mondays." The film's last sequence shows us Henriette and Anatole revisiting the site of Henri and Henriette's rendezvous. The married Henriette sees Henri, and both assert that they have not found happiness since their tryst. "I come here often," Henri says, "My tenderest memories are here." The married Henriette confesses, "And I think of them every night." Husband Anatole calls her away from this brief meeting, and Henri watches as the couple rows away across the river.

The storm separates these two portions of the film and their distinct emotional appeals, but the effectiveness of this device does not depend entirely on the (somewhat cliched) cinematic and cultural associations of rain. The storm can ease the transition from romance to melancholy precisely because the viewer has been prepared for this transition. The emphasis on nature in dialogue and mise-en-scène accentuates the narrational significance of this imminent storm, preparing us for the possibility of a shift in emotional orientation.

The cultural connotations of storms help us to place emotional heartbreak in the realm of likely dramatic possibilities for Henri and Henriette, yet this preparation is fairly subtle. The imminent storm is not emphasized so frequently as to signal that relational tempest is unavoidable, and therefore this preparatory device does not interrupt the romantic mood that Renoir worked to create. The storm is mentioned enough times to introduce the possible genre microscript (one among several) of romantic tragedy. This hint is then activated by the highly foregrounded depiction of the storm. Because we are prepared for the storm (and the turmoil it thematically connotes), we are not surprised by the tonal shift.

Preparing viewers to shift emotional orientations is important to *A Day in the Country*, but so is giving them time to negotiate this change. Emotional inertia requires that it takes time for viewers to change from one mood orientation to a greatly different one, even if they are mentally prepared to make that shift. The storm sequence provides an interval away from the narrative events in Henri's and Henriette's lives, allowing us time to concentrate fully on our work of the moment: changing to a more melancholy mode.

A large part of *A Day in the Country*'s heralded lyricism depends on this smooth emotional transition, and Renoir models one particular way in which such a shift might be accomplished. To summarize: after he establishes a consistent emotional orientation toward the text, he encourages us to hypothesize what will occur later in the narrative. He begins introducing thematic material that prepares us for the coming storm (meteorological and dramatic). Vivid depiction of this storm after the climax of the romantic progression encourages us to depend on the cultural and cinematic connotations of storms, activating the possibility of a sad turn of events introduced earlier. The storm sequence itself provides valuable time for viewers to overcome emotional inertia and make the transition requested of them. In this way, *A Day in the Country* negotiates this emotional transition so that it does not sacrifice dramatic continuity.

Juxtaposing Emotions

A Day in the Country also intermingles components of various genres. Not only does the film contain separate romantic and melancholic sections, but the romantic section integrates both comic and romantic material. How is the comic material intertwined in a way that does not jeopardize the basic romantic orientation? André Bazin notes that this juxtaposition of comedy and tragedy is characteristic of Renoir's best work. Examining how Renoir handled the comic material in A Day in the Country provides a useful comparison to how he integrated material from other genres into The Lower Depths.

Two figures provide the comedy in A Day in the Country: M. Dufours and Anatole. Dufours, a fat, self-important man with a hat and a short necktie, iconically evokes Oliver Hardy. Anatole, a thin, wispy-haired man, mugs confusedly for the camera à la Stan Laurel. Anatole-Laurel gets an uncontrollable case of the hiccoughs and bumbles around trying to find water, and Dufours-Hardy expresses consternation at his ineptness. In their most comic bit, Dufours and Anatole go fishing, only to pull a shoe out of the river.

Although these bumblers are overtly the love interests for Henriette and Juliette, they are tangential to the narrative progression. They are too inept to threaten any possible interference to the boatmen's plans for romantic liaisons with their female partners. Juliette tickles a sleeping Dufours in a vain attempt to engage him in amorous activity, but he refuses to be roused. Fiancés Anatole and Henriette barely speak to each other throughout the picnic. The men seem only interested in fishing (although they didn't bring any fishing equipment). When the boatmen provide them with fishing poles, the men gladly leave the women to amuse themselves with the young locals. The last we see of Dufours and Anatole together is their floundering about with the shoe they caught.

Their lack of centrality to the narrative is crucial to the way A Day in the Country interjects comedy while maintaining its initial emotional orientation. Localizing the comedy in two tangential characters keeps the comic sensibility bounded to a few brief scenes that have minimal impact on the romantic narrative. If Dufours or Anatole had a more direct effect on the narrative outcome (presenting a more effective obstacle to the boatmen's intentions, for instance), their comic antics might threaten the consistency of the primary emotional orientation. Involving them as primary movers of the plot would increase the chances that they would be included in a scene that bolsters the romantic mood. In the time-honored tradition of "comic relief" provided by such tangential characters as *Hamlet*'s gravedigger, the brevity and lack of centrality of Dufours's and Anatole's appearances keep them from jeopardizing the continuity of mood.

Let us contrast *A Day in the Country*'s continuity-preserving strategies with those used in *The Lower Depths*, which begins by introducing us to two characters from seemingly separate worlds: the Baron (Louis Jouvet), a dignified aristocrat who is a calamitously unsuccessful gambler, and Pepel (Jean Gabin), an unsuccessful, small-time thief. We follow the Baron as he loses all his possessions (without losing his bemused upper-crust demeanor). We see Pepel caught up in the interactions at an impoverished flophouse. Pepel fences his stolen goods through his landlord Kostileff (Vladimir Sokolov), while his illicit relationship with Kostileff's wife Vasilissa (Suzy Prim) is turning sour. In hopes of escaping the oppressive poverty of the flophouse, Pepel tries to rob a wealthy home. Unfortunately for him, it is the Baron's home, which has been brought to ruin by gambling losses. When the bankrupt Baron, who is about to take his own life, is interrupted by Pepel, they become instant friends, and their nightlong conversation distracts the Baron from suicide.

Until this point, the film alternates between two vastly different worlds, each occupied by a leading character. On one hand, the Baron presents us with a detached, aristocratic amusement spotlighted from the film's first shot. In this shot Renoir's moving camera occupies the point of view of a government official pacing back and forth before the Baron, whom he confronts (in an obsequious and apologetic manner) about the misuse of public funds. As the unseen official prattles on about the money the Baron has squandered, we see the Baron's mannerly, unapologetic smile that does not betray a single care about the serious charges. Later scenes provide us with more evidence of his detachment from his fiscal crisis. Bystanders tell us that the only way to tell if the Baron has won or lost a fortune gambling is by noting if he lights a cigarette or not (if he does light one, he has lost heavily). Renoir makes the most of this detail by having the Baron leave the gambling tables, nearly light a cigarette, and throw the match away. Although his valet Felix is flustered by the imminent prospect of the furniture being repossessed, the Baron remains unflappable. He clearly belongs to that class of aristocratic Renoir characters who are bred to maintain a mannerly and slightly amused distance from their circumstances, no matter how dire.

In the early portions of *The Lower Depths*, the Baron's bemusement alternates with the bleaker world Pepel occupies at the flophouse. Here the conflicts are a matter of life and death, not a matter for amusement. Activating our expectations through genre microscripts, Renoir prepares us for potential crises later in the film when Vasilissa, spurned by her lover Pepel, threatens to send him to prison if he ever leaves her, and Pepel returns the threat of imprisonment. When Kostileff finds Pepel with Vasilissa his wife, a fight breaks out, and Pepel almost strangles Kostileff. The characters in the flophouse cannot afford the luxury of the Baron's aristocratic bemusement. Instead they are embroiled in a world of crime, betrayal, and worn-out love.

When Pepel's and the Baron's separate narrative trajectories combine, the film establishes its primary emotional orientation, which more resembles the ironic bemusement of the earlier aristocratic sections. When Pepel surprises the Baron in his home, the Baron in turn surprises the burglar with the offer of food and drink. They discuss whether Pepel should accept the unusual offer, and the Baron persuades him that taking food would simply be another kind of stealing, which therefore would not violate the thief's sense of propriety. The Baron further offers Pepel anything he wants in the house, because all his belongings will soon be repossessed anyway. They sit down to an all-night conversation and game of cards as the two thieves from different classes discover their affinity for each other.

This sequence is structurally significant as the convergence between the two primary plotlines and the meeting of the two principals. This narrative significance emphasizes the film's most conspicuously witty dialogue as Pepel and the Baron discuss the proper and improper courses of action for a thief. In this scene, Pepel (who has thus far been embroiled in the potboiler world of the flophouse) is seemingly converted to the Baron's bemused lack of concern for material circumstances, and with this conversion the film signals that it endorses the amusement-in-dire-circumstances orientation toward the diegetic world.

This complex but consistent emotional appeal continues through subsequent sequences. Pepel, carrying some of the belongings the Baron gave him through the streets, is arrested on suspicion of theft, but he maintains the same carefree attitude even when he is behind bars, because he knows he is innocent. The Baron reveals the mistake, and the policeman apologizes profusely. Meanwhile, all of the Baron's remaining goods are being repossessed, and the Baron remains nonplussed. His interactions with his valet are dignified and mannerly with just a bit of humor, even to the end of their relationship. The Baron asks politely if the valet has been able to steal enough to compensate for the wages he is owed, and the valet assures him that he is not to worry. The result is an infectious mix of drollness in difficult circumstances, a quintessentially Renoirian view of the story world.

All this good humor comes suddenly to a halt when Pepel, just released from jail, returns to the flophouse. Although *The Lower Depths* to this point has followed Pepel and the Baron, these principals disappear as the film introduces us to a series of doomed occupants of the flophouse. We are introduced to an actor whose "organism has been poisoned by alcohol." We see an impoverished cobbler, and Kostileff the landlord raises his rent because his work occupies too much space. We see the inhabitants making cruel fun of Nastya, an idealistic young woman caught up in reading a romantic novel called *Doomed Love*. We hear an extended conversation about fear, death, and suffering between a dying woman named Anna and her grandfather Luka, in which Luka says that "Death is mother to us all." The residents are "poor strays" who cannot escape the poverty of the flophouse except through the way Anna and the actor eventually take: death.

This is a far cry from the comedy of manners we have just recently seen as Pepel, the Baron, and the police chief engaged in an elaborate show of etiquette as Pepel was released from jail. The shift is a strongly marked one. Most noticeably, the two characters the film has spent all its time developing have disappeared, leaving us with characters we know little about. The camerawork inside the flophouse during this segment eschews the long tracking shots that characterized the earlier sections, even when these early scenes took place in the flophouse. Visually, narratively, and emotionally, the scenes in the flophouse after Pepel returns signal a radical shift. The juxtaposition of higher and lower classes is certainly no surprise in a film by the director of *Boudu Saved from Drowning*. Yet something more is being asked of the viewer than a simple binary understanding of two social strata. Renoir asks the audience to shift emotional orientations from the bemused to the despairing.

Unlike *A Day in the Country, The Lower Depths* provides almost no cues that help ready us to make the transition. The shift from Pepel's release to the flophouse is smoothed somewhat by music. The Romantic orchestral music that accompanies Pepel's release fades out, followed by diegetic organ grinder music as Pepel walks to the flophouse, where card-playing residents are singing. There is no nondiegetic music in the subsequent scenes in the flophouse as we are introduced to its inhabitants. This gradual progression from lush orchestral music to rough-hewn singing and organ grinding helps audiences make the transition from one diegetic space to another.

In this instance, however, Renoir is asking audiences to make more than just a shift in narrational space to the flophouse (a shift we have made before). The succession of vignettes showing the hopeless lives of the residents calls upon us to revise our emotional orientation toward the text, and a simple progression of musical cues is not sufficient to prepare us to make this shift. Because of emotional inertia, a shift in emotional orientation takes time, and *The Lower Depths* asks us to make this transition without providing the time to do so (as *A Day in the Country* did during the storm sequence). There are insufficient cues to signal to an audience that the film would take a turn toward the despairing.

This film does not only make a single extended shift in its emotional appeal. As is typical for Renoir, *The Lower Depths*'s drama contains overtly comic and melodramatic episodes. Gabriello, the actor who played a bumbling husband reminiscent of Oliver Hardy in *A Day in the Country*, portrays a bumbling suitor in *The Lower Depths*. He plays a police sergeant who ineffectually attempts to woo Natacha (Junie Astor), Vasilissa's sister who has fallen in love with Pepel. His overblown sense of self-importance once again creates a figure who comes to a typically Hardyesque end. Pepel, enraged at his beloved Natacha accompanying the sergeant, punches him, and we last see him as he avoids Natacha, displaying as much dignity as he can muster with an enormous bandage on his head.

Here Gabriello plays a variation on the bumbling windbag he portrayed in *A Day in the Country*, except this time he is a suitor instead of a husband. Gabriello's role as the sergeant is to interject moments of broad comedy into the bemused and despairing emotional orientations that dominate the film.

As in *A Day in the Country, The Lower Depths*'s broad comedy is isolated from the primary storylines, being confined to a single supporting character. By restricting this physical comedy to limited, brief, occasional appearances that do not have lasting impact on the principal characters' progress, Renoir attempts to mix genres while maintaining a clear hierarchy of emotional orientation.

Comic material is not the only genre component Renoir uses in *The Lower Depths* in this limited fashion. The film also contains a character who is caught up in melodramatic narratives of sacrificial love. The flophouse inhabitants make fun of Nastya's absorption in her book *Doomed Love*. When she tells Natacha the book's story of a young couple nobly making great sacrifices all in the name of love, several other flophouse residents are listening, and they frequently interrupt her tale with derisive comments and laughter. Their commentary bounds the overwrought narrative-within-the-narrative with a clearly ironic frame. The film offers us the flophouse characters' world-hardened ironies to provide the audience with a perspective that keeps the melodramatic content in a limited role. As Nastya tells her story of young, idealistic, tragic love, the story never threatens to overturn the film's overall emotional orientation because it is bounded and framed within ironic commentary.

Not all of *The Lower Depths*'s textual shifts are equally responsible for the film's "unevenness." Renoir's strategies for using comic and melodramatic content are consistent with his strategies in *A Day in the Country*. That film demonstrates that bounded, brief, occasional scenes (scenes that do not have a major impact on the primary story arcs) can interject moments of other emotions without jeopardizing the film's overall emotional orientation. The problem with using these devices in *The Lower Depths* is that the lengthy segment in the depressing flophouse has derailed the consistent orientation that the film earlier worked to establish. Without an overall emotional mood well in place, jumping back and forth between emotionally disparate moments can seem disjunctive, scattered. Once the consistency of the film's emotional orientation has been disturbed by the despair of the flophouse scenes, comic and melodramatic moments seem less like brief interjections of emotion within a cohesive whole and more like uneven, erratic appeals to the emotions. André Bazin usually praises Renoir's characteristic "juxtaposition of comedy and tragedy," but he censures *The Lower Depths* for its "improbable game of hide-and-seek between vaudeville and tragedy."[5] The "improbability" here refers to the unpredictability that results when emotions are juxtaposed without preparing the audience for those emotional shifts, as is done in *A Day in the Country*.

Little wonder that critics would describe the first thirty-six minutes of *The Lower Depths* as "almost pure Renoir" and assert that in the following segments (the dark flophouse scenes) that "Gorky's play interrupts Renoir's film."[6] Most have attributed this emotional shift to a tension between Renoir's world view and the pessimism of Gorky's original play. Alexander Sesonske says that the reason *The Lower Depths* is Renoir's most uneven film of the 1930s is "[t]he uneasy imposition of the open Renoir world, with its possibilities for change and hope as well as disaster, upon the closed and desperate world of Gorky's *Lower Depths*."[7] It becomes easy to call the first thirty-six minutes "Renoir's" and the next scenes "Gorky's," 'thus attributing the shift to the problems of a generally optimistic filmmaker adapting a dark original work.

In some ways this recalls the critical strategy of attributing the appeal of Renoir's *A Day in the Country* to its "impressionistic" qualities, providing a clearly linked external source for the material the artist used to create the work. In one case, this external comparison explains the perception of "lyricism." In the other, the comparison provides a convenient straw man to blame for irregularities in the film. Although both explanations have an intuitive sense of fit, they do not provide much specific guidance as to where one film's emotional appeal was well wrought and another was not. These ex post facto explanations remain too rooted in a rigid consistency of personality: Renoir and Gorky are too different, but Renoir *fils* and Renoir *père* are not.

My analysis emphasizes the differences in the way these films signal major upcoming emotional transitions and in the way they hierarchically structure genre components. I do not suggest that the methods Renoir uses are the only methods that can be used to integrate multiple emotional orientations into a single film. This case study has examined two particular ways in which a single filmmaker wrestled with the problems caused by emotional inertia. This chapter demonstrates that the concept of emotional inertia can lead to more specific insights concerning a film's emotional appeal than vaguely intuitive connections to external sources of imagery (such as the influence of impressionism or an auteurist construction of Maxim Gorky).

The other purpose of this chapter was to demonstrate how the mood-cue approach can satisfy the desideratum for explaining how filmic emotions can change over time. The next chapter explores the limits of emotional inertia, examining how a film's emotional appeal can remain consistent over time and yet exhaust the emotion system's capacities.

8　Emotion Work

The Joy Luck Club and the Limits of the Emotion System

The mood-cue approach seems to favor films that try to maintain a consistent emotional tone. Yes, filmmakers can shift tones effectively if they cue an audience to expect such a change (as *A Day in the Country* demonstrates), but navigating such a shift can be tricky (cf. *The Lower Depths*). It seems easier to take advantage of the emotion system's continuity. Once you establish a mood, you just have to keep pouring on a steady stream of congruent emotion cues, and you've got it made, it would seem.

But can a filmmaker simply keep adding cue after cue? We have seen how brief emotion and longer-lasting mood interact to support each other, but are there limits to an audience's ability maintain this consistency? Can a film's emotional appeal wear itself out by trying to evoke too much emotion over time? Again we must remember that different audiences have different expectations for the pacing of their emotion cues. An audience choosing to follow *Stranger than Paradise* cannot expect the same density of cuing they would from *Raiders of the Lost Ark*. But even audience members who have developed a taste for dense emotion cuing rely on the basic emotion system, and that network, like all systems, has its limits. Filmmakers must pace their emotion cues appropriately to maintain a consistent mood. Space the emotion cues too far apart, and the filmmaker is in danger of losing his or her audience's emotions. Pile the cues on indiscriminately, and the audience is in danger of being overwhelmed, even if those cues are emotionally consistent.

Given the variability of different people's emotion systems, it is almost impossible to say that a particular film could exhaust all audiences. We can, however, discuss how a specific film makes it difficult for all but the most dedicated audiences to sustain the emotional appeal across the entire film. By paying attention to the organization and pacing of cues, we can see how a film might test the limits of the emotion system while still maintaining a consistent tone.

Wayne Wang's *The Joy Luck Club* has an admittedly difficult task: to adapt the complexly interwoven stories of Amy Tan's novel to a mainstream film. Classical Hollywood narration is individualistic, tending toward stories about lone protagonists (or occasionally dual heros, as in the musical and the romance). Characters are hierarchically arranged into "lead" and "supporting" roles. Only rarely does this narrational system present the balanced depiction of several, equally dramatically important main characters. To adapt Tan's novel fully, Wang had to tell the stories of four mother-daughter pairs, and each of these characters presents her encapsulated story in her own voice. The film adaptation of *The Joy Luck Club* presents eight self-enclosed flashback stories (each one with its own character narrator), as well as the overall framing story in the present. To do so using the tools of classical narration is not an impossible task, but it certainly is a challenge.

Wang begins his film by openly acknowledging the literary nature of his source. The movie begins with a single storytelling voice, accompanied by a lone flute, telling a fable against a solid black frame. Instantly we are attuned to the importance of words in this film. The film's introduction tells us that we should pay attention to the stories being told and to the voice of the storyteller. After the initial credit sequence, the film opens on a crowded party scene, and the camera at first frames the people at a distance down a hallway. Slowly the camera tracks past businessmen having a conversation in Chinese, and then past a crowd watching football on television. The camera roams, seemingly uncertain of who should be the center of interest, until it begins tracking with June. When it follows her through the house toward a mah-jongg game, the camera tells audiences raised on classical narration that June is the central character here. But when the Chinese-American daughters and mothers pair up for a photograph, the camera leaves June and tracks from one character to another, giving each mother and daughter a foregrounded moment of dialogue.

Using camera movement instead of standard cutting lets the camera embody the trajectory the audience must take through the film. We will be asked to allow each of these women to take control briefly of the film's narration, and then we must pass our interest on to the next character narrator. Although we must pay attention most strongly to June's story (the primary action that resolves the film), we must also be willing to attach ourselves to each of the other characters in turn. The film's initial scenes provide an elegant formal model for the audience, but then it must encourage our emotions to follow this path.

June's expository voiceover informs us about the basic relationships among the characters, and the dialogue during the mah-jongg game sets up one of the film's central issues: the older women's concern that their daughters are ignorant and not respectful of their Chinese heritage. The cuing here is densely verbal, as we've been led to expect from the film's opening moments, but there are few clear emotion cues. The opening fable (which is situated in an exotic past) and the discussion of Chinese heritage alerts us that the past will be important and perhaps calls for a vague sense of nostalgia. Like the camera at the beginning of the party scene, however, the film initially stays at an emotional distance, not settling down on any one particular emotional stance.

During the first flashback, we see the first sharply focused emotion cuing. June (via voiceover and visual flashback) tells the story of her public failure at a childhood piano recital. Her humiliation is compounded because her mother, Suyuan, has been engaging in a bragging contest with Lindo, her best friend and enemy, about whose daughter is the most talented. Lindo boasts about her daughter Waverly's prowess in chess, and Suyuan responds by praising June's musical potential. The beginning of the flashback lets us know the truth: that June is a horrible pianist who butchers Dvorak's "Humoresque."

The stage is set for a scene of horrible embarrassment. As Suyuan boasts, we anticipate the humiliation to come at the piano recital. The camera accentuates the character dynamics by intercutting among the mothers and daughters as June at first successfully plays the piece but then self-destructs. The intercutting provides us with access to all the character's emotional states: June and Suyuan's growing humiliation, Waverly and Lindo's smug triumph. The scene is classically constructed to extend the humiliation, encouraging us to feel embarrassment for our main character, June.

Near the end of this first flashback the film makes the first mention of the sole overarching plot concern. We hear how Suyuan was forced to leave her two babies to die in China. When we return from the flashback to the current day, we learn that those babies survived and that the party is to bid June farewell as she goes to visit her Chinese sisters for the first time. Next we discover that the older aunts have not told the newly found sisters that their mother has died, and that June will bear those sad tidings, although she thinks that the sisters already know about their mother's death. This array of information is necessary to set up the larger plot questions structuring the film. Will June find out that her "aunts" have left it to her to inform the sisters in China that their mother has died? How will the sisters react when they hear the news?

By this point *The Joy Luck Club* has given us a well-constructed emotional sequence (evoking embarrassment) and has established an overall plot question that the film will answer in its closing scenes. Thus far the film's cuing has been well within the norms of classical narrative practice. The difficulty comes when this adaptation starts to do what classical film rarely does: tell separate multiple stories in succession.

There are, of course, omnibus films like *Dead of Night* in which the characters gather for the explicit purpose of telling such stories. In *Dead of Night* the characters assemble in a drawing room and tell a series of horrific tales. After each tale, we return to the drawing room where a bit of dialogue allows the narratorship to pass from one storyteller to the next. The tales are held together by a consistent appeal to horror and by the structure of the overall film. *The Joy Luck Club*, however, attempts a more challenging narrative structure.

After we return from June's flashback and learn of her newly found sisters, we leave the established protagonist to hear and see Lindo's story. This story is not entirely unrelated to June's central concerns (about the babies that June's mother Suyuan left for dead), but neither is it linearly related to those concerns either. When Lindo's voiceover begins, it makes clear the connection between the previous story and the story to come. "How could Suyuan leave those babies? How could my own mother give me up?" she ponders. This voiceover signals a transition to a new story and narrator and sets up a parallel comparison between Suyuan's situation and that of Lindo's mother, providing a continuity that should help smooth the transition.

The connection between the two stories, however, is thematic, not linear. Both deal with loss and seemingly impossible maternal choices that

occurred in the past. Lindo's story, however, does not expand our knowledge concerning the central plot questions about Suyuan leaving her babies.
At best, the story encourages a deeper understanding of how a loving mother
might be led by circumstances to abandon her children. It does nothing to
help us understand what motivated a *particular* mother (Suyuan) to do so.
The curiosity raised by June's story is abandoned during the story presented
immediately thereafter.

Subsequent stories follow the same pattern of making a thematic connection to June's and Suyuan's dilemmas through words heard at the beginning
of the flashback. After Lindo's and her daughter Waverly's stories, we return
to the current-day party, and dialogue once again reminds us of the overall
plot question: "How terrible for Suyuan to lose her babies and not know
if they're alive or dead." Ying Ying turns the narrative inward as she begins
her own voiceover leading to her own story. She says, "Only one thing is
worse," and she goes on to tell what that thing is: killing one's own child.
The next set of mother-daughter flashbacks begins during yet another brief
discussion at the party of June's upcoming visit to see her sisters in China.
An Mei's voiceover begins, "As a little girl I wondered every day. Worst of
all I had to wonder in secret. . . . I had no memory of my mother because
she was kicked out of the house when I was four." An Mei's story gives us
an idea of what it might be like to be a child growing up without knowing
her mother. Again we get a thematic variation on the overall plot concern
without advancing the state of our overall plot knowledge.

You might say that it is unfair to expect a nontraditionally structured
narrative like *The Joy Luck Club* to behave in a linear fashion. Perhaps it
is better to think of this film's structure as being more like a soap opera's
with a set of interrelated but still distinct plotlines that interrupt each other
rather than advancing a single dominant plotline. Perhaps the progress
of *The Joy Luck Club* depends mostly on a deepening understanding of the
overall narrative situation from a variety of perspectives, not on an increasing
knowledge of the particular plight of key characters. There is a good deal
of truth in this objection. And yet the film itself keeps returning us to the
topic of Suyuan, June, and the sisters in China to remind us that this is the
central question. More and more these brief mentions in the dialogue serve to
remind us of how static the overall plot situation is. We know no more about
those Chinese sisters than we did the last time they were mentioned long ago.

The film intermittently picks up its overall plot question only to abandon it quickly without giving us more information. This means that the film more or less abandons one of the primary devices the classical cinema has developed to keep our emotional orientations focused. Mainstream Hollywood narratives tend to be structured around a series of localized questions arranged in a chain that eventually leads to the answer to a global question. At any given moment our emotions may be engaged by a sequence focused on a small question (e.g., "Will the criminals outrun the cops in this car chase?"). The answer to that small question leads us closer to the answer to the overall question posed by the narrative ("Will the couple be reunited happily?"). We do not have to try to force *The Joy Luck Club* into this classical mold, but we should recognize that the film comes to emphasize local questions, not global ones.

The questions that matter most in *The Joy Luck Club* are the questions posed within the individual stories themselves. Will Waverly and Rich (or Lena and Harold, or Rose and Ted) end up together? What will happen to Lindo in her arranged marriage to a boy? Why did An Mei's mother give her up? These questions matter most because they are given the most emotionally concentrated narrative focus, as opposed to the on-again, off-again, static attention to June, Suyuan, and the Chinese sisters. Viewers may put together an overall spin on this film's proceedings, and the film itself provides some *formal* encouragement to do so (the early camera movements, the brief dialogue reminders that connect flashbacks). The film lurches from one story to another, however, with few *emotion* cues to prepare us for these shifts. The simple fact that *The Joy Luck Club* is organized around local stories, questions, and flashbacks does not necessarily damage its emotional appeal, although by choosing this structure the film relinquishes one of the cinema's powerful devices for organizing emotions. The film's emotional task is made even more difficult because of the structure of those flashbacks, which create considerable emotion work for the viewer.

Almost all of the flashbacks in this film takes us to a time and place that we have not visited previously.[1] This, in and of itself, does not pose any particular emotional difficulty to the viewer. But in each new place, we have to be introduced to a new set of characters. We already know the adult versions of Lindo, Ying Ying, An Mei, Waverly, Lena, and Rose from the current-day party scene, and the flashbacks take us back to their childhoods. But when we see and hear Lindo's story, we must be introduced to her mother, her tyrannical mother-in-law, and her child husband. An Mei's story requires that we learn about a dizzying array of characters: her mother, An Mei's dying grandmother, her stepfather, and her stepfather's three other wives. Learning these interrelationships takes an investment of time and effort on the audience's part, and the audience is asked to do this over and over again.

Introducing such characters and defining their basic interrelationships is a process generally called "exposition," and it is the work of almost every film, even sequels. As David Bordwell has noted, this early exposition is one of the moments that classical film narration tends to be particularly communicative. Mainstream films try to tell us who the characters are in as condensed a fashion as possible. Without this knowledge early in the film, it is more difficult for audiences to care about these characters, and so the film has an built-in interest in getting the exposition done quickly and efficiently. For most of the rest of the film, classical narration tends to "play its cards close to the chest," not fully and efficiently divulging information but instead parceling it out bit by bit to keep the audience's curiosity engaged.[2]

These moments of greater communicativeness at the beginning of the film require the audience to attend carefully because the plot information is both rapidly delivered and crucially needed to understand the film. If we are to gain possible emotional pleasure from a film, we recognize that we must initially perform the task of parsing the exposition. This is an investment by the audience, one that is relatively freely given as part of the implicit contract between audience and film. If we want to enjoy the movie, we know from previous experiences that we must learn about the characters' qualities, motivations, and interrelationships. Films may do certain things to encourage audiences to care about the characters initially (for instance, endangering Indiana Jones at the beginning of *Raiders of the Lost Ark*), but generally speaking, filmmakers can count on a certain amount of basic work from their audiences during initial exposition. To obtain the payoff promised by narrative film, we must do some emotion work.

I discuss this phenomenon in rather economic terms ("work," "investment," "contract," "payoff") because those terms make explicit the give-and-take interchange between audience and film. The task of parsing exposition is work, a somewhat tedious effort that films usually try to minimize. If a film asked us to attend to a lengthy period of exposition without providing any emotional payoff, it would exhaust most audiences' initial goodwill. Understanding the exposition may not be much fun, but it opens up the possibility for fun (or other emotional states). One of the appeals of mainstream cinema is that it maximizes our emotional investment. A little emotion work[3] (e.g., attending carefully to the character exposition) can help us reap enormous dividends in emotional experience.

Unlike most mainstream films, *The Joy Luck Club* does not concentrate most of its exposition in its early scenes. Watching the film requires us to engage in the emotion work of comprehending exposition over and over again. This exposition does not pose so large a problem in the original Amy Tan novel because of the different times involved in "reading" print and film. The process of reading the novel takes a significantly longer time than the two-hour-and-nineteen-minute running time of the film, and this time is usually spent in a more dispersed manner. Sizable novels are usually read in doses separated by stretches of nonreading time. To start getting involved with a new set of characters when you pick a novel back up is not as significant an added burden. After all, you're having to focus your attention on the fictional world and resituate yourself vis-à-vis the characters, which is part of the readers' contractual obligation when they return to the novel. Films, however, tend to be viewed in one continuous chunk, and so it seems onerous to ask viewers to reorient themselves toward a new set of film characters over and over, given the norms of mainstream cinema. Of course, the norms for watching a movie on video are different, and many of those who saw *The Joy Luck Club* on tape probably did not watch it continuously from end to end. But the interruptions in watching a video are often structured around phone calls and bathroom habits instead of narrative structure.

It is interesting to consider how a miniseries adaptation of *The Joy Luck Club* might differ from the film experience. If the separate stories were parceled out over separate nights, the difficulty with the multiple expositions would be diminished. This hypothetical experience might be more like reading a chapter a night in the novel. The work of understanding expository introductions of new characters would seem to be part of our expected work when we sit down to watch a new episode. In a continuously running film, however, the emotion work required to reorient ourselves to so many new characters is demanding.

As it tells the multileveled story of these interwoven characters, *The Joy Luck Club* also creates other difficulties for the viewer in the way it handles flashbacks. Classical Hollywood style developed as a way to prevent viewer confusion concerning diegetic space and time. It codified ways to let the audience know when flashbacks began and ended (a zoom into the face, a dissolve, a sound bridge, etc.). Modern Hollywood practice tends not to use such strongly marked devices to delineate flashbacks, but still filmmakers tend to create symmetrical flashbacks. We start with an anchor character in the diegetic present and visit a previous time and place (clearly marked for us by historical objects in the scene). Then time progresses forward from that point, either linearly or in jumps. Modern viewers may no longer need overt cues such as a dissolve to signal a transition, but they can remain confident that a flashback will end by returning us to the same anchor character near our initial departing point in the present.[4]

The Joy Luck Club, however, uses increasingly intricate flashback structures that are difficult to predict with any confidence. We are never quite certain whether we will be returned to the present or whether we will suddenly switch to another character's flashback. We may return to a time that appears to be the contemporary present, only to learn that we are actually in another level of flashback. The elaborate flashback structure asks the viewer to keep several levels of time and space in mind, which is a significant amount of emotion work.

The film's first flashback is classically symmetrical, starting with June at the party, sending us back to her childhood piano debacle, and then returning us to June at the party. Then June hands the narrative reins over to Auntie Lindo, who guides us from the party to the story of her arranged marriage to a boy husband in China. We return to the present-day, or so it appears from the clothing and furniture styles, when Lindo's daughter Waverly is preparing for her wedding. It is now Waverly's turn to tell her story, and we flashback to her career as a chess prodigy in the sixties in the United States. After Waverly's childhood flashback ends, we return to the contemporary wedding preparation scenes with Waverly and her mother Lindo at a beauty salon. Then Waverly has another flashback to the more recent past, in which she tries to smooth over the cultural tensions between her mother and her white fiancé Rich. Waverly's voiceover returns us to the contemporary beauty shop, only to switch us back to her mother's voiceover for a brief glimpse back at her Chinese childhood. After mother and daughter make a limited reconciliation in the beauty salon, we at long last return to the farewell party where we began this entire flashback sequence.

Only then are we sure that the Waverly-Lindo scenes, which seemed to be set in the present, actually took place in the recent past, seemingly a few years before the farewell party. The confusion about which contemporary time frame we are seeing, in addition to the complex and asymmetrical structure of the flashback (unexpectedly handing off to another character's perspective), keeps the audience from feeling settled in the film's time scheme.

The flashback sequence involving An Mei and her daughter Rose makes the Lindo-Waverly flashback look simple. The sequence begins with An Mei at the contemporary farewell party. Her voiceover leads us backward to a glimpse of her prepubescent self reminiscing how her mother was thrown out of the house, but we only see her for a few seconds before we flash *further* back to the moment when the mother accidentally scalds four-year old An Mei with hot soup. Then we move forward to pubescent An Mei, who chooses to go with her mother when she briefly visits the grandmother's household. We lurch forward into contemporary times in which the adult An Mei and her daughter Rose discuss Rose's estranged marriage. Rose's voiceover takes over, and we flashback to see the evolution of Rose and Ted's relationship from their college days through their marriage to their chilly breakup. In a contemporary scene with Rose and her mother, An Mei takes back control of the voiceover and returns to a flashback of her childhood. We follow prepubescent An Mei and her recently reunited mother as they go to live together in her current household, where she is the neglected fourth wife of a rich man. We are introduced to all of the wives and learn their various positions in the house's hierarchy. Then An Mei's nanny tells her the story of why her mother is shunned, and we flash further back to see An Mei's mother being raped and abandoned in disgrace. We return to prepubescent An Mei who discovers her mother's suicide, which gives her a political opportunity to gain power in the household. *The Joy Luck Club* returns to contemporary times where An Mei is telling this story as a lesson for her daughter. Rose then takes responsibility for her own failures in a conversation with her estranged husband Ted, and we at long last return to the farewell party where Ted and Rose are clearly together as a happy couple.

Got that?

Of course it's easy to make such a complicated time scheme seem impenetrable when you summarize it in print. I do not want to argue that Wayne Wang loses his audience's comprehension. To his credit, Wang manages to tell this incredibly complex story in a manner that most audiences can follow. If the sequence was narratively incomprehensible, it would be easy to explain why it would present difficulties for an audience's emotional engagement. Nonetheless, a sequence can be cognitively comprehendible and yet emotionally difficult because it requires a great deal of emotion work.

Of course we have to learn about who An Mei and her daughter Rose are as part of our expected work in parsing this scene. But in addition we have to learn a whole new cast of characters at every change of time period. We familiarize ourselves with An Mei's grandmother's household, with An Mei's mother and the three other wives who share her household, with the husband who rapes An Mei's mother, and with Ted's family situation. We are so busy learning who everyone is that we have little time to feel the strong emotions called for by the story, which deals with suicidal sacrifice, rape, imminent divorce, and deathbed reconciliations. We are too busy performing emotion work to get the full payoff of the story events.

We do eventually parse the exposition and understand who the various characters are. Shouldn't this allow us to feel emotion at the characters' plight, once we get to know them? The difficulty here is rooted in Wang's attempt to condense so much of the novel's plot into the film version of *The Joy Luck Club*. The filmmaker tries to give us almost all the emotional highs and lows packed into the novel. We experience the childhood trauma of public embarrassment, the difficulty of being forced into a child marriage, and the life-and-death intrigues to gain power in a hierarchical household. We witness the complications of having cross-racial marriages, and we see marriages break up and reconcile over domestic quarrels. The film shows us the impossibility of pleasing a demanding mother and the enormous sacrifices mothers make. In *The Joy Luck Club*, mothers lose their children in arranged marriages, by accidental death, by abandoning them in the face of the mother's own imminent death. The story tells us of rape, suicide, unfaithfulness, and in the end a promised reconciliation with long-lost relatives that eventually falls through. This is an enormous number of emotional situations for any film, much less a film that essentially changes its cast of characters so often.

The condensed nature of the storytelling in the film version of *The Joy Luck Club* does not allow much time for the viewer's emotion system to rest and prepare for the next highly charged emotional situation. Once we have done the emotion work of understanding character exposition, we are then immediately asked to feel an emotion that would befit any film's climax: grief at the loss of a child or a mother's suicide, for instance. Once this harrowing emotional appeal has been made, we are then thrown into another character's story to learn another set of characters before we see yet another emotional climax. Instead of building to a central climax, this film creates a climax for each individual storyline, which is an exhausting exercise for the emotion system. All systems shut down when they reach their limits, and *The Joy Luck Club* asks us to push toward the limits of the emotion system's capacity to do emotion work and to feel.

Again we should remember that this difficulty is caused by the time-bound structure of the feature film. The film version of *The Joy Luck Club* is created to be consumed in a single sitting at a pace set by the filmmaker, unlike a book that can be read slowly or quickly and that can be picked up and put down again. Both media have different challenges and advantages in appealing to the emotion system. A film adaptation of a novel is often denigrated because it necessarily has to leave things out that were included in the original story, but I claim that this is not the central distinction in this particular case. The primary advantage of the novel in this instance is that the reader can control the flow of plot information better, allowing us to process the film's emotional appeal at an appropriate pace. The film audience cannot do this. *The Joy Luck Club* does not allow the audience time to "breathe" before it charges ahead with the next set of highly coordinated emotion cues, and this means that many viewer's emotion systems will be overwhelmed.

Certainly there are individual variations in the emotion system, and people have different tolerances concerning how rapidly they can evaluate emotion cues. In addition, audiences differ in how pleasurable they find the rapid-paced emotion cuing of a genre like melodrama. I do not deny some audiences are able to process fully the rapid-fire emotional appeal of *The Joy Luck Club*. Given the flexibility of the emotion system, it is difficult to think of a mainstream film that would alienate absolutely everyone's emotional responses. Nevertheless, it is possible to analyze how *The Joy Luck*

Club is structured to make extraordinary demands on our emotion system. By requiring so much emotion work throughout the film and by condensing so many highly charged events into such a short period of time, the film batters the viewer's emotion system without ever losing our cognitive understanding of the plot. *The Joy Luck Club* provides a case study for how a film might make an emotional appeal that is internally consistent but yet at variance with the structure of the emotions.

9 "I Was Misinformed"
Nostalgia and Uncertainty in *Casablanca*

When I teach my introduction to film criticism course, I sometimes let my students choose to analyze one of a select list of classical Hollywood films as their midterm project. If an individual student wants to examine a particular film that is not on the list, I usually grant permission for him or her to do so (if I am familiar with the text). There is only one film that I have consistently forbidden my introductory students to analyze: *Casablanca*. When students ask, "Why not?" I usually tell them that the film is just too difficult for a beginning critic to analyze. It's too close to the classical ideal of "invisible style" to discuss its visual aesthetic, I argue, and the film depends too much on the "charisma" of the stars, which is another difficult concept to dissect. The remarkable thing about *Casablanca* is that it's difficult to describe what's remarkable about it.

Academics from Umberto Eco to Dana Polan to Robert Ray have tried to pin the film's appeal down. Many accounts foreground the extrafilmic discourses that have depicted the production of *Casablanca* as the Hollywood version of the discovery of penicillin, as a haphazard confluence of several factors that happened to come together to make a classic. For instance, Andrew Sarris has called *Casablanca* "the happiest of happy accidents."[1] Much of this understanding of *Casablanca* as accident is rooted in the allegation (attributed to Ingrid Bergman) that none of the principals involved in making the film knew how it would end during most of the primary shooting. This mythological uncertainty during the production process shows up in the final product, according to many. According to Umberto Eco, the production was "a fairly ramshackle affair" that resulted in a movie that is a "hodgepodge of sensational scenes strung together implausibly." In fact, for

Eco it is the "glorious ricketiness" of the film's construction and the extreme banality of the film that "allows us to catch a glimpse of the Sublime."[2] The reigning wisdom has been that the uncertainty of production created an uncertainty that can be felt by the viewer, and this instability captured in the film can be emotionally reexperienced by the viewer watching *Casablanca* over and over.

Like Rick (Humphrey Bogart) who was lured to Casablanca for the waters, many find the production story's appeal to be seductive, but, like Rick, they have been "misinformed." Knowing what we know about the rigors of the Hollywood studio factory system, it seems unlikely that anything but the lowest of B films would start production without the principals knowing the ending. And in spite of the romanticization of *Casablanca*'s "humble" origins, this was no shoddy production. This film was produced with A-list stars (Bogart and Bergman), an A-list director (Michael Curtiz), and a veteran supporting cast (Claude Rains, Sydney Greenstreet, Peter Lorre). Recent historical work has confirmed that the ending was never in doubt, that everyone knew that Ilsa (Bergman) would take off into the fog on an airplane with Victor (Paul Henreid), not Rick.[3] Richard Maltby has posited that perhaps Ingrid Bergman, still relatively new to the workings of Hollywood and the Production Code, mistook the Hays Office's standard tinkering with the script for true uncertainty about the eventual outcome of the film.[4] In any case, the central extratextual evidence for the ricketiness of the film's production has been disproved, leaving us once again to struggle with the question of what makes *Casablanca* unique. What is the basis of its emotional appeal, which encourages film audiences to return to this text again and again?

Like those academics who have trod this ground before me, I also felt tempted to attempt to find *the* answer to these questions. Unfortunately, these attempts often come up with specious conclusions, such as Eco's assertion that "*Casablanca* became a cult movie because it is not *one* movie. It is 'movies.'"[5] (a claim that is rhetorically forceful but essentially meaningless). Theory often has difficulty explaining the unique individual. While sidestepping the thorny question of *Casablanca*'s uniqueness, I will try to give *an* explanation for both the commonality and the distinctiveness of its emotional appeal to a sense of nostalgia. This involves a reorientation toward the text from the assumptions of Sarris, Eco, et al. I ask you to consider

Casablanca not as a rickety production with charismatic stars and little style, but instead as a coherent, well-made, elegant example of classical Hollywood practice. Unlike Eco, I assert that the well-made narrational structures are more responsible for the pleasures of watching *Casablanca* than are any moments of textual instability.

An Uncertain Start

Following the mood-cue approach, we should examine the opening sections of *Casablanca* to see how the film's narration cues the viewers to orient themselves toward the film. Eco has noted that *Casablanca* has what he calls "an extraordinary long overture," that the film goes for twenty minutes before Ilsa walks into Rick's Café Americain. What purpose do these first twenty minutes serve? Using Eco's words, how does this "overture" set us up for the "symphonic work" to follow?[6]

The factor most apparent to Eco in this early section is that *Casablanca* provides us with many cues concerning what genre scripts we should apply to this film. The music over the opening credits contains Eastern motifs, and several early compositions foreground the exotic touches in the set's architecture. For instance, we witness Major Strasser's arrival at the airport through a distinctively Eastern curved archway. The viewer paying attention to these cues is alerted to the possibility that this might be an exotic adventure film. The use of the *Marseillaise* over the opening credits evokes a historical patriotic film. This genre script is further accentuated when the police shoot a suspect carrying Free French literature immediately beneath a large poster of Petain, tipping us to the relevance of the war propaganda film. Additionally, the spinning globe and the official-sounding voiceover detailing the refugees' trek to Casablanca bring the newsreel to mind.

Eco also notes that *Casablanca* cues us to the relevance of the action film. The sequence in which the police raid the marketplace searching for the stolen papers uses much dynamic figure movement and rapid-fire editing. A policeman blows a shrill whistle, an official car bursts into the marketplace, police accost people, suspects run, police give chase, one suspect is shot in the back. The twenty-minute "overture" ends with another sequence that most clearly evokes the action film, according to Eco. The film carefully and suspensefully lays out the details of the trap being set to arrest

Ugarte: mentioning the imminent capture of the courier's murderer several times, letting us hear the orders to put policemen into position, showing us the forces being deployed at the doors. Ugarte recognizes the trap too late (noticing the guarded doors) and tries to escape but is captured in a rapidly edited action sequence. This sequence, in conjunction with the marketplace raid, alerts the viewer that the action film might be the appropriate genre script to apply to *Casablanca*.

Perhaps the strongest, most sustained set of genre cues encourages us to think of *Casablanca* as a spy story. Almost immediately we hear an announcement concerning two German couriers who have been killed and their papers stolen. As the camera shows us our initial view of Rick's Café Americain, we overhear several clandestine conversations among many plotters. One such conversation stops when a German solder passes by. In another conversation a plotter's overemphasis that the refugees meet him at night with cash in hand tips us that this particular scheme is a swindle. We learn from Senor Ferrari (Sydney Greenstreet) that people are the main commodity bought and sold in Casablanca. We discover that the German papers (letters of transit) are now in the possession of the weaselly Ugarte (Peter Lorre), who seems to be taking credit for the courier's deaths, and that he is planning on selling them for a great deal of money. We see and hear that Rick's is a place where we should be suspicious of what is said, knowing that deception and covert violence are main courses served at the café.

Captain Renault's (Claude Rains) meeting with Rick in his office finishes the primary groundwork for *Casablanca*'s spy story. We discover the history of Victor Lazlo's struggle for the French underground, including his several escapes from Nazi captors. Renault also recounts a bit of Rick's resume, letting us know that he was once a gun-runner and a soldier for hire in the Spanish Civil War. This shows us that Rick is no mere bar owner but is well qualified to participate in the illicit dealings of the spy world. Everything we need for the spy story is here: missing papers, shady characters, underground heros, corrupt officials. And all this with only the slightest hint of the romance as a possible frame for interpreting the action. All this before Ilsa walks into Rick's and introduces the romantic plotline in earnest.

There's a fairly straightforward way to interpret this set of intersecting genre cues in the opening 20 minutes of *Casablanca*. One could argue that the primary cognitive and emotional orientation called for in the initial sequences of the film is uncertainty; not uncertainty brought about by the production's indecision about how to end the film, but the viewer's initial uncertainty concerning the film's genre. This is a variation on what Eco means when he says that *Casablanca* is not one movie but is "movies," that the film's genius is in mixing together "the repertoire of stock formulas . . . used wholesale."[7] Putting a slightly more cognitivist spin on this argument, by intermingling several genre microscripts, the initial sequences keep us uncertain about the appropriate emotional orientation to use in watching the film.

According to this particular interpretation, the mood of uncertainty makes it difficult for us to feel certain about Rick's possible course of action. Will Rick keep Ilsa in Casablanca and send Victor to Lisbon? Will he turn Victor over to the Nazis and flee Casablanca himself with Ilsa in tow? This initial mood of uncertainty is sustained by a series of scenes that reinforce our doubts about Rick's actions. At times he seems to be on the verge of selling Victor out, at other times he appears to withhold the letters of transit vindictively to punish Ilsa. The uncertainty over the ending is set up by the uncertainty established in the film's opening moments, and this state is both a cognitive orientation that encourages us to weigh the veracity of narrative information and an emotive orientation that helps make the film's progress suspenseful.

And so, if you want to follow this interpretation, I've sketched the outline for you. You can fill in the details and come up with an interpretation hinted at by Eco but better supported in cognitivist terms by the mood-cue approach. I don't want to denigrate this interpretation, which I think has much to afford it. Nonetheless, I feel it applies much better to the first-time viewer of *Casablanca*. Unless you assume that the repeated viewer has some sort of cognitive-emotional amnesia, the person watching *Casablanca* again already has a dual set of genre expectations in mind. They know that *Casablanca* is not a newsreel or a political propaganda film as much as it is a romance and a spy story.

Certainly most of the film output of the classical Hollywood studios was designed with a single viewing in mind, but *Casablanca* is one of the relatively rare films of that period to attain a widespread "cult" following of repeated viewers. Eco thinks that *Casablanca*'s citation and evocation of other films and genres is key to its cult status, that because it is so densely "intertextual" it invites multiple readings. But we have seen, as we enter into a more densely intertextual media age, that intertextuality is no strong indicator that a film will repeatedly provide pleasures. A densely intertextual film such as Disney's *Hercules* does not indicate that it is seen as repeatedly as *The Lion King*. Although this conglomeration of intertextual references and genre microscripts is significant, I would like to follow another line of interpretation with a slightly different emphasis on *Casablanca's* cues.

Throughout the early sequences of the film, *Casablanca* cues us to look ahead expectantly and to anticipate payoffs. The film elegantly leads us from one time and place to another by hinting at what is to come, training us to look forward in the story. When an official orders for police to "Round up all suspicious characters and search them for stolen documents," we immediately see those orders being carried out as the film cuts to the police raid on the marketplace. When the suspect who has been shot is searched, the officers discover Free France literature on the body, and we immediately cut to the motto *Liberté Egalité Fraternité* above the Palais du Justice where the next scene occurs. After a man realizes his pocket has been picked, he looks up and offscreen, and we see an airplane descending, closely watched by a crowd of refugees, which helps make the transition to the airport for Strasser's arrival. At the airport Strasser and Renault discuss the imminent capture of the courier's murderer ("Tonight he'll be at Rick's. Everybody comes to Rick's."), which leads to the exterior establishing shot of Rick's Café Americain. At Rick's we overhear bits of conversation among café patrons plotting their future escapes from Casablanca.

When introducing Rick himself, *Casablanca* further encourages our anticipation by using a dramatic trick as old as Greek tragedy: withholding our access to the hero. Before we see Rick, we hear Karl tell people that Rick never drinks with customers and that he would not be impressed by the customer's status. The film teases our desire to see Rick, first showing his hand signing a check, then showing his cocktail glass, then him fingering a chesspiece, then his cigarette before the camera tilts up to reveal his face. First verbally, then visually, the film encourages us to look forward to the introduction of the hero.

After giving us a series of coordinated cues to encourage us to anticipate immediately following events, *Casablanca* then encourages us to look further forward to major plot events. Picking up on earlier hints about the murderer's arrest, the film then sets up the arrest a bit at a time. We find out that Ugarte has the papers, letting us know who will be arrested. Renault boasts about the arrest to Rick and to Strasser. We see the police preparations for the arrest. Finally we see Ugarte dragged off in custody. *Casablanca* first trains us to anticipate what scene will immediately follow. Then it encourages us to look forward to larger plot events, such as Ugarte's arrest. Then we are appropriately prepared to anticipate the film's overall outcome: will Rick and Ilsa be together, and will Victor escape Casablanca?

None of this is too surprising as a narrational strategy. These are fairly straightforward examples of what Noël Carroll calls erotetic narration, the tendency for classical narration to pose a series of questions that it then answers, only to open up more questions. As David Bordwell has argued, classical narration sets up a series of goals that encourages the viewer to look forward, hypothesizing whether these goals will be met or not.[8] The anticipatory narrational strategies in *Casablanca*'s early sequences are well-wrought, if somewhat standard, practice.

The urgency of the narrational expectations called for in the first sequences is heightened by the rapid editing pace. In the opening five minutes, after the credits and before we enter Rick's, the average shot length is a snappy 5.3 seconds. Not only do these scenes provide local payoffs for the viewer's expectations but they also provide these payoffs quickly, giving a sense of urgency to the proceedings and letting us know that we need to be hypervigilant if we are to stay on top of the film's plot. The practice of encouraging the viewer to look forward in anticipation is fairly standard; the pace of *Casablanca*'s early sections accentuates and foregrounds this practice.

Casablanca further encourages the viewer's forward-looking anticipation by showing us a universe where events seem to be bound by rules, helping us to make accurate predictions. *Casablanca* swiftly establishes the rules of how Rick's café works. We hear Karl tell a bank owner that Rick never drinks with the clientele as a matter of policy. Ugarte asks Rick to share a drink with him and then he apologizes for his blunder before Rick can refuse as Ugarte remembers Rick's interdiction. When Victor asks Rick to join him and Ilsa for a drink, Renault quickly answers for Rick, explaining Rick's policy. This shows us that everyone in Rick's universe understands the rule. Only newcomers such as Victor, the banker, and we the audience need to be reminded of how things work at Rick's.

Renault is helpful in informing us of other rules that govern Rick's life. When Major Strasser questions Rick, Renault tells him that "Rick is completely neutral about everything, and that includes women." Rick has already demonstrated that he alone seems to be impervious to the charms of a French woman who has fallen for him, and he demonstrates considerable political diplomacy when Strasser tries to tie down Rick's politics (Rick claims that he understands the perspective of both the fox and the hound). Rick himself lets us know another principle of neutrality: "I stick out my neck for nobody." He states this tenet just before Ugarte's arrest, and he reiterates it as he puts the principle into action by refusing to interfere in Ugarte's arrest. Once you understand the rules, Rick's café seems to be a predictable universe in which people behave according to those well-defined and blatantly stated rules. Or so we are told.

Once these carefully established precedents are set, we see many of them almost immediately overturned. Rick violates his no-exceptions rule about not drinking with customers when Victor invites him to have a drink. Just in case we did not note the violation, Renault expresses his surprise aloud at the reversal. When Rick picks up the check for Victor and Ilsa, Renault again notes aloud that there is "another precedent gone." The film carefully trains us to understand how the diegetic present works, and then almost immediately violates those rules. The things we know about the diegetic present are proven wrong, which makes us suspicious about how reliable those other rules are (about Rick's neutrality in politics and love).

The uncertainty discussed by other critics is definitely there in the text of *Casablanca*, but it is not there because of any remnant of alleged uncertainties in the production process. The uncertainty results from being trained to understand the rules of the universe and then immediately having to throw those rules out.[9]

Of course there are many films that establish a protagonist interacting with the world in an orderly, predictable fashion, only to then introduce an element (Ilsa, in this case) that turns the protagonist's world upside down, making him or her rethink and refashion the rules for behavior. Perhaps this is a description of one of the basic story arcs of character change in the classical cinema. Most films, however, take almost the entire film's length to overturn fully the protagonist's initial behavior patterns. *Casablanca* is distinctive in that the protagonist begins refuting his former behavior almost immediately after those patterns are established for the audience. This unusual move causes us to ask, "Why?" and the new variable introduced into the universe seems clear: Ilsa.

Still we have to figure out what is it about Ilsa that has brought about this change, and here *Casablanca* tries its most distinctive strategy: it evacuates the diegetic present as a clear source of information about how the characters will behave in the future. Slowly we learn not to trust what we see unfolding before us in the diegetic present. We have seen that kind of information prove unreliable. What can be relied on, it seems, is the past. The Rick defined for us in the diegetic present does not seem capable of the heroic action that ends the film. But the Rick of the past, the lover and supporter of lost causes, *is* capable of the noble sacrifice at the airport.

At best, the film's diegetic present provides partial and conflicting evidence concerning Rick's possible future choices. Because other precedents have been overcome, we suspect that Rick's stalwart "I stick out my neck for nobody" is similarly in jeopardy. When Victor first approaches Rick for help, we see Rick bitterly denying any assistance, seemingly as a vindictive refusal to help the woman who once hurt him. After an appeal from Ilsa, he makes arrangements to deliver both letters of transit to Victor. Meanwhile Rick arranges for Renault to arrest Victor, enabling Rick to leave with Ilsa. Given these mutually exclusive plausible possibilities presented by Rick's actions, how do we judge among them? How do we interpret events such as Rick's sale of his club to Ferrari, events that could lead to several different futures? The primary evidence lies in the diegetic past.

If there is anything particularly distinctive about *Casablanca*, it is that the film, after having clearly established our forward-looking narrative expectations, then leaves us with no seemingly dependable clues in the diegetic present actions to allow us to predict the outcome. Instead, we are asked to delve deeper and deeper into the past to find a way to predict the outcome. Having trained us to look forward, the film then asks us to look back.

Misunderstanding this narrational switch, many critics have accused *Casablanca*'s characters of behaving implausibly. Eco calls the characters "psychologically incredible," and as proof of the variable nature of the character traits, he oddly cites the fact that Victor orders four different drinks, which Eco finds unbelievable in a man with an "ascetic temper."[10] Pauline Kael says that "you're never really pressed to take its melodramatic twists and turns seriously."[11] What both may be responding to is that the actions in the diegetic present do not give us the clear, consistent picture of character change that we have grown to expect in the classical cinema. *Casablanca* asks us to distrust what we see in the present and concentrate on finding out more about the past, which seems to be the best and most consistent determinant of these characters' future.

Before I get into the details of this argument, let me first anticipate an objection. Certainly there is nothing particularly distinctive about a film that progresses forward by uncovering more and more of a character's hidden past. In this case the "what will happen next?" question becomes "what will we next discover about the past?" I want to argue something stronger for *Casablanca*. In *Casablanca* we learn to ignore the primary evidence on display in the diegetic present as being less trustworthy than the events in the characters' past. It is not merely that the past has an effect on the present; instead, the past overwhelms the present in forging the future.

As much as almost any film in the classical Hollywood period, *Casablanca* is about the importance of the past on the outcomes of the future. There is a feeling of nostalgia built into the film's narrative structure as it encourages us to interrogate the long-gone past. While we are cognitively discerning these past events, the film simultaneously elicits a longing for a more clear-cut time when romantic and political forces were not so entangled. This nostalgia is created by a shift from "forward-looking" to "rear-driven" narration.

"Forward looking" and "rear driven" refer to two broadly defined ways to describe and predict human behavior. To one way of thinking, the best way to predict what people will do is to understand what they have done before. Such a perspective is "rear driven." One of the revolutions of Freud's writing was the discovery that a person's long-ago psychic traumas can have effects on their present and future life, and for Freud the best way to understand a person's behavior is to delve deeper into his or her past. To another way of thinking, the best way to understand a person is to understand the goals he or she is pursuing. Know what people want, and you can better predict what they will do. This is "forward looking." Behaviorism embraces this kind of thinking, asserting that reinforcers and goals tell us more about what an experimental subject will do than does knowledge of the subject's past.[12]

Bordwell has discussed the classical Hollywood cinema in "forward-looking" terms. Given characters' initial states and their goals, we follow their actions as they pursue those goals until they either win or lose. Although this forward-looking mechanism drives the cinema, classical narration often tries to give the appearance that it is rear driven. In the classical cinema, the characters must have a coherent psychological motivation that drives them toward achieving a goal, and this motivation frequently comes from the characters' past. The importance of the characters' past in most Hollywood films is to show why the characters are the way they are. Once those traits are well established, the classical Hollywood film can get on with the major business at hand: the protagonist's pursuit of a goal. Although the film has its entire length to pursue the eventual goal or outcome, it generally devotes only a limited amount of time to exploring past events that led up to the current dilemma.[13]

When classical narration wants to delve deeply into a character's past, it often does so by structuring the entire film as an extended flashback or series of flashbacks within a narrative frame. *Citizen Kane, Sunset Boulevard,* and *Double Indemnity* begin at the deaths or near-deaths of their protagonists, and so the forward-looking impetus of the narration chronologically reveals the past as it progresses toward the first scene we glimpsed. In these cases, Hollywood makes the diegetic past into the presentational present of the film, which then proceeds according to standard erotetic narration within the flashbacks.

While the initial portions of *Casablanca* teach us to anticipate future events, the film also begins to make us curious about the past. In their first scene, together Renault begins his probing into Rick's past, which he will continue throughout the film: "I've often speculated on why you don't return to America. Did you abscond with the church funds? Did you run off with the senator's wife? I'd like to think that you killed a man." Over and over in *Casablanca* characters ask about each other's pasts, and over and over their inquiries are stymied. Rick answers Renault's speculations about church funds, senators' wives, and killing by refusing to confirm any one explanation ("A combination of all three" led him to leave America, he says). Ilsa turns away Rick's probing of her pre-Paris life by reminding him that curiosity about the past is outside the rules of their relationship ("We said no questions"). When we do get direct answers to questions about Rick's and Ilsa's past, those answers are useless. The answers to the question "Where were you, say, ten years ago?" are trivial; Ilsa was getting braces on her teeth, Rick was looking for a job. As the characters stonewall each other's interrogation about the past, this hones the viewer's own curiosity about the characters' back story.

Casablanca begins giving us significant information about Rick's past by using a standard expository device: having supporting characters tell his story. Renault informs us (and later both Strasser and Victor reiterate) that Rick was involved on the losing sides of conflicts in Ethiopia and Spain and that Rick cannot return to America. True to the norm of classical narrational practice, *Casablanca* begins to parcel out a little disclosure about the past, followed by a little more, and a little more. We learn that Rick and Ilsa knew each other in Paris, and we discover that they share emotional associations about the song "As Time Goes By." When Ilsa returns to Rick's after it closes, we get the film's only flashback: an extensive re-creation of their last day in Paris, seen through Rick's perspective. When Rick bumps into Ilsa at a laceseller's stall, he demands an explanation for her leaving him, but she defers. Only later at a dark rendezvous in his office does Ilsa break down and deliver a full explanation for her actions. The past is now fully disclosed, and we are ready to shift again into forward-looking mode as we head toward the film's final outcome.

The film clearly loads the dice by evacuating our trust in the present events and seeming to promise a more trustworthy past. The film prods us further toward a romantic outcome by clearly foregrounding Rick the lover over Rick the patriot. If we can't trust what we see of his actions in the present, surely we can trust what we see of his past, and that points us toward a romantic reconciliation for Rick and Ilsa.

The trick is that the past is not as straightforward a determinant of the future as we are led to think. Rick the freedom fighter emerges in the end, not Rick the lover. We are partially prepared for the freedom fighter's appearance by several sly reminders. While concentrating on Rick's romantic past, the film also slips in brief mentions of his heroic past. Several times (in the flashback and in subsequent conversation) Ilsa refers to "his record" and to what the Nazis would do to him if they discovered his past. It is this deemphasized but still mentioned past that influences the final outcome.

So in the end the seemingly straightforward past is shown to be almost as difficult to interpret as the present is. The film privileges the explanatory power of these characters' past, and it encourages us to feel nostalgic for their Parisien romance. At the same time, however, it denies us the clear access to history that we desire. Questions are stymied, and when they are answered, we misread the significance of events. *Casablanca* foregrounds Rick the lover in the past, making barest mention of Rick the patriot, and yet it is Rick the patriot who emerges in the end. The simpler past we longed for becomes as difficult to read as the convoluted present. *Casablanca* cues us toward the safety of nostalgia and then makes the past seem unpredictable.

So what potentially reliable evidence is left to interpret? The character's faces. From the early moments in the film, *Casablanca* alerts us that we should watch and interpret faces. In particular we see characters examine Rick's face and then fill in the words assumedly left unspoken by Rick's mute mug. Ugarte seems to try to read Rick's mind and comes to the conclusion that Rick despises him. Why? Ugarte asks, but Rick provides no answer, so Ugarte provides it for him: "Oh, you object to the kind of business I do." Renault in particular seems to model for us how we should peruse and read Rick's unspoken meanings. When Renault accuses Rick of being a sentimentalist, he pauses to examine Rick's face for a reaction. There is none. Undeterred, Renault reads a reaction into Rick's impassive expression. "Don't laugh," he says, but Rick doesn't seem to be in any danger of laughing. Over and over characters analyze Rick's face and come to their own conclusions, modeling the process that the film wants to encourage in us the audience. If we can't trust present events, and if we can't in the end trust our biased reading of the past's significance, perhaps we can see hints of the future in the characters' faces.

This is the promise that is held out to the repeated viewer of *Casablanca*. One of the central problems with Carroll's concept of erotetic narration is the difficulty of explaining why viewers might watch a film repeatedly. Once viewers knows all the answers to the questions posed in the film, why should they return to the film? Once we know Rick's choice at the airport, why watch *Casablanca* again? There are several possible answers, but one of the pleasures offered the repeat *Casablanca* viewer is the opportunity to observe the faces once again in light of what you now know has happened in the diegetic past and what will happen in the film's denouement. Can you see hints of what is to come in the actor's faces? In subsequent viewings one can look for clues about how the past impinges on the present, knowing how important that information is to driving the plot.

There are other factors that perhaps make *Casablanca* even more open to repeated film viewings. For instance, certain repetitions are key to the film's construction. As highly foregrounded catch phrases are repeated in different circumstances ("Here's looking at you, kid"), they accumulate associations and therefore gain affective power. Of course one of the central repeated elements is the song "As Time Goes By," which is built up through anticipatory dialogue. Just as Rick is not forthcoming when questioned about his history as a soldier for hire, Sam (Dooley Wilson) plays a similar stonewalling game before playing Ilsa's or Rick's request. "Play it, Sam," Ilsa asks. "I don't know what you're talking about." "Play 'As Time Goes By.'" "I'm rusty." "Then I'll hum it." Finally, as Ilsa hums, Sam joins in, ending the audience-teasing game. A similarly drawn-out interchange between Rick and the reticent Sam gives us the second rendition of the song. After its third repetition, "As Time Goes By" is incorporated into the nondiegetic music as a repeated leitmotif to evoke emotive associations later in the film. Such repeated elements (catch phrases, songs) in *Casablanca* clearly rely on the associative structure of the emotion system.[14]

I am not trying to provide an exhaustive explanation for *Casablanca*'s emotional appeal, and certainly there are other important factors in the film's construction. Linking the film's intimate story to broader political themes is vital to its force, as are the age-old struggle between love and duty, Michael Curtiz's elegant camera movements, and the exotic imagery. In this chapter, I offer a partial explanation, arguing that a blend of forward-looking and rear-driven narration gives *Casablanca* both a strong narrative drive and an overriding sense of nostalgia for the past. If this explanation does not get exactly at what is unique about *Casablanca*, it provides a better explanation for the "uncertainty" in the text while suggesting how *Casablanca* can appeal to viewers over and over.

Casablanca's use of narrative time invites us to become nostalgic for times gone by, times when love was simpler than it currently appears to be. This is certainly true of the appeal of this film in the twenty-first century, but it was also true of this film in 1942 because of the way this film teaches us to pursue a phantom past. The song "As Time Goes By" is particularly well chosen for a film as timeless as this one, or rather a film in which time is so dispersed. Out of all the gin joints in all the world, we return to Rick's to reread the importance of a bygone and bittersweet past on the future.

PART THREE

AFTERWORD

10 An Invitation to Interpret

My primary desideratum for an approach to filmic emotions was a desire to explain the specific emotional appeals of particular films. I also called for an approach that could analyze a wide range of films and that encouraged critics to examine the full range of cinematic signification. By producing new interpretations of the emotional appeals of *Raiders of the Lost Ark, Ghostbusters, Local Hero, Stranger than Paradise, Casablanca, Strike, A Day in the Country, The Lower Depths, The Joy Luck Club,* and *Stella Dallas,* I have demonstrated the mood-cue approach's capacity to explain such a broad range of filmic appeals using both local and global structures. By examining how films such as *Local Hero, The Lower Depths,* and *A Day in the Country* change their emotional appeals, I have also shown how the mood-cue approach can satisfy the desideratum for an explanation of how filmic emotions change over time. Analyzing *Strike, The Lower Depths,* and *The Joy Luck Club,* I have demonstrated several ways in which this approach can discuss a film's failure to evoke emotion.

Along the way, this approach has also produced several neologisms that may be useful in future analysis of film's emotional appeals, thus satisfying one of the desiderata that called for such terminology. In addition to the basic terms of the approach (cues, mood), I have proposed other terms as explanatory mechanisms for particular texts, for example, emotion markers, feeling for or with, forward looking and rear driven, sparsely and densely informative texts. When this approach is applied to particular films, it seems to encourage articulating and labeling heretofore unnamed narrative structures that are designed to elicit emotions. This is an additional advantage of this approach, because new terminology produces new questions for research. Viewers recognize the differences between the emotional appeals of *Raiders of the Lost Ark* and *Stranger than Paradise*, but critics have only had a language borrowed from common usage to explain such differences. Such concepts as sparsely versus densely informative emotion cuing can provide a basis for comparing the way texts structure their appeals. What kinds of films tend to be more densely informative emotionally? How does this density vary within a text? Are there patterns of alternation between densely and sparsely informative segments?

Articulating new terms may open up new avenues for genre study in particular, because genres are so frequently organized around their dominant feeling tone (horror, thrillers, etc.). How does a particular genre structure its use of emotion cues and mood? Which emotion channels of access are preferred in the genre? What quantity of cues characterize a genre? How frequently must mood be reinforced, and in what characteristic ways? How do these vary over historical periods (musical conventions of melodramas of the thirties versus those of fifties melodramas, for instance)? Do different auteurs have patterns of emotion cuing (e.g., does Spielberg rely heavily on emotion markers?)?

The distinction between feeling *for* and feeling *with* also opens up possibilities for further investigation. How does this distinction vary across genres? Are there gender tendencies at work (as Nancy Chodorow might suggest) that encourage women to feel *for* characters more often than men? Are there ideological ramifications to feeling *for* versus feeling *with*?

This approach can also help us provide closer descriptions of narrational techniques that are all too frequently examined using broad humanist terminology. *Film Structure and the Emotion System* has demonstrated how the mood-cue approach can give more specific insight into *Casablanca*'s "uncertainty," Jean Renoir's "impressionism," and Sergei Eisenstein's "psychologism." The approach in this book might also be used to articulate more specifically Hitchcock's distinction between surprise and suspense, for example, or Sirk's use of "distanciation." We have long recognized the emotional appeals of such broadly described techniques, but we have needed a way to talk about them in more precise ways. If producing new questions and new terminology provide a measure of a new approach, then this approach is abundantly productive.

And yet, in applying this approach to films, I became quite aware of its current limitations. Rooting this approach in current study in cognitive psychology and neuropsychology necessarily duplicates those fields' current research emphases on lower-level emotion processes. Researchers schooled in explanations of object recognition and visual perception do not tend to examine high-level emotion processes. In using this body of research, my system tends to be able to provide more specific explanations of how films make emotional appeals at the microlevel than at the broader level. Too often my explanations of narrational structures such as emotion markers leans too heavily on low-level emotion-related processes such as surprise or startle instead of providing explanations for more complex emotional experiences.

In part, this reliance on lower-level processes is entirely appropriate for explaining a film's emotional appeals. If a filmmaker wants to elicit emotional responses from a wide variety of individuals in a mass audience, he or she will probably rely heavily on "lowest common denominator" emotion cues, such as those that evoke the surprise or startle reflex. My application of this approach explains fairly well film's reliance on such dependable cuing structures. Nonetheless, this approach is currently limited in its ability to explain more complex emotional phenomena that cognitivism has not examined closely. My discussion of nostalgia in *Casablanca* is probably about as high level an emotion as the mood-cue approach can examine with any degree of confidence.

Cognitivism's emphasis on lower-level processes has a bearing on this book's concept of "mood." Cognitivists such as Nico Frijda have provided useful explanation for what a "mood" is; few, however, have helped us to define and distinguish between different "moods." Because the field has tended to shy away from exploring the subtler conscious emotion scripts people carry, my approach currently leaves critics to their own devices in coming up with appropriate labels for movie moods, relying largely on common usage of such terms. The moods I have discussed (e.g., the "suspenseful" mood in *Raiders of the Lost Ark*'s opening) are clearly open to alternative labels by other critics (one might argue that "fear" is a better descriptor). Of course any interpretation is open to alternative readings, but the theories currently provided by cognitive psychology and neuropsychology do not provide a strong basis for judging the appropriateness of various labels for moods.

To overcome my approach's primary limitations (the imprecision of labeling specific emotional states), this approach needs to be bolstered by research in a young field: the sociology of emotion. Sociologists are beginning to make inquiries concerning how people conceptualize emotion. What are the widely held prototypes of fear, jealousy, embarrassment, and so forth? What real-world scripts do people carry concerning emotional experience? What features do people call upon when labeling other people's emotions? Cognitive psychology and neuropsychology can teach us much about the basic framework of the emotion system, but to explain how films might elicit more complex emotional states, we need to draw on empirical research into higher-level emotion scripts and prototypes. Although the sociology of emotion still continues to be shaped by other earlier research agendas (emphasizing how social expectations encourage us to modify our emotional expressions and experiences), it is the field best positioned to articulate the many scripts that organize individuals' emotional experiences.

There are limits, however, to how far this approach can go in examining the emotional interaction between text and viewer. The model in this book is first and foremost concerned with texts and narrational structures. Texts offer invitations to feel, and individual viewers can accept or reject these invitations. Textually centered critics who understand the makeup of the emotion system can create useful readings of how a film makes its emotional appeal. What this approach can never do, however, is to predict and explain individual viewers' emotional responses to films. The emotion system that is being studied by cognitive psychologists is too complex, too flexible for it to be possible to explain all possible responses in a mass audience. This book shows that in spite of the emotion system's flexibility, textually based critics can still provide specific insight into the way cinematic narrational structures encourage us to feel. A textually based approach to analyzing the interaction between text and viewer can only provide an explanation for half of the interaction, but that does not mean that explanation is any less important. In fact, I hope that this approach will be useful to reception theorists who want to explore viewer's emotional responses to films. Better understanding how films are constructed to appeal to the emotions can only help a reception theorist explain the nuances of what actual viewers are doing when they laugh and cry at the movies. This book only takes a step toward a better understanding of the role of emotion in film, but I believe it is a necessary step.

This book is an example of Theory discussing how Film is structured to elicit Emotion in viewers. The intent here is to provide an empirically grounded framework for future work on *films* and *emotions*. In examining how particular films try to elicit particular emotional responses, we need an understanding of the broader processes at work, an understanding of the basic architecture of the emotion system. This book translates theoretical knowledge from cognitive psychology into a more practical approach that can be applied to individual films. I extend an invitation to critics to use the flexible critical approach outlined in this book to interpret cinematic emotional appeals in particular films, hoping they might feel confident that this approach is congruent with our best current understanding of the emotions.

The Neurological Basis of Psychoanalytic Film Theory

Metz's Emotional Debt to Freud the Biologist

> We are not used to feeling strong emotions without their having any
> ideational content, and therefore, if the content is missing, we seize as a
> substitute upon some other content which is in some way or other suitable,
> much as our police, when they cannot catch the right murderer, arrest a
> wrong one instead.
>
> – Sigmund Freud[1]

Psychoanalytic film theory has become the dominant theoretical approach for investigating the pleasures of the cinema, and yet there is some question even among psychoanalytic critics whether this body of theory has given us much insight into filmic emotions per se. Can psychoanalytic theory indeed provide a useful way to understand the specific emotions that film texts elicit? After surveying landmark psychoanalytic writings on film, this appendix examines the foundations of those writings in the Freudian-Lacanian assumptions about emotion. Looking at Freud's central conceptions concerning emotion can tell us whether psychoanalysis can provide a strong theoretical anchor for discussions of filmic emotion.

In psychoanalytic film criticism's discussion, there is a conspicuous absence of the word "emotion" in favor of the terms "pleasure" and "desire." Distinctions among pleasure, desire, and emotion are not purely terminological; the choice of pleasure and desire over emotion is symptomatic (to use a Freudian term) of a larger theoretical neglect of the emotions. By discussing "desire" and "pleasure," psychoanalytic film theory can appear to be dealing with questions of emotion while it continues academia's traditional neglect of the emotions as too "messy."

"Pleasure" in the Freudian sense is a kind of emotional experience, and so to address pleasure is in some way to address emotions. But the Freudian concept of pleasure is both more and less than the concept of emotion used in this book. "Pleasure" and "unpleasure" are feeling tones that characterize certain emotions; for instance, anxiety is marked by unpleasure and love by pleasure. In this sense, pleasure is primarily the somatic component of particular emotional experiences, the discharge of tension. This unsubtle somatic sense of pleasure is what psychoanalytic film theory has inherited from Freud, making it less well equipped to discuss the particulars of cinematic emotional response beyond a general understanding of bodily arousal and discharge. At the same time, the concept of Freudian pleasure used by Christian Metz, Laura Mulvey, and their followers is also a principle that is larger than emotion. Freud posited the existence of a "pleasure principle" that induces people to seek out the experience of pleasurable bodily discharge. The pleasure principle becomes a governing mechanism for human behavior. It is not merely an emotion; instead, the existence of this positive feeling tone becomes a governing mechanism for human behavior.

Ironically, the enshrinement of pleasure as a central motivating factor enabled Freud to forego specific attention to the emotions. Pleasure becomes a universally desired reward, and therefore does not require much more analysis than a carrot placed on a stick in front of a horse. What Freud was much more interested in was the origins of behavior, not the rewards that motivate it. The concept of pleasure inherited from Freud and enshrined by psychoanalytic film theorists is at once too small (describing an unnuanced bodily reaction) and too large (describing a general principle motivating behavior) to be useful in theorizing emotion or describing particular emotions. Treating pleasure as a reward that the cinematic apparatus offers to those who occupy subject positions, psychoanalytic film theory appears to discuss emotional response while it shifts the focus toward what it considers to be more fundamental mechanisms: processes of identity, identification, and ideology.

The error psychoanalytic film theory has made is to mistake the emotional nature of Freud's data (dreams, nightmare, hysterical symptoms, etc.) and his terms "pleasure" and "desire" for a coherent theory of emotion. My central case against Freudian psychoanalysis as a basis for a theory of filmic emotions is that Freud was primarily a theorist of instincts and drives, concepts that are too broad to provide specific insights into particular films and their emotional appeals. This leads psychoanalytic film theory toward asking entirely different questions. A theory of drives can investigate what leads audiences to the movie theater, a question that this study does not broach. Such a theory of drives does not lead us toward precise answers concerning how individual films evoke emotion, however. Although Freud, Metz, Mulvey, and their successors appear to be talking about emotion when they discuss "pleasure" and "desire," they are actually talking past the concept of emotion toward matters they consider more important.

Metz and Mulvey: Setting the Terms

Contemporary psychoanalytic film theory is primarily concerned with spectatorship, investigating how the cinema positions us as subjects. According to such theory, the cinema recreates many of the conditions in which we first recognized ourselves as individual, unified persons. As children looking at a mirror, we discover a unified image of our bodies. This recognition allows us to constitute an "I," an ego that can both be a position for perceiving others (a "subject") and an "object" for others to see. By identifying with the whole image seen in the mirror, we gain a sense of wholeness and mastery over the body. The cinema relies on this early developmental experience and restages it through its emphasis on perspectival visual imagery. Without this positioning, it is impossible for spectators to make sense of the imagery they see. This positioning is not purely cognitive, according to theorists. To lure us into subject positions, films must offer us the emotional experience of pleasure.

What pleasure does the cinema offer? Why do we go to the movies? When Christian Metz investigates these questions in *The Imaginary Signifier*,[2] he establishes a framework for poststructuralist psychoanalytic investigation into the cinema. Metz locates the Freudian mechanism of identification at the center of the spectator's pleasure. Metz argues that the cinema first offers the appeal of primary identification, of identifying with the camera. This fundamental building block of the cinema allows us to become immersed in the diegetic world as if it were real. Film can only offer audiovisual representations of a world, not the world itself. The cinematic signifier necessarily reminds us of its lack because the depicted object is absent. Identifying with the camera gives these representations a sense of presence, which gives film its reality effect. The film promises a cohesive experience for those who occupy the subject position, and this substitution provides temporary satisfaction for our desire for wholeness. By restaging the process of our earliest identifications with images (the Lacanian mirror stage), film asks us temporarily to reconstitute our identities by taking up the pleasurable, cohesive, all-seeing position offered to us by the film.

This is not the only pleasure that the cinema yields, Metz argues. Film also gives us the possibility of identifying with onscreen characters, which Metz labels "secondary identification" (because it occurs after the spectator's "primary identification" with the camera). Laura Mulvey[3] emphasizes the way that these two identifications frequently coincide to give subject positioning in the Hollywood cinema a particular ideological force. Mulvey notes that the two "looks" of the cinema (the camera's and the character's) frequently join forces to ally us with certain characters, paralleling our desires with theirs. She emphasizes how the ideological mechanism of the Hollywood cinema positions spectators with active males looking at passive "to-be-looked-at" females. Hollywood offers the pleasures of voyeurism (particularly looking at women) and of fetishistic scopophilia (allying our gaze with the male gaze). According to Mulvey, one cannot isolate the narrative structures of classical cinema from their history of ideological usage, making the desire for Hollywood pleasures complicit in structures of domination.

Importing a Freudian vocabulary, Metz and Mulvey set the terms for the discussion of film spectatorship – identification, mirror stage, displacement, condensation, fetishism, scopophilia, narcissism, and voyeurism – thus laying the groundwork for future applications of psychoanalytic theory. Of course Metz and Mulvey did not originate these terms; they borrowed them from Lacan and Freud. Their innovation lies in the application of these existing Freudian and Lacanian concepts to the cinema. Metz and Mulvey do not, however, significantly nuance or enhance the basic concepts that they borrow from Freud. When they discuss voyeurism or fetishism, they use the terms in their Freudian sense. The act of applying these terms to the cinema did not fundamentally alter their meaning. The interchange between Metz and the psychoanalysts Freud and Lacan is one-way: Freud enriches our understanding of the cinema without the cinema significantly changing the Freudian system.[4] I therefore focus on the original concepts that Metz relies on in discussing cinematic pleasure. By going to the original source of these conceptions, I hope to reveal the assumptions about emotion that Metz and psychoanalytic film theorists borrow when they borrow their terms for analysis.

The first problem with drawing on Freud to explain cinematic emotions is straightforward. Psychologists generally agree that Freud's writings do not contain a well-developed theory of the emotions. Freud provided a comprehensive theory of the instincts and sexuality, but there is no correspondingly rigorous body of Freudian theory dealing with emotion,[5] creating an absence that Jerome Wakefield calls "the Achilles heel of theoretical psychoanalysis."[6] As the founding figure for psychoanalysis, Freud helped set the agenda that would guide the field for decades. By situating emotion as a secondary factor in explaining human behavior, Freud actually prevented emotion from becoming a central object of study for psychology.

To better understand Freud's neglect of the emotions, I revisit his intellectual project, examining how his initial neurologically based approach forged central assumptions that would become foundational for his later theories. I situate Freud's writing as a lifelong attempt to assert the centrality of instincts as the key to understanding human behavior. I argue that, for Freud, the emotions[7] were a symptom of the more important instinctual system. If our desiderata call for an approach rooted in a coherent theory of *emotion*, psychologists would generally agree that Freud would make a poor choice.

Freud's Neurophysiology of the Psyche

Freud began his career as a neurologist, seeking to explain behavior in neurophysiological terms, and this early mode of viewing the world strongly shaped his subsequent career. Some have argued that Freud may best be seen as a biologist[8] who sought scientific explanations for mental phenomena, which were not traditionally considered to be part of biology's concern. Trained in the natural sciences, Freud sought to bring the irrational into the hard light of rationalism. His early writings (from around 1888 to 1895) are peppered with references to the nervous system, revealing an attempt to produce a neuropsychological explanation for human behavior. In the *Project for a Scientific Psychology* (I), Freud tried to produce the beginnings of a theory that could explain psychological phenomena based on the current understanding of neurophysiology.

Project posits the existence of "key neurones" (I, 320) that, when activated, secrete some unknown chemical product that stimulates an excitation of the central nervous system, producing a conscious feeling tone. The way these "key neurones" would operate, Freud posited, was comparable with the current understanding of how motor neurons produce a physical response in the muscles. The motor neurons build up a certain quantity of excitation that, when it reaches a threshold level, seeks to discharge that energy into the muscles, producing motion. Whenever motor neurons gain energy, they seek to discharge it (or at least to maintain a steady state), following a basic principle for neural functioning. Increasing excitation is an anathema for nerves. Freud saw the key neurones as similarly seeking to discharge the energy accumulated by emotional stimulation.

These key neurones are stimulated when a person encounters an emotion-producing stimulus in the outside world (for example, a threatening event). Key neurones are excited at the same time as central nerves that are processing the idea of the emotional stimulus. Because these nerves are stimulated simultaneously, they cause an associative connection between the idea and the feeling tone. In this way, the memory of an experience can bring back the original emotion without the original stimulus having to be present, in the manner of a conditioned response. For early Freud, the concept of the conditioned response provided the primary model for explaining emotional behavior.[9]

Freud eventually abandoned this attempt to explain high-level emotional experiences based on explicitly neurological constructions, and his later writings contain fewer and fewer overt references to neurology. The gap between the kinds of psychological phenomena he was interested in studying and the neurological base of knowledge he learned through his training was simply too great. As Holt notes, Freud's neurons increasingly took on the properties of homunculi, performing high-level mental proceses instead of remaining the simple building blocks of those processes.[10] Rather than sacrifice his interest in high-level mental and physical phenomena such as hysteria, he ostensibly abandoned his connection to his initial discipline to create a theoretical apparatus that was psychical, not physiological.

And yet these early neurologically based assumptions about the emotions continue to exert their presence throughout the course of Freud's writing. The same principles that he used to explain the inner workings of the emotions as a neurological system form the basis for his psychological system. Although he shifts his entire approach to an emphasis on the psychical, this new system operates remarkably like his initial conception of the physiology of the emotions. In Freud's metapsychology one can see, according to McIntyre, "the ghost of the central nervous system sitting crowned upon the grave thereof."[11]

For Freud the emotions were part of an economy of psychic energy:

[Our theory] introduced a dynamic factor, by supposing that a symptom arises through the damming-up of an affect, and an economic factor, by regarding that same symptom as the product of the transformation of an amount of energy which would otherwise have been employed in some other way. (XX, 22)

He referred to the quantity of energy that is processed through the emotion system as "quota of affect" (*Affekt-betrag*) or "sum of excitation" (*Erregungssumme*; he used the terms roughly interchangeably).[12] He posited the following:

a quota of affect or sum of excitations which possesses the characteristics of quantity (although we have no means of measuring it), which is capable of increase, diminution, displacement, and discharge, and which is spread over the memory-traces of ideas somewhat as an electric charge is spread over the surface of a body. (III, 60)

The economy of psychic energy governs the emotions using rules Freud learned from neurology. When repeatedly stimulated, neurons (either motor neurons or the hypothetical emotional "key" neurons) accumulate an electric charge that is maintained until a threshold is reached. At this point, the neuron fires, discharging the accumulated energy and causing a response in the associated system (the muscles, the brain, the emotion system, etc.). Energy may be expressed in a variety of ways depending on which path it takes (making the biceps or the triceps contract, causing the eyes to tear), but the mechanism of excitation and discharge remains the same whether it is a quota of affect or a simple neurological activation that is being processed.

The "ghost of the central nervous system" can be seen clearly in Freud's emphasis on emotional discharge. For Freud, emotions were discharge phenomena. Whenever a significant quota of affect exists, it seeks to be released through some expressive behavior. A human will maintain a quota of affect only if the channels by which it could be discharged are all blocked. This description of the emotion system follows a basic principle governing the function of neurons. The preferred state of the system is at a low level of energy, making the system seek to discharge energy whenever possible (XVIII, 9; XX, 265; II, xx).

Discharge is so central to Freud's conception of emotion, he believed that if emotional energy was not discharged, there would be no emotion. Emotions are conscious experiences of the body, according to Freud. There are no unconscious emotions, as he made clear in the following key passage:

It is surely of the essence of an emotion that we should be aware of it, i.e., that it should become known to consciousness. Thus the possibility of the attribute of unconsciousness would be completely excluded as far as emotions, feelings, and affects are concerned. (XIV, 177)

Only when the emotion system expresses its energy through the body do emotions exist. Emotions, following the pattern observed in nerves, only influence human behavior when they are discharged.

At this point we can now sketch a three-stage process that describes Freud's understanding of the way emotions function. In stage one, an instinct attaches itself to an idea (usually through association), transferring instinctual energy into a "quota of affect." The second stage begins when this quota of affect starts to discharge its energy as bodily arousal. Note that both of these stages can occur as unconscious processes, which means that for Freud these steps were not yet emotion per se. In the final stage, the bodily arousal is sensed, reaching conscious experience and creating emotion. Awareness transforms a physical state into a psychic experience, similar to the way that a simple physical lack of food is changed to the sensation of hunger.[13] It is this experience that Freud called emotion.

This description of the Freudian emotion process relies heavily on Jerome Wakefield's admirable work in reconstructing Freud's understanding of emotion.[14] At no point in his writings did Freud give such a straightforward description of the step-by-step process of emotion, which raises a question: Why didn't this incredibly systematic thinker lay out a systematic explanation of the emotions, instead of leaving it to later writers to piece together a coherent account based on scattered writings?

The answer is reflected in Freud's concept of the quota of affect. As we have seen, processing a quota of affect can result in a variety of outputs. This quota can be discharged through any number of actions or conscious thoughts. Although his choice of terminology misleadingly implies that a quota *contains* affect, Freud used the term "quota of affect" to describe a *tendency* to express affect, a potential emotion and not an emotion per se. A quota of affect was not affect for Freud because this energy can release its potential in various ways, many of which would not be described as emotion by most people. For example, a quota of affect can be expressed just as well through a thought as it can through a physical action such as crying. Both are highly effective, healthy means of discharging the quota of affect, but only one of them (a consciously experienced bodily arousal) would Freud have considered an emotion.

A quota of affect is only a quantity of energy that has no qualities that distinguish it as being emotional. It tends to be expressed in ways that would be considered emotional, but this is merely a tendency, not a predictive fact. The quota of affect remains a potential emotion, which for Freud meant that it is no emotion at all, as Schafer notes.[15] Jerome Wakefield says that "[f]or Freud, affect is more an occasional side-effect than a central function or inevitable outcome of instinctual energy."[16]

Here we begin to see the weakness of Freud's system in providing a nuanced explanation of the emotions. Freud's central emotion concept, the quota of affect, is not necessarily tied to the experience of emotions; it can just as easily be discharged through nonemotional expression. This concept led Freud away from a more specific consideration of the nature of emotion, because emotions were only one of numerous side effects. Freud never assembled a cohesive description of his understanding of the emotion system because it never seemed particularly crucial to his work.

I argue that to reduce emotions to a discharge phenomenon is to reduce their particularity, and particularity is a key quality for our desiderata. An emphasis on discharge makes all emotions look the same. Accordingly, Freud seemed to be telling the same story over and over again with regard to the emotions: a quota of energy is mobilized only to be dissipated. This story makes sense when applied to microlevel phenomena such as the firing of neurons; when applied to larger phenomena such as emotional functioning, it makes such complex systems seem simple.

Associations and Functionality

Neurology is not the only important influence on Freud's emotional energy system. Energy interchanges involving Freud's quota of affect also operate based on a principle from thermodynamics. Recall that in the definition of the quota of affect cited earlier, Freud compared this quantity of energy to "an electric charge... spread over the surface of a body" (III, 60). As the electricity metaphor suggests, this quantity of psychic energy follows the laws that govern Newtonian physics. For example, it may be converted or transferred into different forms. Just as electricity can become light or heat, the quota of affect can find expression through a range of behaviors: tears, wailing, or trembling. This commutability of emotional energy represents a departure from the purely neurologically based conception of emotion.

Freud believed that the quota of affect follows a basic principle of conservation of energy. The energy remains constant unless more energy enters the system or leaves the system. A quota of affect accumulates as excitations increase, just as an electric charge increases when energy is added. Once the quantity reaches a threshold point, it attempts to exit the system by being discharged through one of several possible paths and entering into consciousness. If the paths of release are somehow blocked, the energy remains in steady state until it can be discharged.

This is the primary change between Freud's psychic emotion system and his earlier neurophysiologically based explanation of emotion.[17] A neuron does not maintain a charge for long periods of time; it discharges the stimulation as soon as possible. Neurophysiologists would reject the idea of a neuron holding onto a charge for a lengthy period, but the psychic equivalent of this idea becomes crucial for Freud's understanding of the emotions. This principle of the conservation of emotional energy is central to the entire list of emotional disorders that Freud enumerated.

This conservation of energy operating in the emotion system makes it possible for an emotion to be associated with thoughts or bodily functions.[18] Freud posited that the quota of affect remains resident in the individual until it is released, even if this involves a long period of time. When a thought is separated from its associated emotion and repressed into the unconscious, the quota of affect can stay active in the emotion system, finding connections to bodily states (as in conversion) or making connection with other contiguous thoughts (as in obsessions, fetishes, and phobias):[19]

If someone with a disposition [to neurosis] lacks the aptitude for conversion, but if, nevertheless, in order to fend off an incompatible idea, he sets about separating it from its affect, then *that affect is obliged to remain in the psychical sphere.* The idea, now weakened, is still left in consciousness, separated from all association. *But its affect, which has become free, attaches itself to other ideas which are not in themselves incompatible; and, thanks to this "false connection," those ideas turn into obsessional ideas.* This, in a few words, is the psychological theory of obsessions and phobias. (III, 51–52, emphasis in original)

Association is key to the way thoughts are consciously worked over, to the way they are stored in conscious memory or the unconscious, to the way they are reactivated from the unconscious, and to the way they may be expressed through conversion.

Although the associative mechanism may obscure the link between affect and symptom, the analyst can be confident nevertheless that the link exists. At the heart of Freud's psychoanalysis is a faith that there is a rational connection between the emotional situation that causes a symptom and the symptom itself (even if the original situation is far removed in time and place), just as there is a rational connection between an insult and an angry blow. For Freud the connection between a trauma and the resulting hysterical symptom is as firm as the tie between a trauma and an immediate action response. The difference is that association and repression obscure the link in hysteria, requiring analysis to make this clear again. The work of the analyst is to follow the trail of associations leading from the symptom to its cause. For Freud, the emotions remained just as directly functional as Darwin believed they were, although association could obscure the causal connection to the untrained eye.[20]

The importance Freud attached to association in his emotion system, however, opened up possibilities that extend far beyond the functional explanation of emotions that he initially adopted from Darwin. If the individual did not have the resources to deal with the emotion adequately at the time, he or she could choose to repress the emotional idea, according to Freud. Repression pushes the idea into the unconscious, freeing the conscious mind from the burden of the emotion. It splits the emotion from the thought, setting the quota of affect loose to be attached to other ideas that are related not through logical causality but through mere contiguity or similarity. Freud's practice of analysis led him to muse that perhaps

"the release of affect and the ideational content do not constitute the indissoluble organic unity as which we are in the habit of treating them, but that these two separate entities may be merely *soldered* together and can thus be detached from each other" (V, 461–2).

The belief that a quota of affect can be transferred from one idea to another, loosely related idea breaks the strong tie between the thought and the quota of affect that is at the heart of a functional account of the emotions.[21]

When such emotion does attach itself to a thought, the flexibility of possible attachments sometimes allows the quota of affect to "misattach" itself to the wrong thoughts. Anxieties can become connected to thoughts that are marginally related to their cause, creating phobias, obsessions, or fetishes. While Freud's psychiatric practice presents a catalog of the ways that the quota of affect can become disconnected from the original thought, Freud's overall theoretical goal was to assert their connectedness, to show the rationality behind seemingly irrational behavior. As Sachs notes,

Freud's psychoanalytic interpretations of incongruities of affect *always* try to show that the incongruities are real appropriateness, behind what is taken to be the facade of every apparently discrepant feeling. . . . [This] functioned for him as *one* of the criteria for the correctness of psychoanalytic interpretations of affective disorders.[22]

There are two unintuitive findings presented by these emotional disorders, and these two findings present two very different directions for pursuing research. One is that there is a hidden rational explanation for seemingly illogical states, if one can find the connection obscured by associative mechanisms. The other surprising finding is that emotion (which usually appears to be rooted in specific situational factors and tied to specific objects) is transferable, mobile.

Freud was clearly invested in exploring the ramifications of the former, not the latter. For Freud, emotion remained a clue that the detective-analyst could follow to find the same answer over and over: that emotional disorders only seem to be disorderly, when in actuality they are not. As Lewis says, "[a]lthough the affects always played a major role in his subsequent clinical accounts, they were always secondary in his theoretical formulations."[23] Although some of his clinical observation brought up possibilities of emotion loosed from its moorings to thought, Freud did not explore this possibility in a systematic way because of the focus of his larger project, thus leaving the Freudian explanation of emotion rife with contradiction. At times he seemed to come close to situating a central place for associations in the emotions (as I do in my account of the emotions), but he never fully integrated these thoughts into a cohesive system.

The question still nags: Why did Freud, whose case studies are rife with emotional data, pay so little specific attention to the phenomenon of emotion itself? Why did Freud devote only 27 of 621 pages of his most important work (*The Interpretation of Dreams*) specifically to emotion when emotion plays such a large part in the experience of dreams?[24] Why this assumption that emotion is a symptom, not a foundational basis for human behavior?

For Freud, the foundation of human behavior was the instincts, particularly the sexual instincts. These instincts provided the energy that drove his psychic economy: "psychoanalysis derives all mental processes (apart from the reception of external stimuli) from the interplay of forces . . . . All of these forces are originally in the nature of *instincts*; thus they have an organic origin" (XX, 265). Libido (sexual energy) is the motive force behind dreams, creative expression, and attachments to other people. Although he nuanced his description of the instincts across his career (for instance, the conception of "life" and "death" instincts that emerged in his later work), his work can be seen as a longstanding defense of the importance of sexuality and the instincts as the key factors explaining human behavior.

With the instincts and sexuality at the core of the being, Freud found little room for the emotions as another foundational concept. So emotions became less central to his research agenda to provide the most powerful explanations of human behavior. They became symptoms of the more basic factors,[25] which are the more important object of study. As Wakefield argues,

since emotions can be readily exchanged for each other and for other reactions due to defensive maneuvers, there is no "conservation of affect" for each affective tone, so affects do not seem in the end to be very important in themselves; they are only of interest as a side-effect of instinctual processes.[26]

To Freud's mind, the instincts were a more dependable and consistent explanatory factor than the malleable energy of the quota of affect. This orientation in his practice led Freud to confine himself to reporting the emotional details of the clinical data, theoretically neglecting them in favor of "deeper" explanations.

Theorists of Instincts and Drives

Considering how large Metz's figure looms over discussions of cinematic pleasure, it is initially surprising that he does not refine Freud's understanding of emotion when he imports psychoanalytic concepts into film theory. However, one must remember that Metz is primarily a semiotician, not a psychoanalyst. He chooses psychoanalysis as a mechanism for explaining cinematic pleasures because he perceives it to be compatible with semiotics: "linguistics and psychoanalysis are both sciences of the symbolic and are even, come to think of it, the only two sciences whose immediate and sole object is the fact of signification as such."[27] Lacan saw that the Freudian unconscious was structured like a language, and Metz sees that this language could also be a language of film. That Metz does not update or challenge Freud's understanding of the emotions is not surprising if one sees Metz's lifelong project as an examination of the semiotics of cinema. His first priority is to explain cinematic signification, and cinematic pleasure is an important but still secondary subproblem.

Once one understands Freud as primarily a theorist of instincts and sexuality, it becomes easier to see that Metz in *The Imaginary Signifier* explains why we go to the cinema in terms of instincts and drives, not in terms of the emotions it elicits. Because Metz believes the world has "universal affective features"[28] that people can apprehend, he need not articulate a new model of the emotions specifically for the cinematic situation. He can concentrate on the nature of the cinematic signifier that is constructed to elicit these emotions, leaving the description of that emotion system to Freud.

Metz asserts that the pleasures of the cinema are rooted in what he calls the "perceptual passions:" the scopic drive (the desire to see) and Lacan's invocatory drive (the desire to hear).[29] Cinematic pleasure offers an "instinctual satisfaction,"[30] balancing the needs of the pleasure principle with the requirements of the reality principle.

This pleasure operates in a distinctively Freudian fashion. Cinematic pleasure is a discharge phenomenon that operates using the same rules Freud outlined for his economy of emotional energy. Metz says:

The primary process rests on the 'pure' pleasure principle, uncorrected by the reality principle, and therefore aims at the maximal and immediate discharge of psychical excitations (affects, representations, thoughts, etc.). It will thus use any of the itineraries of energy discharge, and this is the basis of condensation and displacement.[31]

According to *The Imaginary Signifier,* the pleasure principle in the cinematic spectator "always seeks to liquidate stases."[32] Pleasure, for Metz and for contemporary psychoanalytic film theory, is a release of a quota of affect, following Freud's assumptions. It is a phenomenon that is important not because it is *emotional* but because it disperses instinctual energy. The drive to see and hear brings us to the cinema, and cinematic pleasure (temporarily) satisfies this desire by releasing and extinguishing this instinctual energy.

If Metz can be understood as a theoretician who incorporated Freud's psychoanalysis into his semiotic framework, Laura Mulvey can be seen as a writer interested in symptomatic readings of films for the insights they can yield into the workings of society. Her later work increasingly emphasizes the mythic underpinnings that are not specific to the cinema but that are shared by other mass-culture forms. Such works are "collective fantasies" containing clues that can be deciphered to uncover the hidden underpinnings of the culture.[33] By investigating the Oedipal dimensions of *Blue Velvet,* for instance, Mulvey can discuss how this particular reworking of the Oedipus story sheds light on Enlightenment thought and the fascination with the hidden and archaic in modern American culture. The Hollywood melodrama is particularly productive for her because of the way melodrama uses a historical myth while it simultaneously "symptomises the history of its own time."[34] Melodrama, with its emphasis on what is hidden and unspoken, becomes central for Mulvey less because of its emotional content and more for what it can reveal about what a society represses.

The process of deciphering the melodrama became a two-step process:

To notice that lighting, colour, or framing, for instance, inflected meaning would be the first stage. The next would be to work out why and whether the figure in the pattern referred to disguised social symptoms. Although the first stage is integral to any reading of the cinematic image, and open to anyone who cares to see with their mind's eye, the second stage is, obviously, more difficult. The melodrama, however, revolves so openly around sexuality and emotion that anyone who cares to do so can sense their symptomatic connection with social constraints, ideology, or collective fantasy.[35]

Emotion is important as a symptom, as an indication that important ideological work is being done in a film. The emotion, like the reading of the cinematic image, is "open to anyone who cares to see with their mind's eye." The real work of the critic, like the Freudian psychoanalyst, is to go beyond such surface manifestations and to investigate the deeper structure of repressed meaning. Emotions are important not in and of themselves but for what they hide.

When Mulvey does investigate film and emotion with some specificity, she emphasizes the emotional states exhibited by characters, not the emotions in the spectator. She acknowledges that it is "dangerous" to elide the world of onscreen characters with the real world of the film viewer. Nonetheless, she notes in her discussion of *Duel in the Sun* that "the emotions of those women accepting 'masculinisation' while watching action movies with a male hero are illuminated by the emotions of a heroine of a melodrama." The emotions of an onscreen character are more easily readable than those of the film spectator, and so she uses these emotions to illuminate the emotions of the real-world viewer. Ingrid Bergman's look as she investigates the house in *Notorious* becomes "an emblem of female curiosity" that "mobilizes the spectator's curiosity."[36] Mulvey relies on character's emotions almost exclusively when discussing particular emotional responses.

The seeds of this emphasis on the characters' emotions can be seen in her landmark essay on "Visual Pleasure and Narrative Cinema." What gives the scopophilia and narcissism of the cinema their ideological punch is the fact that Hollywood organizes our primary identification with the camera in alliance with particular characters' looks. Historically speaking, we are asked to identify with the active gaze of a man at the passive figure of a woman. Quickly Mulvey shifts the focus from the spectator's look to the onscreen look between characters as the determining factor in a symptomatic reading of Hollywood ideology. The male character models how we should look at the woman, and to reject this look is to refuse to participate in the narrative and the pleasure it offers. Therefore, we can read the spectator's emotional responses from the characters, because our pleasure depends on following their lead. When Mulvey examines filmic emotion, she frequently assumes that the character onscreen is a model for our own spectatorial responses, which allows her to treat them interchangeably.

In an essay investigating film theory's fascination with melodrama, Mulvey metaphorically describes the interrelationships among her central areas of interest:

The Hollywood cinema of the studio system had as many separate but intermeshed layers as an onion. Peel away the outer skin of a conformist, censored cinema addressing an immigrant audience on the aspirations of the American Dream; you then find an energetic form of popular entertainment, mass producing the finest-tooled spectacle of the modern age for commodity consumption. Peel away the modernist gloss and the industrial base and you find recycled versions of folk stories. . . . Peel away the insistence on a surface sexuality, the eroticisation of the screen as spectacle and woman as sexualised spectacle and you find traces of everyday anxieties or collective fantasies that defy conscious expression. Right in the center is emotion and its eternal, external, physical symptoms: laughter, horror, the thrill of suspense . . . and tears.[37]

The metaphor of the onion is particularly apt because when one peels away an onion, one finds nothing at the center. Similarly, Mulvey's system seems to place emotion at its center but spends all its time working outward toward the surrounding layers: toward collective anxieties, the sexualized spectacle of the woman, and the commodification of mythology. Mulvey, like Metz and Freud, finds other layers of meaning to be more important than the allegedly central issue of emotion.

Just because Metz and Mulvey echo Freud's deemphasis on emotion does not necessarily mean that subsequent psychoanalytic film theorists share the same inheritance. Perhaps more current psychoanalytic criticism, with its more specific focus on particular genres and historical eras, has overcome the Freudian lack of specificity concerning emotions. Perhaps if psychoanalytic film critics pay attention to a more specific object of study, they can give more nuanced insight into filmic emotions than Metz did when he tried to describe the entire cinematic apparatus. Let us briefly survey some of Metz's and Mulvey's descendants in search of a more subtle understanding of what emotion is.

Claire Johnston's *Notes on Women's Cinema*[38] framed the questions that feminist scholars would pursue using Mulvey's combination of ideological criticism and psychoanalytic investigation. What pleasures does Hollywood offer to women, and what are the ideological ramifications of these pleasures? Can women filmmakers free cinematic technique from its patriarchal heritage and produce a truly alternative cinema by and for women? As Constance Penley says,

Even if one believes that the only lesson feminists can learn from Hollywood is a negative one (how not to make films that depend on voyeuristic responses and a sadistic subjection of the woman to male fantasy), a working knowledge of the mechanisms of pleasure and modes of power of this dominant institution would seem to be indispensable.[39]

Because pleasure and power are so imbricated together in the cinema, scholars pursued a better knowledge of their interworkings using ideological criticism and a psychoanalytic vocabulary.

Later scholars have pursued this investigation in several ways. Some have imported psychoanalytic mechanisms articulated by post-Freudian thinkers and have posited these mechanisms as explanations for the emotional and political power of spectatorship. Gaylyn Studlar places her emphasis on theories of the pre-Oedipal (such as the writings of Nancy Chodorow) and presented the desires of masochism as an alternative to Mulvey's mechanisms. Mary Ann Doane looks to Joan Rivière's concept of femininity as a masquerade and argues that the cinema asks female spectators to engage in a kind of transvestitism as they occupy subject positions.[40]

Others have pursued psychoanalytic explanations of the pleasures that other portions of the cinematic signifier provide. Metz and Mulvey maintain an almost exclusive emphasis on the visual, but later scholars discuss the importance of sound in processes of spectatorship. Mary Ann Doane and Kaja Silverman discuss how the synchronized human voice is valuable in constituting a cohesive subject position in the cinema. Claudia Gorbman argues that film music also greatly contributes to satisfying the spectator's desires in the way Metz and Mulvey articulated.[41]

Some have followed Roland Barthes's argument that pleasure (*jouissance*) exceeds the limited pleasures (*plaisir*) offered by an ideological subject positioning, turning pleasure from the ideologically complicit player initially articulated by Mulvey into an element that can destabilize structures of power. Other scholars have argued that discussions of spectatorship cannot operate across a wide range of times but must be bound to a specific set of historical norms. Patrice Petro, Miriam Hansen, and others discuss narrational and ideological norms operating in a particular era to make historically specific arguments about the nature of desire and spectatorship in that era. Yet another body of work rejects Metz and Mulveys attempt to discuss the pleasures offered by the Hollywood cinematic apparatus as a whole, instead choosing to concentrate on spectatorship in one particular genre. The largest body of such scholarship investigates melodrama and the women's film (for example, Mary Ann Doane's *The Desire to Desire* and Christine Gledhill's *Home Is Where the Heart Is*) as alternative forms of narration presenting a distinctive vision of female desire. Scholars have also posited psychoanalytic mechanisms as explanations for the pleasures of horror (Carol Clover) and pornography (Linda Williams).[42]

As psychoanalytic film theory gains more specificity in its discussion of particular genres and historical eras, this seems to promise more specific attention to the primary task of enlarging "the working knowledge of the mechanisms of pleasure" (in Penley's phrase). As psychoanalytic scholars discuss particular women's films, for instance, they are reminded that filmic appeals depend not only on ideological positioning but also on the experience of emotion:

The woman's film as a genre also produces a certain representation of spectatorship which is powerful in its effects. Spectating becomes an affective rather than cognitive activity (voyeurism, in contrast, is associated with an epistemological drive), and it is infused with the negativity of longing and mourning. The films activate a pathos which embraces and celebrates loss, reconciling the spectator to the terms of the given social order. Such readings have been denounced as pessimistic, disallowing the possibility of pleasure on the part of the female spectator. This is far from true. Tears and pleasure are by no means incompatible and signal the complicity of women in the cinematic mechanics of the organization of vision, desire, and sexual difference. I think the problem of complicity, of participation and even enjoyment, announces the necessity for a psychoanalytic inquiry.[43]

For Mary Ann Doane (quoted here) and others, dealing with pleasure and unpleasure necessarily calls for a psychoanalytic approach. Specific work on limited objects (such as particular genres or eras) seems to provide the best hope for psychoanalytic scholarship trying to explain pathos and participation, complicity and crying.

Psychoanalytic scholarship rarely talks about the particulars of filmic emotion, however, and instead concentrates on articulating the filmic mechanisms of subject positioning and on labeling the mechanisms of desire (masochism, scopophilia, etc.). As E. Ann Kaplan notes as she looks back on her participation in an extended dialogue about *Stella Dallas* (discussed in Chapter 5 of this book),

> I did not deal sufficiently with the issue of emotional connection that identifying involves, and which came up in admitting that *Stella Dallas* continues to make me cry. The tears happen because I identify with Stella's loss of her daughter at the end of the film – her inability to share in the wedding, her self-denying self-relegation to a sphere outsider her daughter's new life. I would now argue that, along with desiring identity via identifying, we also desire emotional connectedness. Identity is constructed in the process of establishing emotional connection. We respond to being "hailed" because the process of subject-formation offers both identity and emotional connectedness.[44]

Psychoanalytic film theory, with its joint emphasis on identification and ideology, has tended to discuss the politics of identity in much more detail than it does the nuances of a film's emotional appeal. Kaplan recognizes that this reticence toward talking about emotion has deep roots:

> It was largely our anti-realism theory that made it difficult to use the word "emotional" in recent feminist film theory: we have been comfortable with the "cool," theoretical sound of "desire." But identificatory processes involve emotional needs for symbiosis, wholeness, becoming one with an Other. In arguing that such processes in realist texts inevitably enmeshed the spectator in oppressive ideologies, we were led to advocate a cerebral, non-emotional kind of text and corresponding spectator response.[45]

The "cool, theoretical sound of 'desire'" lures feminist film criticism away from specific consideration of the emotions and leads them back to more cerebral matters such as ideology.

Because it came forward during the heyday of Althusserian-based criticism, such psychoanalytic theory linked ideology to identification. This linkage provided a political punch that energized film feminism, but it also led to the relative neglect of the emotions that Kaplan described. In the work following Metz and Mulvey, one sees the same lack of specific attention to the emotions. Psychoanalytic film theory is deeply indebted to its Freudian roots, which provide many productive metaphors and concepts. Unfortunately, the centrality of instincts and drives in Freud leads these theorists toward pleasure (not emotion as a whole) and toward an understanding of emotions as side effects (not as vital mechanisms).

The difficulty of a theory of cinematic emotions based on instincts and drives is that it lacks specificity. Such a theory tells the same story over and over again, regardless of differences between particular examples. Either a quota of affect is discharged (pleasure) or it is increased (unpleasure). To understand a cinematic pleasure in such a model, it is ultimately more important to understand the instincts and drives behind the emotion than the specifics of the emotional situation itself. Ultimately Metz's *The Imaginary Signifier* is more concerned with *why* we gain pleasure from the cinema than it is with cinematic pleasures themselves. Psychoanalytic film theory fails to encourage specific explanations of filmic emotion in particular films, and so it fails our first desideratum.

Notes

1. An Invitation to Feel

1. For more information about Eisenstein's prescient intuitions about the nature of emotion, see Greg M. Smith, *Movie Moods: The Emotion System and Film Structure* (Ph.D. dissertation, University of Wisconsin—Madison, 1998), chapter 3.

2. David Bordwell, *Narration in the Fiction Film* (Madison: University of Wisconsin Press, 1985); Noël Carroll, *The Philosophy of Horror, or Paradoxes of the Heart* (New York: Routledge, 1990); Gregory Currie, *Image and Mind: Film, Philosophy, and Cognitive Science* (Cambridge: Cambridge University Press, 1995); Murray Smith, *Engaging Characters: Fiction, Emotion, and the Cinema* (Oxford: Oxford University Press, 1995); Joseph Anderson, *The Reality of Illusion: An Ecological Approach to Cognitive Film Theory* (Carbondale: Southern Illinois University Press, 1996); Edward Branigan, *Narrative Comprehension and Film* (New York: Routledge, 1992); Torben Grodal, *Moving Pictures: A New Theory of Film Genres, Feelings, and Cognition* (Oxford: Oxford University Press, 1997); Ed S. Tan, *Emotion and the Structure of Narrative Film: Film as an Emotion Machine*, trans. Barbara Fasting (Mahwah, NJ: Lawrence Erlbaum, 1996).

3. Kristin Thompson, *Breaking the Glass Armor: Neoformalist Film Analysis* (Princeton, NJ: Princeton University Press, 1988), 3.

4. For an intriguing introduction to issues around cognition, emotion, and film music, see Jeff Smith, "Movie Music as Moving Music: Emotion, Cognition, and the Film Score," in *Passionate Views: Film, Cognition, and Emotion*, eds. Carl Plantinga and Greg M. Smith (Baltimore: Johns Hopkins University Press, 1999).

5. It is possible that portions of the discussion in this book may also apply to other audiovisual narrative media that unfold uninterrupted in real time (for instance, certain kinds of theater). This is not to say that there are no differences between the two media (for instance, the theatrical convention of a greater emphasis on language) and their emotional appeals, but that their narrational structure may call on very similar principles.

2. The Emotion System and Nonprototypical Emotions

1. For an overview of these issues, see Howard Gardner, "How Rational a Being?" *The Mind's New Science: A History of the Cognitive Revolution* (New York: Basic Books, 1987), 360–80.
2. Noël Carroll, *The Philosophy of Horror, or Paradoxes of the Heart* (New York: Routledge, 1990).
3. The most accessible introduction to fuzzy logic is Bart Kosko, *Fuzzy Thinking: The New Science of Fuzzy Logic* (New York: Hyperion, 1989).
4. For instance, Robert M. Gordon, *The Structure of Emotions: Investigations in Cognitive Philosophy* (Cambridge: Cambridge University Press, 1987).
5. Because cognitivism has long treated its subject as if it were independent of the bodily "hardware" and therefore could be modeled on a computer, it is this somatic component of emotion that has discouraged traditional cognitive researchers from approaching the subject. Emotions were obviously highly dependent on the "hardware" and thus were outside the computer-centered model of cognitive processing. The most well-known criticism of cognitivism's emphasis on the computer is John Searle, "Minds, Brains, and Programs," *The Behavioral and Brain Sciences* 3 (1980): 417–57.
6. Pamela K. Adelmann and R. B. Zajonc, "Facial Efference and the Experience of Emotion," *Annual Review of Psychology*, vol. 40, eds. M. R. Rosenzweig and L. W. Porter (Palo Alto, CA: Annual Reviews, 1989), 249–80; Paul Ekman, Robert W. Levenson, and Wallace V. Friesen, "Autonomic Nervous System Activity Distinguishes among Emotions," *Science* 221, no. 4616 (1983): 1208–10; Carroll E. Izard, "Facial Expressions and the Regulation of Emotions," *Journal of Personality and Social Psychology* 58, no. 3 (1990): 487–498.
7. Walter Cannon, "The James-Lange Theory of Emotions: A Critical Examination and an Alternative Theory," *American Journal of Psychology* 39 (1927): 106–24; Walter Cannon, "Again the James-Lange and Thalamic Theories of Emotion," *Psychological Review* 38 (1931): 281–95.
8. Magda B. Arnold, *Emotion and Personality*, 2 vols. (New York: Columbia University Press, 1960); Stanley Schachter and Jerome E. Singer, "Cognitive, Social, and Physiological Determinants of Emotional State," *Psychological Review* 69 (1962): 379–99.
9. Nico Frijda, *The Emotions* (Cambridge: Cambridge University Press, 1980).
10. For James R. Averill, emotions *are* a special kind of role we inhabit briefly. We are socialized to know that the experience of sadness is like and when we should inhabit this "role." See "A Constructivist View of Emotion," *Emotion: Theory, Research, and Experience*, vol. 1, eds. Robert Plutchik and Henry Kellerman (New York: Academic Press, 1980), 305–39.
11. Catherine A. Lutz, *Unnatural Emotions: Everyday Sentiments on a Micronesian Atoll and Their Challenge to Western Theory* (Chicago: University of Chicago Press, 1988).
12. Silvan S. Tomkins, *Affect, Imagery, and Consciousness: Vol. 1, The Positive Affects* (New York: Springer, 1962); Silvan S. Tomkins, *Affect, Imagery, and Consciousness: Vol. 2, The Negative Affects* (New York: Springer, 1963); Frijda (1980).

13. Studies indicate that Western women experience and express more emotionality, with certain exceptions (for instance, anger and contempt), than do their male counterparts. For a review of gender differences in emotional experience, see Leslie R. Brody and Judith A. Hall, "Gender and Emotion," *Handbook of Emotions*, eds. Michael Lewis and Jeannette M. Haviland (New York: Guilford Press, 1993), 447–60. For a survey of research on gender differences in emotional expressivity, see Judith A. Hall, *Nonverbal Sex Differences: Communication Accuracy and Expressive Style* (Baltimore: Johns Hopkins University Press, 1984).

14. Richard S. Lazarus, "On the Primacy of Cognition," *American Psychologist* 39, no. 2 (February 1984): 124–9; Robert B. Zajonc, "On the Primacy of Affect," *American Psychologist* 39, no. 2 (February 1984): 117–23.

15. This distinction is closely related to Cannon's description of emotional experience versus emotional behavior. See Cannon, "Again the James-Lange and the Thalamic Theories of Emotion," 285.

16. For instance, Schachter and Singer (1962) and Frijda (1980).

17. For instance, Joseph E. LeDoux, "The Neurobiology of Emotion," *Mind and Brain: Dialogue in Cognitive Neuroscience*, eds. Joseph E. LeDoux and W. Hirst (New York: Cambridge University Press, 1986), 301–54; Jaak Panksepp, "The Anatomy of Emotions," *Emotion: Theory, Research and Experience, Vol. 3: Biological Foundations of Emotion*, eds. Robert Plutchik and Henry Kellerman (New York: Academic Press, 1986), 91–124.

18. For information on children's emotional development, see Michael Lewis and Carolyn Saarni, eds., *The Socialization of Emotions* (New York: Plenum, 1985). For a review of the literature on animals and emotions, see Terry R. McGuire, "Emotion and Behavior Genetics in Vertebrates and Invertebrates," Lewis and Haviland, 155–66.

19. Cannon, "The James-Lange Theory of Emotions," 106–24; Larry A. Normansell and Jaak Panksepp, "Play in Decorticated Rats," *Society for Neuroscience Abstracts* 10 (1984): 612; W. J. Jacobs and L. Nadel, "Stress-Induced Recovery of Fears and Phobias," *Psychological Review* 92, no. 4 (October 1985): 512–37.

20. Laura Mulvey, "Visual Pleasure and Narrative Cinema," *Movies and Methods*, vol. 2, ed. Bill Nichols (Berkeley: University of California Press, 1985), 304.

21. Frijda (1980).

22. A. Öhman, U. Dimberg, and F. Esteves, "Preattentive Activation of Aversive Emotions," *Aversion, Avoidance, and Anxiety*, ed. J. P. Aggleton (Hillsdale, NJ: Lawrence Erlbaum, 1989), 169–93.

23. Richard S. Lazarus, James R. Averill, and E. M. Opton, Jr., "Toward a Cognitive Theory of Emotions," *Feelings and Emotions*, ed. M. B. Arnold (New York: Academic Press, 1970).

24. William James, "The Emotions," *The Principles of Psychology*, vol. 2 (New York: Holt, 1890).

25. Ekman, Levenson, and Friesen, 1208–10.

26. Glenn E. Higgins, "Sexual Response in Spinal Cord Injured Adults: A Review of the Literature," *Archives of Sexual Behavior* 8, no. 2 (1979): 173–96.

27. John M. Cleghorn, George Peterfy, E. J. Pinter, and C. J. Pattee, "Verbal Anxiety and the Beta Adrenergic Receptors: A Facilitating Mechanism?" *Journal of Nervous and Mental Disease* 151 (1970): 266–72; Gisela Erdmann and Beatrix van Lindern, "The Effects of Beta-Adrenergic Stimulation and Beta-Adrenergic Blockade on Emotional Reactions," *Psychophysiology* 17, no. 4 (1980): 332–8.

28. Gregorio Marañon, "Contribution a L'etude de L'action Emotive de L'adrenaline," *Revue Francais d'endocrinologie* 2 (1924): 300–10.

29. Tomkins, *Affect, Imagery, and Consciousness*, vols. 1 and 2.

30. Fritz Strack, Leonard L. Martin, and Sabine Stepper, "Inhibiting and Facilitating Conditions of Facial Expressions: A Non-Obtrusive Test of the Facial Feedback Hypothesis," *Journal of Personality and Social Psychology* 54, no. 5 (1988): 768–77.

31. Paul Ekman and Wallace V. Friesen, *The Facial Action Coding System* (Palo Alto, CA: Consulting Psychologists, 1978).

32. Ekman, Levenson, and Friesen, 1208–10.

33. Carroll E. Izard, "Facial Expressions and the Regulation of Emotions," *Journal of Personality and Social Psychology* 58, no. 3 (1990): 496.

34. Ekman, Levenson, and Friesen, 1208–10.

35. Paul Ekman, "A Set of Basic Emotion Families," unpublished paper.

36. Gellhorn is an important early exception. See "Motion and Emotion: The Role of Proprioception in the Physiology and Pathology of the Emotions," *Psychological Review* 71 (1964): 457–72. Also see Michael Argyle, *Bodily Communication* (New York: International Universities, 1975).

37. Susan Folkman and Richard S. Lazarus, "Coping as a Mediator of Emotion," *Journal of Personality and Social Psychology* 54, no. 3 (1988): 466–75; John H. Riskind and Carolyn C. Gotay, "Physical Posture: Could It Have Regulatory or Feedback Effects on Motivation and Emotion?" *Motivation and Emotion* 6, no. 3: 273–98.

38. B. Pasquarelli and N. Bull, "Experimental Investigation of the Body-Mind Continuum in Affective States," *Journal of Nervous Mental Disorders* 113 (1951): 512–21.

39. Tomkins, *Affect, Imagery, and Consciousness*, vols. 1 and 2. See Klaus Scherer and Paul Ekman, eds., *Handbook of Research on Nonverbal Behavior* (New York: Cambridge University Press, 1982) for a description of pitch and frequency variation as vocal signals of emotion.

40. An instructive and thorough study can be found in Klaus R. Scherer, Rainer Banse, Harald G. Wallbott, and Thomas Goldbeck, "Vocal Cues in Emotion Encoding and Decoding," *Motivation and Emotion* 15, no. 2 (1991): 123–48. The study's generalizability must be questioned, however, because it examines affective vocalization in radio actors.

41. Klaus R. Scherer, "Vocal Affect Expression: A Review and a Model for Future Research," *Psychological Bulletin* 99, no. 2 (1986): 143–65.

42. Robert W. Frick, "Communicating Emotion: The Role of Prosodic Features," *Psychological Bulletin* 97, no. 3 (1985): 412–29; Leda Cosmides, "Invariances in the Acoustic Expression of Emotion during Speech," *Journal of Experimental Psychology: Human Perception and Performance* 9, no. 6 (1983): 864–81.

43. Lois Bloom, "Developments in Expression: Affect and Speech," *Psychological and Biological Approaches to Emotion*, eds. Nancy L. Stein, B. Leventhal, and Tom Trabasso (Hillsdale, NJ: Lawrence Erlbaum, 1990); Lois Bloom and Richard Beckwith, "Talking with Feeling: Integrating Affective and Linguistic Expression in Early Language Development," *Cognition and Emotion* 3, no. 4 (1989): 313–42.

44. Judy Dunn, Inge Bretherton, and Penny Munn, "Conversations about Feeling States between Mothers and Their Young Children," *Developmental Psychology* 23, no. 1 (1987): 132–39; Peggy J. Miller and Linda L. Sperry, "The Socialization of Anger and Aggression," *Merrill Palmer Quarterly* 33, no. 1 (1987): 1–31.

45. For a discussion of the normative societal "pull effects" that interact with the "push effects" of forceful internal states, see Arvid Kappas, Ursula Hess, and Klaus R. Scherer, "Voice and Emotion," *Fundamentals of Nonverbal Behavior*, eds. Robert Stephen Feldman and Bernard Rime (Cambridge: Cambridge University Press, 1991), 200–38.

46. Joseph LeDoux, *The Emotional Brain: The Mysterious Underpinnings of Emotional Life* (New York: Simon & Schuster, 1996).

47. "The amygdala, in this view, is a common, modality-independent way station that assigns significance to cortical sensory inputs and discharges through the hypothalamus in the guidance of behavior on the basis of the emotional significance of environmental events" (Panksepp, "The Anatomy of Emotions," 101).

48. Cannon, "Again the James-Lange and Thalmic Theories of Emotion," 281–95.

49. This model is similar to those found in Leonard Berkowitz, "On the Formation and Regulation of Anger and Aggression: A Cognitive-Neoassociationistic Analysis," *American Psychologist* 45, no. 4 (1990): 494–503; Gordon Bower and P. Cohen, "Emotional Influences in Memory and Thinking: Data and Theory," *Affect and Cognition*, eds. M. Clark and S. Fiske (Hillsdale, NJ: Erlbaum, 1982), 291–331; Peter J. Lang, "A Bio-Informational Theory of Emotional Imagery," *Psychophysiology* 16, no. 6 (1979): 495–512; and H. Leventhal, "A Perceptual-Motor Theory of Emotion," *Advances in Experimental Social Psychology*, vol. 17, ed. Leonard Berkowitz (New York: Academic Press, 1984), 117–82.

50. Walter Cannon discusses examples of the "as if" phenomenon in Marañon's work of the 1920s. See Cannon, "The James-Lange Theory of Emotions," 113.

51. I do not believe that there are actual physical entities corresponding to a "fear" node or a "joy" node; however, the interconnectivity of the physical emotion system supports a theoretical model such as the one I propose.

52. So this model's answer to the Lazarus-Zajonc argument over whether cognition precedes emotion or emotion precedes cognition is that both are initiated parallel to each other.

53. Cognitive researchers have found that much subtle information processing goes on below the level of logical "if-then" consciousness. For instance, David Marr's landmark work on seeing and object recognition argues that visual data undergo some rather sophisticated transformations before calling on conscious knowledge of the world when recognizing an object. We are learning that much processing goes on before we make conscious decisions, even on such basic matters as object recognition. See David Marr, *Vision: A Computational Investigation into the Human*

Representation and Processing of Visual Information (San Francisco: W. H. Freeman, 1982).

The conscious mind does not act on unfiltered data provided by the senses. Instead, much of our information about the world comes to consciousness "preprocessed" by "bottom-up" mechanisms that function below the level of our awareness. Conscious mechanisms of attention and expectation guide our perceptual apparatus, working in conjunction with lower-level processes. Understanding such simple phenomena as object recognition (or "being afraid") is no longer a matter of merely defining a logical category ("the fearsome") and making conscious yes-no decisions concerning an object's membership status in that category.

54. Scientists have nominated different dimensions as the primary denominator of emotions: positive-negative, good-bad, approach-withdrawal, pleasant-unpleasant. Although most researchers split their classification of emotions into commonsensical "positive" and "negative" categories, we can rely less on common sense and more on neurological evidence.

Davidson's and Tomarken's neurological research indicates that approach-withdrawal is likely the basic dimension of affect. (See Richard J. Davidson and Andrew J. Tomarken, "Laterality and Emotion: An Electrophysiological Approach," *Handbook of Neuropsychology*, vol. 3, eds. Francois Boller and Jordan Grafman [Amsterdam: Elsevier, 1989], 419–41.) In most cases the approach-withdrawal dimension is very similar to the positive-negative dimension that most researchers assume underlies emotive systems. Usually we want to get closer to objects we believe are positive and to distance ourselves from negative things. Loving someone (a positive state) involves wanting to be close to them, and fearing a person (negative) usually means wanting to get away from them.

The advantage of the approach-withdrawal dimension over the positive-negative dimension can be seen by considering anger on both dimensions. Anger tends toward an approach response, to strike or attack the object that makes you angry. Most researchers unproblematically place anger among the "negative" emotions, which seems intuitively correct when viewed in the abstract sense. Why would anyone want to be angry? This reflects the common sense of most of American (and much of Western) society. Yet anger can be exhilarating. We acknowledge that there are situations in which anger is an appropriate response, and we admit that anger is necessary in those situations, yet we as a society cast anger as an unpleasant experience. By labeling anger as negative, we reflect our society's fear of anger more than we reflect knowledge of internal affect.

I propose that we can consider the positive-negative distinction as a socialized recategorization of approach-withdrawal. We are taught by our parents and others which emotional states are "good" and which ones are "bad." The process of socialization involves translating biological approach-withdrawal into good-bad. The good-bad dimension is built into our associative emotion network at a very low level, often below consciousness, but it is never below the biological approach-withdrawal.

55. Robert N. Emde, "Toward a Psychoanalytic Theory of Affect: II. Emerging Models of Emotional Development in Infancy," *The Course of Life: Psychoanalytic*

Contributions toward Understanding Personality Development. Vol I: Infancy and Early Childhood, eds. Stanley I. Greenspan and George H. Pollock (Adelphi, MD: National Institute of Mental Health, 1980), 85–111.

56. Carroll E. Izard, Elizabeth A. Hembree, and Robin R. Huebner, "Infants' Emotion Expressions to Acute Pain: Developmental Change and Stability of Individual Differences," *Developmental Psychology* 23, no. 1 (1987): 105–13.

57. Emde, 85–111.

58. At seven to nine months the infant learns to recognize a "visual cliff," the edge of a surface on which he or she is crawling. Previous to this stage a child will crawl off the edge without recognizing the danger of falling. Visual recognition of this edge is an important stage in the child's developing coordination.

59. M. L. Hoffman, "Affect, Motivation, and Cognition," *Handbook of Motivation and Cognition: Foundations of Social Behavior*, eds. E. Tory Higgins and Richard M. Sorrentino (New York: Guilford Press, 1985), 244–80.

60. Marvin Minsky, *The Society of Mind* (New York: Simon and Schuster, 1987).

61. Because psychology's epistemological stance toward the world emphasizes the individual, much of the research has investigated the question of "basic" emotions, emotions that cross cultural boundaries, as in Andrew Ortony and Terence J. Turner, "What's Basic about Basic Emotions?" *Psychological Review* 97, no. 3 (1990): 315–31. For more on the controversial issue of basic emotions, see Paul Ekman, "An Argument for Basic Emotions," *Cognition and Emotion* 6, no. 3/4 (1992): 169–200.

62. For an overview of anthropological studies of emotion across cultures, see Catherine A. Lutz and Geoffrey M. White, "The Anthropology of Emotions," *Annual Review of Anthropology* 15 (1986): 405–36.

63. Nancy L. Stein and Tom Trabasso, "The Organisation of Emotional Experience: Creating Links among Emotion, Thinking, Language, and Intentional Action," *Cognition and Emotion* 6, no. 3/4 (1992): 225–44.

64. Lutz, *Unnatural Emotions*.

65. For an interesting debate on the difficulties of comparing one culture's version of "anger" with another's, see Michael Z. Rosaldo, *Knowledge and Passion: Ilongot Notions of Self and Social Life* (Cambridge: Cambridge University Press, 1980); M. E. Spiro, "Some Reflections on Cultural Determinism and Relativism with Special Reference to Emotion and Reason," *Culture Theory: Essays on Mind, Self, and Emotion*, eds. Richard A. Shweder and Robert Vine (Cambridge: Cambridge University Press, 1984); Anna Wierzbicka, *Semantics, Culture, and Cognition* (New York: Oxford University Press, 1992).

66. Geoffrey M. White argues for an approach to emotion study that is less tied to Western conceptions of the individual in "Emotions Inside Out: The Anthropology of Affect," Lewis and Haviland, 29–39. Also see Hazel Rose Markus and Shinobu Kitayama, "Culture and the Self: Implications for Cognition, Emotion, and Motivation," *Psychological Review* 98, no. 2 (1991): 224–53.

67. Paul Ekman and Wallace V. Friesen call these "display rules." See "The Repertoire of Nonverbal Behavior: Categories, Origins, Usage, and Coding," *Semiotica* 1 (1969): 49–98.

68. Now that geneticists are positing explanations for incredibly subtle differences in human functioning, it is difficult to maintain definitively that complicated emotional functions are not genetically encoded. Nonetheless, I believe that we should be careful in assuming too much genetic and biological causality in the composition of the emotion system. Certainly it is possible that we may arrive at more strictly biological determinations of high-level emotional functioning, but the burden of proof remains with biologically based research that has yet to be performed.

69. Davidson and Tomarken (1989); John M. Gottman and Robert W. Levenson, "Assessing the Role of Emotion in Marriage," *Behavioral Assessment* 8, no. 1 (1986): 31–48.

70. Ekman, "Argument"; Paul Ekman, "Expression and the Nature of Emotion," *Approaches to Emotion*, eds. Klaus R. Scherer and Paul Ekman (Hillsdale, NJ: Lawrence Erlbaum, 1984).

71. Pio Ricci-Bitti and Klaus R. Scherer, "Interrelations between Antecedents, Reactions, and Coping Responses," *Experiencing Emotion: A Cross-Cultural Study*, eds. Klaus R. Scherer, Harald G. Wallbott, and Angela B. Summerfield (Cambridge: Cambridge University Press, 1986), 129–41.

72. Elisha Y. Babad and Harald G. Wallbott, "The Effects of Social Factors on Emotional Reactions," Scherer, Walbott, and Summerfield, 154–172.

73. Nico H. Frijda, "Moods, Emotion Episodes, and Emotions," Lewis and Haviland, 381–403. The largest body of psychological research on mood examines how mood affects memory tasks. For a summary of this research, see Gordon H. Bower, "Mood and Memory," *American Psychologist* 36, no. 2 (1981): 129–48.

74. Frijda, "Moods."

75. Another emotional term with an even longer temporality than those mentioned here is temperament, which can last a lifetime. Temperament is a long-term trait tendency toward the expression of a particular emotion or emotion set. This book does not deal with such long-term states.

76. W. N. Morris, *Mood: The Frame of Mind* (New York: Springer-Verlag, 1989); Alice M. Isen and Joyce M. Gorgoglione, "Some Specific Effects of Four Affect-Induction Procedures," *Personality and Social Psychology Bulletin* 9, no. 1 (1983): 136–43.

3. The Mood-Cue Approach to Filmic Emotion

1. The partial case studies in this chapter do not explore the full potential usage of the narrational terminology introduced here. These short case studies are meant to be indicative of how the analytical approach to film analysis outlined here can help explain the particulars of a film's emotional appeal; subsequent chapters dealing with complete films provide more fleshed-out examples of this approach.

2. This emphasis on emotive redundancy echoes the Hollywood cinema's tendency toward narrational redundancy of story information. Mainstream cinema repeats its commentary through character, event, environment, and so forth, to ensure that viewers comprehend the necessary plot information. Just as narrational redundancy exists because viewer attention frequently varies, emotive redundancy exists because the viewer's emotion system can be accessed through a variety of associative channels.

3. Kristin Thompson, "The Concept of Cinematic Excess," *Narrative, Apparatus, Ideology: A Film Theory Reader*, ed. Philip Rosen (New York: Columbia University Press, 1986).

4. David Ansen, "Highland Fling," *Newsweek*, 28 February 1983, 79; *Variety*, 16 February 1983; Pauline Kael, *New Yorker*, 21 March 1983, 115–18; Stanley Kauffmann, "Highland Fling, French Flummery," *New Republic*, 21 March 1983, 24; James M. Wall, "Local Hero," *Christian Century*, 22–29 June 1983, 622; *USA Today*, May 1983, 68; Richard Schickel, "Scotch Broth," *Time*, 21 February 1983, 80; Janet Maslin, "Oily Fairyland," *New York Times*, 17 February 1983, 25; Vincent Canby, "Vitality and Variety Buoy New Movies from Britain," *New York Times*, 6 March 1983, A2.

5. Umberto Eco, *The Role of the Reader: Explorations in the Semiotics of Texts* (Bloomington: Indiana University Press, 1979).

6. I do not argue that "open" texts create deeper emotional responses than do "closed" texts, or vice versa. Having fewer emotion cues does not necessarily make the viewing experience more actively participational and therefore more deeply moving, nor does an overtly proscriptive work guarantee a stronger response. Just as different people have different preferences for channels of emotional access, they also can prefer different levels of cuing intensity.

7. This is another way that the film positions itself as "alternative" by playing with our preconceptions about the very nature of film narration.

4. Other Cognitivisms

1. Noël Carroll, "Prospects for Film Theory: A Personal Assessment," *Post-Theory: Reconstructing Film Studies*, eds. David Bordwell and Noël Carroll (Madison: University of Wisconsin Press, 1996).

2. Noël Carroll, *The Philosophy of Horror, or Paradoxes of the Heart* (New York: Routledge, 1990).

3. Noël Carroll, "Film, Emotion, and Genre," *Passionate Views: Film, Cognition, and Emotion*, eds. Carl Plantinga and Greg M. Smith (Baltimore: Johns Hopkins University Press, 1999), 25.

4. Carroll, "Film, Emotion, and Genre," 26.

5. Carroll might argue that his relative independence from empirical psychological research could be an advantage to his system. One could assert that because cognitive psychology, like most empirical fields, is particularly susceptible to periodic revolutions in thought based on new empirical findings, too closely tying one's assertions about film to such research might mean that the film theory would become obsolete if the psychological research is overturned. Carroll could argue that by staying at a level of abstraction that does not commit itself to a particular set of cognitive theories, his doctrinally uncommitted cognitivism is creating a theory of filmic emotions that has more longevity. Below this level of abstraction, everything is merely an issue of the details of system architecture.

I believe that there is no such thing as a doctrinally uncommitted cognitivism. As I argue in this chapter, Carroll's assumption that cognition is a necessary component for emotion places him in a particular camp within cognitivism. This assumption is not merely a matter of details; instead, it has fundamental ramifications for the shape of his theory. Within cognitivism, there are few matters of "detail" that can be clearly labeled as not having ramifications for the system as a whole. Such details have a way of fundamentally reshaping our theoretical systems. By seeming not to choose one particular cognitive camp versus another, one ends up actually making a choice, as Carroll does. I believe that, in spite of the partial and evolving nature of scientific inquiry, it is better to make that choice based on the best available empirical work.

6. Carroll, "Film, Emotion, and Genre," 27.

7. Carroll's argument about identification is the distinction between a thought and a belief. An audience's emotional response to a monster is different from an onscreen character's response to that monster. The character believes that the villain is monstrous, whereas the audience merely entertains the thought of its monstrosity. Carroll understands "identification" to mean that audience members believe that they are "identical" or "one with" the character. He argues that this is clearly not the case. We do not believe we are the protagonist, although we can entertain thoughts similar to the protagonist's.

   While agreeing with the thrust of Carroll's argument, I believe he is vulnerable to charges from psychoanalytic film theorists that he is taking the concept of identification too literally. I doubt that any psychoanalytic film theorist would go so far as to assert that audience members "believe" they are "identical" to the protagonist, and so Carroll's argument against identification (see *The Philosophy of Horror*, 79–96) has the sense of defeating a straw man.

8. Carroll's fundamental assumptions lead him to consider the microprocesses of style to have primarily a supporting role. This tendency can be clearly seen in his discussions of the function of movie music. In these discussions, stylistic factors such as music can accentuate the central tendencies, but they remain subordinated to the primary emotional appeal of characters trying to achieve goals and overcome obstacles. Music in most suspense scenes is merely a "temporal correlate" of more important emotion processes (Noël Carroll, "Toward a Theory of Film Suspense," *Persistence of Vision* 1 [1984]: 77). In Carroll's largest statement on film music, he emphasizes music's capacity to "modify" more primary narrational process, much as an adjective modifies a noun. Film music "fills in" or "enhances" what is said through situational cues and character. See Noël Carroll, "A Contribution to the Theory of Movie Music," *Mystifying Movies: Fads and Fallacies in Contemporary Film Theory* (New York: Columbia University Press, 1988), 213–25.

9. Carroll notes:

   I am not preoccupied with the actual relations of works of art-horror to audiences, but with a normative relation, the response the audience is supposed to have to the work of horror. I believe that we are able to get at this by presuming that the work of art-horror has built into it, so to speak, a set of instructions about the appropriate way the audience is to respond to it. (Carroll, *The Philosophy of Horror*, 31)

10. Ed S. Tan, *Emotion and the Structure of Narrative Film: Film as an Emotion Machine*, trans. Barbara Fasting (Mahwah, NJ: Lawrence Erlbaum, 1996).

11. Tan, 204.

12. Tan's project is broader than my own, attempting to supply not only an approach for analyzing films but also an explanation for the cinema's appeal, and his central concept of interest is crucial for this larger argument.

13. Tan, 38.

14. Torben Grodal, *Moving Pictures: A New Theory of Film Genres, Feelings, and Cognition* (Oxford: Oxford University Press, 1997).

15. These fictional simulations can be quite forceful at the local level of processing; in fact, a fictional representation can provide a more strongly focused stimulus than many real-world phenomena. For Grodal, this experience of the strength of the representation is independent of its reality-status. It is not that real objects more forcefully present themselves to us than fictional simulations do. Instead, one mental module judges the reality-status of a representation, whereas a separate but interacting module responds to the strength of the representation. We can respond emotionally to a fictional stimulus such as a film because the mind is not a single functional unit judging whether things are "true" or "false." Different mental modules allow us to feel emotions in the theater without confusing fiction with reality.

16. Grodal, 90.

17. Grodal, 95.

5. "Couldn't You Read between Those Pitiful Lines?" Feeling for *Stella Dallas*

1. E. Ann Kaplan, "The Case of the Missing Mother: Maternal Issues in Vidor's *Stella Dallas*," *Issues in Feminist Film Criticism*, ed. Patricia Erens (Bloomington: Indiana University Press, 1990), 126–36; Linda Williams, "Something Else Besides a Mother: *Stella Dallas* and the Maternal Melodrama," *Issues in Feminist Film Criticism*, 137–62; Ann Kaplan, "Dialogue: Ann Kaplan Replies to Linda Williams's 'Something Else Besides a Mother: *Stella Dallas* and the Maternal Melodrama,'" *Cinema Journal* 24, no. 2 (1985): 40–3; Patrice Petro and Carol Flinn, "Dialogue: Patrice Petro and Carol Flinn on Feminist Film Theory," *Cinema Journal* 25, no. 1 (1985): 50–2; E. Ann Kaplan, "Ann Kaplan Replies," *Cinema Journal* 25, no. 1 (1985): 52–4; Christine Gledhill, "Dialogue: Christine Gledhill on *Stella Dallas* and Feminist Film Theory," *Cinema Journal* 25, no. 4 (1986): 44–8; E. Ann Kaplan, "E. Ann Kaplan Replies," *Cinema Journal* 25, no. 4 (1986): 49–53.

2. Kaplan, "The Case of the Missing Mother," 134.

3. Williams, 137.

4. I am relying on Mary Ann Doane's distinction between the maternal melodrama and the love story articulated in *The Desire to Desire: The Woman's Film of the 1940's* (Bloomington: Indiana University Press, 1987).

5. The concept of feeling with or for is closely related to the distinctions Murray Smith articulates in *Engaging Characters: Fiction, Emotion, and the Cinema* (Oxford: Oxford University Press, 1995). In Smith's terms feeling for involves "alignment" (access to character information such as feelings and actions) and "allegiance"

(responding emotionally to the character's situation but not experiencing the same feelings as the character). Feeling with is the empathic phenomenon that Smith calls "emotional simulation." I have chosen the terms "feeling for" and "feeling with" partially because of the benefit of their straightforwardness. In addition, feeling with or for better captures a sense that a text, merely by varying the information provided to the viewer, can call for two distinctly different modes of emotional expression.

6. Feeling with or for is related to Bordwell's concept of how knowledgeable the narration is concerning the fabula or diegesis (*Narration in the Fiction Film* [Madison: University of Wisconsin Press, 1985], 57–61). Feeling with is comparable to his concept of restricted range of knowledge, in which the spectator's and the character's knowledge are virtually congruent. Feeling *for* can only happen when the narration is (a) knowledgeable of important emotional data that the character is not and (b) communicative about that knowledge. The concept of feeling with or for attempts to emphasize the viewer's emotional activity in response to the range of knowledge proffered by a text. Feeling for or with is based on the narration's knowledge, but it cannot be reduced to the text alone. The text's control of knowledge offers an invitation to the viewer to feel, although it cannot compel the viewer to do so.

This concept also attempts to emphasize the shifting nature of our knowledge and the accompanying emotional responses. As Bordwell notes, "narrative films are constantly modulating the range ... of the narration's knowledge" (58), and my use of the feeling with or for concept tries to be sensitive to these important shifts.

On a related note, Thomas Elsaesser notes that melodrama tends to manipulate the difference between our awareness and that of the characters to "activate very strongly an audience's participation, for there is a desire to make up for the emotional deficiency, to impart the different awareness, which in other genres is systematically frustrated to produce suspense: the primitive desire to warn the heroine of the perils looming visibly over her in the shape of the villain's shadow. But in the more sophisticated melodramas this pathos is most acutely produced through a 'liberal' mise-en-scène that balances different points of view, so that the spectator is in a position of seeing and evaluating contrasting attitudes within a given thematic framework – a framework that is the result of the total configuration and therefore inaccessible to the protagonists themselves." ("Tales of Sound and Fury: Observations on the Family Melodrama," *Movies and Methods*, vol. 2, ed. Bill Nichols [Berkeley: University of California Press, 1985], 187.)

7. Doane notes that "Music is the register of the sign which bears the greatest burden in the love story" (*The Desire to Desire*, 97).

8. There are two other key leitmotifs in *Stella Dallas*. One is a slower, more meditative romantic theme associated with the Morrisons's warm society home (and in particular with Helen Morrison):

The other is an upbeat theme associated with exuberantly happy times as when Laurel is actively participating in upper-class society (riding bicycles with the socialites, playing ping-pong with the Morrisons, etc.):

This happy music could be considered to be the narration's straightforward endorsement of the blissful upper-class utopia that the Morrisons seem to inhabit (particularly in comparison with Laurel's home with Stella). When examined in context, however, this music's function is complicated somewhat. We first hear the upbeat theme immediately after the gut-wrenching birthday party scene. The appearance of this suddenly sprightly music makes a strong contrast to the overall mood that has just been bolstered by the dense cuing of the birthday party scene. The juxtaposition of this insistently perky music with the preceding pathos is striking, calling on the viewer to make too great an emotional shift. Because the film music seemingly asks us to make a larger emotional shift than is humanly possible, the happy music becomes suspect. It is too good to be true. Such an insistently upbeat tone must be fated to return to the predominant orientation of impending social doom. By this strong juxtaposition, the film calls on the viewer to continue to anticipate social disaster, asking us to read the upbeat theme as only a temporary shift in tone.

The melodramatic mode depends on such reversals, according to Thomas Elsaesser (174), but my model suggests that viewers may interpret these reversals as localized departures from the dominant emotional orientation. Such a model of the return to a dominant orientation after localized departures may help explain the apparent inevitability that seems to guide characters in melodrama back to their doom.

For a discussion of leitmotifs and classical film scoring, see Claudia Gorbman, *Unheard Melodies: Narrative Film Music* (Bloomington: Indiana University Press, 1987); Kathryn Kalinak, *Settling the Score: Music and the Classical Hollywood Film* (Madison: University of Wisconsin Press, 1992); Caryl Flinn, *Strains of Utopia: Gender, Nostalgia, and Hollywood Film Music* (Princeton, NJ: Princeton University Press, 1992).

9. When Laurel learns that it was after their train trip back from the Hotel Mirador that Stella approached Helen Morrison and offered to give up custody of Laurel, she realizes that Stella must have overheard the girls' gossip as they were in the sleeping car. The film helps emphasize this realization with a musical fragment of the main theme, which now is so strongly associated with Stella that it can be used to signal that Laurel is thinking of her.

10. Kaplan, "Dialogue," *Cinema Journal* 24, no. 2, 41.

11. When we shift to feeling *with* during Stella's final sacrifices, our emotional reaction is no longer based on what we think Stella might do if she knew what we knew. Instead, she demonstrates what one person might do with this knowledge. Individual viewers can refuse this appeal, saying that the viewer would never give

up her child as Stella does. Nonetheless, the text does invite us to feel *with* Stella as she makes her ultimate sacrifice.

12. Historical genre research could be done to determine if such a strategy (placing the moment of greatest overdetermination by multiple emotion scripts at the end of the film) is typical of the melodrama or of the woman's film.

13. Peter Brooks, *The Melodramatic Imagination: Balzac, Henry James, Melodrama, and the Mode of Excess* (New York: Columbia University Press, 1985), 10.

14. An important subfield of psychoanalytic film theory emphasizes the importance of sound in spectator positioning, particularly in dealing with female spectators. See Kaja Silverman, *The Acoustic Mirror: The Female Voice in Psychoanalysis and Cinema* (Bloomington: Indiana University Press, 1988); and Mary Ann Doane, "The Voice in the Cinema: The Articulation of Body and Space," *Movies and Methods*, vol. 2, ed. Bill Nichols (Berkeley: University of California Press, 1985), 565–75. Recent writings on film music have underscored the function of music in subject positioning, particularly Gorbman's *Unheard Melodies* and Flinn's *Strains of Utopia*. Neither branch of theory has entered into the *Stella Dallas* debate, however.

15. Noël Carroll, *Mystifying Movies: Fads and Fallacies in Contemporary Film Theory* (New York: Columbia University Press, 1988), 213–25. The most widely known case for the aesthetic use of film sound as counterpoint is Sergei Eisenstein, Vsevolod Pudovkin, and Grigori Alexandrov, "Statement on Sound," *S. M. Eisenstein, Selected Works: Volume I, Writings, 1922–34*, ed. and trans. Richard Taylor (Bloomington: Indiana University Press, 1988), 113–14.

16. Michel Chion, *Audio-Vision: Sound on Screen*, ed. and trans. Claudia Gorbman (New York: Columbia University Press, 1994), 8.

17. Gorbman, 160.

6. *Strike*-ing Out: The Partial Success of Early Eisenstein's Emotional Appeal

1. My analysis of *Strike* relies on the Soviet version of the film that was "stretch-printed" to add a soundtrack. This is the version that circulates most widely in the United States.

2. Sergei Eisenstein, *S. M. Eisenstein, Selected Works, Vol. 1: Writings, 1922–34*, ed. and trans. Richard Taylor (Bloomington: Indiana University Press, 1988), 176.

3. Eisenstein, *Writings, 1922–34*, 68.

4. Eisenstein, *Writings, 1922–34*, 67–8.

5. The norm of rapid editing in Soviet montage cinema can potentially make it more difficult for a filmmaker to foreground certain passages as more highly marked. Because the norm involves such quick cutting, this means that a filmmaker cannot simply use quick cutting to signal an emotionally significant moment (an option open to traditionally classical filmmaking with its longer average shot lengths). Because the standard of editing pace expectations has been raised so high, it is difficult to differentiate significant moments through pace alone (although the Soviet montage cinema is certainly capable of doing this, using shots for only a fraction of a second). Montage cinema has to turn to other means to differentiate certain segments as emotionally, stylistically, and narrationally significant, as the "police agent

introduction" example (with its montage of animals and grotesque actors and its flashy wipes) illustrates.

6. David Bordwell, *Narration in the Fiction Film* (Madison: University of Wisconsin Press, 1985), 239–40.

7. Historical-materialist narration does not always vault from one vastly different diegetic space and time to another. Some of its most notable achievements occur in sequences in which the scene takes place within one location (such as *Potemkin*'s Odessa steps sequence). Of course, Soviet montage cinema handles such sequences differently than a classical film would, often violating the rules of spatial continuity. Such continuity violations can create "impossible" spaces, but this does not prevent the viewer from being able to recognize that the shots belong to a sequence (e.g., are physically bound to the Odessa steps). In this way historical-materialist narration can create sequences that are identifiable as such without resorting to the strictly classical unities of time and space.

8. Bordwell, 240.

9. Kristin Thompson, *Breaking the Glass Armor: Neoformalist Film Analysis* (Princeton, NJ: Princeton University Press, 1988); Herbert Eagle, ed., *Russian Formalist Film Theory* (Ann Arbor: Michigan Slavic Publications, 1981); Lee T. Lemon and Marion J. Reis, eds., *Russian Formalist Criticism: Four Essays* (Lincoln: University of Nebraska Press, 1965).

10. Sergei Eisenstein, *S. M. Eisenstein, Selected Works, Vol. 2: Towards a Theory of Montage*, eds. Michael Glenny and Richard Taylor, trans. Michael Glenny (London: BFI, 1991), 232.

11. One could assert that the emotional orientation is provided by the audience's knowledge of the events of these strikes in Soviet history. Bordwell notes that because Soviet audiences knew the history portrayed in montage cinema, there was no doubt about the overall narrational outcome. The curiosity, then, was to see how this particular film would arrange its signifiers to arrive at the foregone conclusion. Perhaps *Strike* depended on the audience knowing what the outcome of these resistant struggles was to orient the viewer toward the tragic happenings, and so Eisenstein worked more to establish a formal orientation toward the diegesis than he did to establish an emotional orientation. In any case, the first part of the *text* itself remains relatively ineffective on its own terms at coordinating an effective emotional appeal without reliance on an emotional orientation brought by the audience into the theater.

12. Eisenstein, *Works, 1922–34*, 59.

13. Bordwell, 235–6.

14. When historical-materialist narration shifts toward the classical, the shift is not complete. The section centered on Stronghin does not look like a Hollywood film, although it shares some of the qualities of such narration (restriction to one character, easily recognizable genre situations). As Bordwell notes, even when historical-materialist cinema tells familiar stories that are predictable at the global level, it tells them using a style that is unpredictable at the local level (241–3). It is difficult to predict when the Stronghin segment will use direct address, although the overall dramatic situation is familiar enough to encourage a predictable emotional response.

15. Eisenstein, *Works, 1922–34*, 68–9.
16. Eisenstein, *Works, 1922–34*, 61.
17. Sergei Eisenstein, *Film Form: Essays in Film Theory*, ed. and trans. Jay Leyda (Cleveland: Meridian, 1957), 234–5, 254.
18. Eisenstein, *Works, 1922–34*, 68, 69.
19. Eisenstein, *Works, 1922–34*, 43–4, 174–6.
20. Eisenstein, *Works, 1922–34*, 63.

7. Lyricism and Unevenness: Emotional Transitions in Renoir's *A Day in the Country* and *The Lower Depths*

1. Pauline Kael, *5001 Nights at the Movies: A Guide from A to Z* (New York: Holt, Rinehart, & Winston, 1982), 136; Alexander Sesonske, *Jean Renoir: The French Films, 1924–1939* (Cambridge, MA: Harvard University Press, 1980), 260.
2. By referring to the characters by name throughout this chapter, it makes it seem more obvious which characters should be paired romantically. It is a romantic cliche for a character named Henri to fall in love with a character named Henriette. Renoir, however, avoids the awkward possibility of a viewer anticipating the narrative's progression based on a triviality such as the characters' names. Following de Maupassant's lead, Renoir withholds the first names of his characters, so that only after it is clear from their interactions that Henri and Henriette are a couple do we realize that their names are also connected. Then *A Day in the Country* makes a less obvious connection apparent for us when Rodolphe, upon learning Juliette's name, traces his own name to Romeo. If we had known at the beginning of the romance that the four characters were named Henri, Henriette, Romeo, and Juliette, the narrative would be utterly and banally predictable.
3. For example: "Renoir honours the spirit of impressionism by forgetting all but its subject matter and paraphrasing its means in terms of the film sequence" (Raymond Durgnat, *Jean Renoir* [Berkeley: University of California Press, 1974], 136).
4. Jean Renoir, *Renoir on Renoir: Interviews, Essays, and Remarks*, trans. Carol Volk (Cambridge: Cambridge University Press, 1989), 250.
5. André Bazin, *Jean Renoir*, ed. Francois Truffaut, trans. W. W. Halsey II and William H. Simon (New York: Da Capo Press, 1992), 19, 55.
6. Sesonske, 269.
7. Sesonske, 260.

8. Emotion Work: *The Joy Luck Club* and the Limits of the Emotion System

1. Except for the flashback to Waverly's childhood, which shares the same basic time and place as her childhood friend June's.
2. David Bordwell, *Narration in the Fiction Film* (Madison: University of Wisconsin Press, 1985), 59–60, 160.
3. My notion of "emotion work" is not to be confused with the way Arlie Hochschild uses the term in *The Managed Heart* (Berkeley: University of California Press, 1983). Hochschild refers to emotion work as the effort expended to make your emotional

expressions appear in the way expected of your role or job. *The Managed Heart* argues that more and more employers pay not just for the actual physical labor required to perform the job but also for the corresponding correct attitude of their workers. It is not enough for airline stewards to serve drinks; they must also do so with a pleasant attitude, regardless of the passengers' actions.

This notion of "emotion work" is not engaged in freely but is bought and paid for by one's employer. The person gains money, not emotional experiences, in exchange for his or her efforts. In my concept of emotion work, there is a certain level of effort expended (either purely emotional, purely cognitive, or both), and the payoff for that work, if successful, is emotional experience (a desired emotional state).

4. For more on flashback structure, see Maureen Turim, *Flashbacks in Film: Memory and History* (New York: Routledge, 1989).

9. "I Was Misinformed": Nostalgia and Uncertainty in *Casablanca*

1. Andrew Sarris, *The American Cinema: Directors and Directions* (New York: E. P. Dutton, 1968), 176.
2. Umberto Eco, "*Casablanca*: Cult Movies and Intertextual Collage," *Travels in Hyperreality*, trans. William Weaver (San Diego: Harcourt Brace Jovanovich, 1986), 197, 198, 209.
3. Frank Miller, *Casablanca: As Time Goes By. . . .* (Atlanta: Turner, 1992), 140.
4. Richard Maltby, "'A Brief Romantic Interlude: Dick and Jane Go to 3-1/2 Seconds of the Classical Hollywood Cinema," *Post-Theory: Reconstructing Film Studies*, eds. David Bordwell and Noël Carroll (Madison: University of Wisconsin Press, 1996), 453–4.
5. Eco, 209 (emphasis in original).
6. Eco, 203.
7. Eco, 202.
8. Noël Carroll, "The Power of Movies," *Daedalus* 114, no. 4 (fall 1985), 96–9; David Bordwell, *Narration in the Fiction Film* (Madison: University of Wisconsin Press, 1985), 157, 164–5.
9. *Casablanca*, of course, does not use all of its characters equally to create an uncertain universe. Some of the characters (Laszlo, Strasser) behave in consistently predictable ways. This account emphasizes the same characters that the film privileges (the protagonists), and these characters largely create the uncertainty.
10. Eco, 197, 201.
11. Pauline Kael, *5001 Nights at the Movies: A Guide from A to Z* (New York: Holt, Rinehart, and Winston, 1982), 96.
12. Similarly, artificially intelligent processes may be designed as either forward looking or rear driven. Once a forward-looking process is given an initial state, it can proceed toward a defined goal by looking ahead, checking how close a legal operation will move it toward the goal, and then moving consistently closer to that goal. A rear-driven process, on the other hand, may be more useful if the goal is not so clear. A rear-driven process chooses operations based on its current state and on the previous states, while operating according to the rules governing the environment.

13. For most classical films, then, we only need to know enough about the characters' past to help us understand their present state. A forward-looking artificial intelligence program doesn't need to know much about how it got to its initial state, and similarly the classical film doesn't need much background information about the character to set its apparatus into motion. It only needs to provide a little background exposition to give the characters the appearance of being coherently motivated by their pasts.

14. For more on the music in *Casablanca*, see Martin Marks, "Music, Drama, Warner Brothers: The Cases of *Casablanca* and *The Maltese Falcon*," *Michigan Quarterly Review* 35, no. 1 (winter 1996): 112–42.

Appendix

1. James Strachey, ed., *The Standard Edition of the Complete Psychological Works of Sigmund Freud*, vol. 10 (London: Hogarth, 1966), 175. Emphasis in original. All subsequent references to the *Standard Edition* will be noted parenthetically (volume, page) in the text.

2. Christian Metz, *The Imaginary Signifier: Psychoanalysis and the Cinema*, trans. Celia Britton, Annwyl Williams, Ben Brewster, and Alfred Guzzetti (Bloomington: Indiana University Press, 1980).

3. Laura Mulvey, "Visual Pleasure and Narrative Cinema," *Movies and Methods*, vol. 2, ed. Bill Nichols (Berkeley: University of California Press, 1985), 303–15.

4. Perhaps Metz places more emphasis on the scopic drive than may be found in Freud, but the operation of this drive is no different from the Freudian conception of drives and instincts.
   Metz uses the term "primary identification" in a way that is specific to the cinema (meaning the spectator's identification with the camera). This should not be confused with Freud's use of the same term to indicate an early connection to or with the mother. Metz's understanding of the mechanism of identification is squarely within the Freudian tradition, and his choice to give a Freudian term a purely cinematic meaning is meant to emphasize the similarity between the cinematic spectator and the Freudian child.

5. Otto Fenichel, "The Ego and the Affects," *Psychoanalytic Review* 28 (1941): 47–60; Stuart Hampshire, "Notions of the Unconscious Mind," *States of Mind*, ed. Jonathan Miller (New York: Pantheon, 1983), 100–15; David Rapaport, "On the Psychoanalytic Theory of Affects," *Psychoanalytic Psychiatry and Psychology, Clinical and Theoretical Papers*, eds. Robert P. Knight and Cyrus R. Friedman (New York: International Universities Press, 1954), 274–310.

6. Jerome C. Wakefield, "Freud and the Intentionality of Affect," *Psychoanalytic Psychology* 9, no. 1 (1992): 2.

7. Freud's preferred term to denote the emotions is *affekt* (usually translated as affect), although he also uses other words, such as *empfindung* (sensation) and *gefühl* (feeling), to refer to emotional states. The translators of the *Standard Edition* note that "Freud himself had flexible view on the use of these words" (I, xxiii). Most consider that Freud uses these terms in a roughly interchangeable way and that

differences in his usage of these terms are not significant. For more on Freud's use of the word *affekt*, see David Sachs, "On Freud's Doctrine of Emotions," *Freud: A Collection of Critical Essays*, ed. Richard Wollheim (Garden City, NJ: Anchor Press, 1974), 138.

8. Frank J. Sulloway, *Freud, Biologist of the Mind: Beyond the Psychoanalytic Legend* (New York: Basic Books, 1979).

9. Cornelis Wegman discusses this model in some detail in *Psychoanalysis and Cognitive Psychology: A Formalization of Freud's Earliest Theories* (Orlando, FL: Academic Press, 1985), 73–8.

10. Robert R. Holt, "Beyond Vitalism and Mechanism: Freud's Concept of Psychic Energy," *Historical Roots of Contemporary Psychology*, ed. Benjamin B. Wolman (New York: Harper & Row, 1968).

11. Alasdair C. McIntyre, *The Unconscious* (London: Routledge & Kegan Paul, 1958), 23.

12. Helen Block Lewis, *Freud and Modern Psychology, Vol. 1: The Emotional Basis of Mental Illness* (New York: Plenum, 1981), 3.

13. Freud described the onset of anxiety as being similar to becoming aware of other bodily sensations, such as hunger:

> picture the endogenous tension as growing either continuously or discontinuously, but in any case as only being noticed when it has reached a certain *threshold*. It is only above this threshold that it is turned to account *psychically*, that it enters into relation with certain groups of ideas, which thereupon set about producing the specific remedies. (I, 192–3, emphasis in original)

14. This account of the three-stage model of Freudian emotions is based on Jerome C. Wakefield, "Why Emotions Can't Be Unconscious: An Exploration of Freud's Essentialism," *Psychoanalysis and Contemporary Thought* 14, no. 1 (1991), 29–67.

15. Roy Schafer, "Emotion in the Language of Action," *Psychology versus Metapsychology: Psychoanalytic Essays in Memory of George S. Klein*, eds. Merton M. Gill and Philip S. Holzman (New York: International Universities Press, 1976), 130.

16. Wakefield, "Why Emotions Can't Be Unconscious," 53.

17. As Wegman notes, this quota of affect acts as

> a defilement, or literally, a quantity of excitation that since it formed has become permanent and is waiting to be removed. Now this does not accord with the theory of affect, as Freud develops it in a neurophysiological level. . . . An implicit assumption is that, once associated with a high excitation level, ideas acquire the power to produce excitations again and again. (88–9)

18. For instance: "It is the idea which is subjected to repression and which may be distorted to the point of being unrecognizable; but its quota of affect is regularly transformed into anxiety – and this is so whatever the nature of the affect may be, whether it is aggressiveness or love" (XXII, 83).

19. Earlier I noted that, because the quota of affect could be expressed as a variety of emotional or nonemotional thoughts or actions, Freud did not assert that the emotions are a crucial determinant of behavior. The range of pathologies noted

here (conversion, fetishes, obsessions, phobias, etc.) extend the potential options for expressing the quota of affect, making the quota of affect even less strongly connected to emotional experience.

20. "When there is a *mesalliance*, I began, between an affect and its ideational content, ... The affect is justified. . . . But it belongs to some other content, which is unknown (*unconscious*), and which requires to be looked for. The known ideational content has only got into its actual position owing to a false connection." (X, 175)

21. Freud's clinical observations concerning anxiety show that emotions are not necessarily attached to objects, as his functionalist emotion system would seem to indicate. Freud's description of anxiety as having "a quality of *indefiniteness and lack of object*" (XX, 165, emphasis in original) threatens to destabilize the connection between thought and quota of affect found in his assumptions about emotion. When anxiety finds an object to attach to, Freud called it fear. If it does not become attached, anxiety can become "free anxiety" that is not tied to the original thought nor to any other thought. Such free anxiety is a highly mobile quota of affect that is not directed toward anyone or anything in particular. Freud discussed a transitional period in which Little Hans's sexual desire for his mother was changed into anxiety, which becomes so detached that it does not respond to any object, even the original object of desire. Once the bond between thought and emotion has been broken, the quota of affect can become fully autonomous in extreme cases.

22. Sachs, 144–5 (emphasis in original).

23. Lewis, *The Emotional Basis of Mental Illness*, 103.

24. In *The Interpretation of Dreams*, Freud admitted that "dreams insist with greater energy upon their right to be included among our real mental experiences in respect to their affective than in respect to their ideational content" (V, 460).

25. Freud said, "all comparatively intense affective processes, including even terrifying ones, trench upon sexuality" (VII, 203).

26. Wakefield, "Why Emotions Can't Be Unconscious," 63.

27. Metz, *The Imaginary Signifier*, 18.

28. Christian Metz, *Film Language*, trans. Michael Taylor (Chicago: University of Chicago Press, 1991), 27.

29. Metz, *The Imaginary Signifier*, 58.

30. Metz, *The Imaginary Signifier*, 111.

31. Metz, *The Imaginary Signifier*, 122. See chapter 11, endnote 4 for Metz's explicit articulation of Freud's energy system.

32. Metz, *The Imaginary Signifier*, 118.

33. Laura Mulvey, "Netherworlds and the Unconscious: Oedipus and *Blue Velvet*," *Fetishism and Curiosity* (Bloomington: Indiana University Press, 1996), 137–54.

34. Laura Mulvey, "Americanitis: European Intellectuals and Hollywood Melodrama," *Fetishism and Curiosity*, 24.

35. Laura Mulvey, "Social Hieroglyphics: Reflections on Two Films by Douglas Sirk," *Fetishism and Curiosity*, 29.

36. Laura Mulvey, "Pandora's Box: Topographies of Curiosity," *Fetishism and Curiosity*, 62.

37. Mulvey, "Americanitis," 25.

38. Claire Johnston, ed., *Notes on Women's Cinema*, British Film Institute pamphlet, 1973.

39. Constance Penley, *Feminism and Film Theory* (Routledge: New York, 1988), 6.

40. Gaylyn Studlar, *In the Realm of Pleasure: Von Sternberg, Dietrich, and the Masochistic Aesthetic* (Urbana: University of Illinois Press, 1988); Nancy Chodorow, *The Reproduction of Mothering: Psychoanalysis and the Sociology of Gender* (Berkeley: University of California Press, 1978); Mary Ann Doane, "Film and the Masquerade: Theorizing the Female Spectator," *Issues in Feminist Film Criticism*, ed. Patricia Erens (Bloomington: Indiana University Press, 1990).

41. Mary Ann Doane, "The Voice in the Cinema: The Articulation of Body and Space," in *Movies and Methods*, vol. 2, 565–76; Kaja Silverman, *The Acoustic Mirror: The Female Voice in Psychoanalysis and Cinema* (Bloomington: Indiana University Press, 1988); Claudia Gorbman, *Unheard Melodies: Narrative Film Music* (Bloomington: Indiana University Press, 1987).

42. Roland Barthes, *The Pleasure of the Text*, trans. Richard Miller (New York: Hill and Wang, 1975); Patrice Petro, *Joyless Streets: Women and Melodramatic Representation in Weimar Germany* (Princeton, NJ: Princeton University Press, 1989); Miriam Hansen, *Babel and Babylon: Spectatorship in American Silent Film* (Cambridge, MA: Harvard University Press, 1991); Mary Ann Doane, *The Desire to Desire: The Woman's Film of the 1940's* (Bloomington: Indiana University Press, 1987); Christine Gledhill, ed., *Home Is Where the Heart Is: Studies in Melodrama and the Woman's Film* (London: BFI, 1987); Carol J. Clover, *Men, Women, and Chain Saws: Gender in the Modern Horror Film* (Princeton, NJ: Princeton University Press, 1992); Linda Williams, *Hard Core: Power, Pleasure, and the Frenzy of the Visible* (Berkeley: University of California Press, 1989).

43. Mary Ann Doane, *Camera Obscura*, 20–21 (1989): 144.

44. E. Ann Kaplan, *Camera Obscura*, 20–21 (1989): 197.

45. Kaplan, 198.

Index